COUNTRY WALKS
NEAR BALTIMORE

Revised and expanded fourth edition

by Alan Fisher

RAMBLER BOOKS

Baltimore

COUNTRY WALKS NEAR BALTIMORE

By Alan Fisher
Maps and photographs by the author

Rambler Books
1430 Park Avenue
Baltimore, MD 21217

If you notice errors in the text or maps, please point them out in a letter to the publisher.

Printed in the United States of America

FOURTH EDITION

ISBN 0-9614963-8-X

On the cover: Pot Rocks at Big Gunpowder Falls (Chapter 8).

CONTENTS

Preface   7

Comfort and Safety   9

1 Hereford Area of Gunpowder   13
    Falls State Park: Gunpowder
    South and North Trails

2 West Hereford at Gunpowder   25
    Falls State Park: Gunpowder
    South Trail, Highland Trail,
    and Mingo Forks Trail

3 East Hereford at Gunpowder   33
    Falls State Park: Gunpowder
    South Trail and Panther
    Branch Trail

4 Sweet Air Area of Gunpowder   41
    Falls State Park

5 Little Gunpowder Trail and Ma & Pa   53
    Trail between Bottom Road
    and Pleasantville Road at
    Gunpowder Falls State Park

6 Little Gunpowder Trail between   61
    Route 1 (Belair Road) and Inter-
    state 95 at Gunpowder Falls
    State Park

7 Sweathouse Branch Wildlands at   69
    the Central Area of Gunpowder
    Falls State Park

8 Lost Pond Trail and Sawmill Trail at   81
    the Central Area of Gunpowder
    Falls State Park

9 Big Gunpowder Trail between   89
      Route 147 (Harford Road) and
      Route 40 at the Central Area of
      Gunpowder Falls State Park

1 0 Loch Raven   99

1 1 Northern Central Railroad   107

1 2 Oregon Ridge Park   123

1 3 Soldiers Delight Natural Environ- 131
      ment Area

1 4 McKeldin Area of Patapsco Valley   141
      State Park

1 5 Patapsco Valley State Park   151
      between the McKeldin Area
      and Dogwood Road

1 6 Avalon and Orange Grove Areas   173
      of Patapsco Valley State Park

1 7 Gwynns Falls Trail   185

1 8 Cylburn Arboretum   201

1 9 North Point State Park and Fort   211
      Howard Park

2 0 BWI Trail and the Baltimore &   225
      Annapolis Trail Park

2 1 Savage Park and Savage Historic   239
      Mill Trail

2 2 National Wildlife Visitor Center at 247
      the Patuxent Research Refuge

2 3 North Tract of the Patuxent   261
      Research Refuge

      Index of Featured Sites and Trails 268

MAP 1 — Orientation

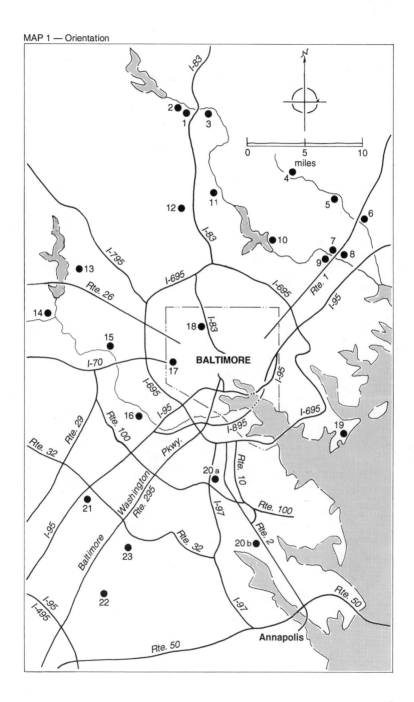

PREFACE

THIS BOOK IS FOR PEOPLE who want an outing in a country setting without wasting half the day getting there and back. If you live in the Greater Baltimore region, the excursions described here are close at hand. The walks show the best of our area's parks and trails, some of which are suitable also for ski touring and bicycling. The excursions cover the gamut of the region's landscapes. Successive visits during different seasons—to see the changing foliage, views, wildflowers, and birds—provide an added dimension of enjoyment.

Each chapter of this book includes a brief introduction, a discussion of natural or social history, detailed directions, and one or more maps. For this fourth edition, the commentary and directions have all been updated, and all the maps have been re-drawn in a larger format. In addition, a half-dozen new walks have been added.

Automobile directions: Because readers will be driving from different places to reach the sites described here, the automobile directions sometimes outline different avenues of approach. Necessarily, there is much repetition, so focus on the set of directions that applies to you and skip the others. Also, you may find it helpful to use **Map 1** on page 5 in conjunction with each chapter's more detailed map or inset showing local roads.

The following people helped me with this book in various ways, including providing information and making suggestions: Fraser Bishop, Jennifer Cline, Kimberly Lloyd, John McGrain, Chip Price, and Mike Strawbridge. Many, many thanks.

Alan Fisher
Baltimore

Where is this covered bridge? See Chapter 6.

COMFORT AND SAFETY

PLEASE READ THIS. It is customary, in guidebooks such as this, to include a catalog of cautions about possible nuisances and hazards. Such matters do not make for scintillating reading, but really, I think that you will be glad to focus here on a few potential problems, so that you can avoid them, rather than remember them belatedly through uncomfortable (or even dangerous) experience. Please also read the introductory matter for each excursion before you go.

First, about footwear: The main thing is to wear shoes that can withstand getting wet and that have thick soles to protect your feet. Walking shoes with waterproof liners really work and are fine spring though fall, but ankle-high boots are better because they are more likely to prevent water from spilling in at the tops. Particularly during winter, wear hiking boots with lug soles to provide traction in snow, which may occur unexpectedly on shaded slopes even though, in our mild climate, the ground is mostly bare.

Other gear for a comfortable outing includes a small knapsack or pouch containing a snack and drink, insect repellent, and an extra layer of clothing, such as a windbreaker or rain parka. Kids in particular will be glad when the food appears.

Some of the trails described in this book traverse steep, rocky slopes, so control your children closely. Bear in mind that boulders and ledges presenting little difficulty when dry can be treacherous when snowy or icy. And unlike some people I have encountered, don't undertake impromptu rock climbing, only to find yourself clinging to a cliff and unable to extricate yourself.

Every year the newspapers carry stories about people who pick up a squirrel, a raccoon, or some other animal and get bitten. They then have to undergo a series of painful anti-rabies shots. Don't be one of these people; don't handle *any* wild animals. In somewhat the same vein, copperhead snakes are not unheard of in the Baltimore region. In rocky areas where snakes might sun themselves, be careful where you place your feet and hands.

During winter, all too often drownings occur when people fall through the ice after venturing out onto frozen ponds and rivers. I am sure that you have heard this before; everybody has. And yet each winter a few more people die in this manner. Don't be one of them; stay off the ice. And tell your kids.

Other sound advice that is ignored with puzzling regularity concerns lightning. If you are in an exposed or elevated area and a storm approaches, return to your car immediately. That is the safest place to be. And if lighting occurs before you get back to your car, hunker down in a low spot. Don't worry about getting wet or feeling stupid as you crouch there with the rain pouring down. Clearly it is better to get wet and yet be safe than to try to stay dry by huddling under an isolated tree or park pavilion or some other target for lightning.

Where the trails follow roads for short distances, walk well off the road on the shoulder to minimize the risk of being hit by a car, and use caution, especially at dusk or after dark, where the trails cross roads. Studies show that in poor light conditions, motorists typically cannot even see pedestrians in time to stop, so your safety depends entirely on you.

Finally, one of the pitfalls of writing guidebooks is that conditions change. Just because this book recommends something does not mean that you should forge ahead in the face of obvious difficulties, hazards, or prohibitions.

ABOUT TICKS: Virtually all parks and wildlife refuges in the Baltimore region now post warnings about ticks and Lyme disease. The chances of being bitten by a tick are minimal if you stick to wide, well maintained trails. But if you walk through tall grass or brush, you can easily pick up ticks, which are active from early spring through autumn, or even during mild weather in winter. Some ticks may carry Lyme disease, which can cause swelling of the knees and hips, arthritis, and other disorders. The main carriers of Lyme disease are tiny deer ticks (about the size of a caraway seed in spring and summer, slightly larger in fall and winter). One simple precaution is to wear long pants and a long-sleeved shirt and to tuck your pant legs into your socks and your shirt into your pants in order to keep ticks on the outside, where you can pick them off. Spray your clothes, especially your shoes, socks, and pant legs, with insect repellent containing DEET (N-diethylmetatoluamide) applied according to the directions on the label. If your clothes are light colored, it will be easier to spot any ticks that may get on you. Inspect yourself occasionally during your outing and when you return to your car. And when you get home, wash your clothes and examine your body closely. Pay particular attention to your lower legs, the backs of your knees, your groin, back, neck, and armpits, which are all places where ticks are known to bite.

If you are bitten by a tick, remove it immediately. Grasp the tick with sharp-pointed tweezers, as near to your skin as possible, and gently but firmly pull straight out until the tick comes off, then blot the bite with alcohol. Some authorities say to save the tick in alcohol for identification and to make a note of when you were bitten. If the tick's mouthparts break off and remain in your skin, call your doctor to have the pieces removed. Research suggests that ticks must feed for a day in order to transmit Lyme disease, so there is a fairly big margin of safety if you remove the tick promptly.

The main early symptom of Lyme disease is a circular, slowly expanding red rash, often with a clear center, that may appear a few days or as long as two months after being bitten by an infected tick. Flu-like symptoms are also common, perhaps accompanied by headache, swollen glands, a stiff neck, fever, muscle aches, nausea, and general malaise. If you develop any of these symptoms after being bitten by a tick, see your doctor promptly so that one of a variety of blood tests can be conducted. Don't put it off, because Lyme disease in its early stages is easily treated with some antibiotics.

1

GUNPOWDER FALLS STATE PARK

Hereford Area: Gunpowder South and North Trails

As shown on **Map 2** on page 21, a circuit of 10.5-miles (16.8 kilometers) follows the valley of Big Gunpowder Falls at the Hereford Area north of Baltimore. This is the region's best opportunity for a long walk that does not require retracing your steps to get back to your car. Sometimes the route follows the Big Gunpowder's bank, and at other times the trail climbs high above the river along the side and rim of the valley. With its wooded bluffs, rock outcrops, and dramatic twists and turns, the gorge provides constant variety. Of course, you can shorten the trip by crossing the river at Masemore Road or York Road, but why would you want to do that? If it's a shorter walk you're looking for, Chapters 2 and 3 discuss other outings at the Hereford Area.

The Hereford Area is open daily from sunrise to sunset. Dogs must be leashed. The park is managed by the Department of Natural Resources, Maryland Forest, Park and Wildlife Service; telephone (410) 592-2897.

For automobile directions, please turn to page 20. Walking directions are on pages 20-23.

LONG STRETCHES of Big and Little Gunpowder Falls have been developed into a linear park. Most of the park follows the valley of Big Gunpowder Falls diagonally across Baltimore County from northwest to southeast—from just below Prettyboy Reservoir to the river's mouth at Chesapeake Bay. Another arm follows the roughly parallel course of Little Gunpowder Falls, which forms the boundary between Baltimore and Harford Counties. Some sections of the park, notably at Hereford, provide an outstanding opportunity for walking in a rocky and wild setting.

Compared to Baltimore City's basic park system, which was created about the turn of the century, Gunpowder Falls State Park is relatively new, having been planned and acquired in response to the rapid suburbanization of Baltimore County after World War II. Since 1958, when the Maryland State Planning Commission first recommended a system of unconnected parks along both branches of Gunpowder Falls, the state has acquired nearly 15,000 acres for the project, plus more land at other areas, including the Northern Central Railroad, North Point, and Hart and Miller Islands, all of which are administered through Gunpowder Falls State Park.

With the exception of the Hammerman Area, which has many large parking lots and swimming and picnicking facilities for thousands of people, most of Gunpowder Falls State Park is undeveloped for uses other than hiking, horseback riding, and fishing. Some areas have been designated as "wildlands," meaning that except for trails, there is to be no development at all. Visitors to the Hereford Area in particular (which I think is a model of what a wilderness-style, stream-valley park should be) would never guess at the many years of controversy, of planning and reconsideration, and of patient negotiation and compromise that have gone into creating the simple and beautiful park seen today.

Although highly popular with the general public, state park projects are often the subject of vociferous local opposition. For example, when the immensely successful Northern Central Railroad Trail was being planned in the mid-1980s, several hundred people residing near the old railroad right-of-way signed a petition to quash the project on the grounds that it would increase traffic, noise, litter, and crime in their vicinity. At hearings in the early 1990s on the plan for North Point State Park, many residents expressed dismay and outrage that the state would spend tax money to attract *outsiders* from the city to their remote bayside corner of Baltimore County. As one speaker at a similar hearing on the development of the Hereford Area of Gunpowder Falls State Park once asked, "Why can't they go to places that are *closer in?*"

By holding a series of public hearings—sometimes occurring

over a period of years—and enlisting the suggestions and cooperation of a local citizens advisory committee, the state's park planners try to diffuse prejudice and to address legitimate concerns and requests. If nearby residents feel that they are not being adequately consulted, however, the reaction can be sharp. In 1977, when the Maryland Park Service tried to develop an equestrian center and a large complex of picnic pavilions and toilets for three thousand visitors at Bunker Hill Road in the heart of the Gunpowder's Hereford Area, local residents formed a group called the Northern Baltimore County Citizens Committee and, with the help of their state senator, succeeded in having funds for the project deleted from the state's budget. They pointed out, accurately, that smaller crowds were already problematic at Bunker Hill, where gatherings sometimes continued into the night and where the covered bridge that once spanned the river had been burned down. When the state put forward a new park plan in 1978, the Northern Baltimore County group attacked it too, and then, at the invitation of the Secretary of the Department of Natural Resources, prepared its *own* park plan for the Hereford Area.

In the fall of 1979 the Northern Baltimore County Citizens Committee released its counter-plan, and during the following year a series of meetings were held to resolve, point by point, the differences between it and the state's plan. No proposed structure or improvement was too small for scrutiny. Among the issues debated was whether toilets should be built at the parking lots upstream from Bunker Hill (suggested by the park planners but opposed by the community), whether parking lots should be provided near bridges downstream from Bunker Hill (opposed by the community), and whether camping should be allowed at Bunker Hill (again opposed by residents of the area). A local bow-and-arrow club wanted an archery range, and joggers suggested that an exercise course be built. Owners on Bunker Hill Road wanted a new access road to bypass their houses that occupy small inholdings within the park. An entire meeting was devoted to canoeists and "tubers"—kids of all ages who float down the river in inner tubes. Local fishing groups, which by this time had joined the fray, wanted part of the river closed to boats. Even owners of streamside property below the park took the occasion to complain of canoeists and tubers trespassing on what they viewed as their river and wanted to know what the Department of Natural Resources was going to do about it. Finally, there was much ado about picnicking. The Department of Natural Resources favored building group picnic pavilions at Bunker Hill, but the citizens committee adamantly opposed any feature that might attract partying crowds, produce litter, provide targets for vandals, or detract from the natural appearance of the park.

Although trying for all concerned, this lengthy process of negotiation has resulted in a substantially better park at Hereford than either the state or the Northern Baltimore County Citizens Committee would have arrived at on its own. All the essential ingredients for public use of the area are present. And absent—happily—are over-designed and inappropriate features that were contemplated at one time or another. In addition to the main parking lots on both sides of the river at Bunker Hill Road (where there is no longer an automobile bridge), smaller lots have been developed at the four roads that cross the river. Contributing to the park's low-keyed tone and natural appearance is the fact that all the parking lots are paved with gravel rather than asphalt. Bunker Hill Road has been maintained as a narrow country lane rather than upgraded to the exalted and sometimes ridiculous standards seen at other state parks. Camping by supervised youth groups is permitted at Bunker Hill, and areas of grass accommodate any number of picnickers without marring the scene with playground equipment and cookie-cutter pavilions. Stocked with trout, the river attracts fishermen from throughout the region, and canoeists and tubers float down the stream without troubling anyone. An archery range has been tucked away in a corner. Finally, at the Hereford Area a network of hiking trails traverses more than 3,300 acres of twisting gorge, tributary ravines, and adjacent highlands.

ACQUIRING THIS LAND for public use is another facet of the protracted process of park creation. The work begins as soon as the proposed boundary is approved by the Secretary of the Department of Natural Resources and may continue for decades as funds become available, as negotiations mature, as unanticipated opportunities present themselves, as some parcels are lost to development, and as the boundary (or "take line") is changed to include more land—or at any rate different land—than was originally planned. It is a painstaking and sometimes painful process. So far Gunpowder Falls State Park has been pieced together from about four hundred different parcels. Most owners, particularly owners of vacant, unproductive valley slopes, have been amenable to selling, but some unhappiness is inevitable when the states sets out to purchase nearly 25 square miles and as many as three dozen houses—although the state tries to avoid buying houses unless absolutely necessary for a viable park.

Price, of course, is the principal issue. To protect the interests of both the property owner and the state, the Department of General Services, the agency that handles land acquisition for Maryland's parks, is required to hire two independent appraisers to make separate determinations of fair market value of each property. The appraisals are reviewed by the Department's staff and if one or the other is approved, an offer in that amount is made to the owner. Sometimes a third appraisal is necessary if the first two figures are far apart, for the evaluation of real estate is not a precise technique. Occasionally an owner will obtain yet another appraisal which may convince the state's reviewers and the Board of Public Works (which must approve all acquisitions) that a higher price is justified.

If a price cannot be agreed upon, the Department of General Services in consultation with the Department of Natural Resources may simply wait in order to try again later with a new appraisal and offer. Or, in a very few cases, the matter may be turned over to the Attorney General's Office for condemnation, so that eventually the value of the property is determined in court unless the case is first settled by agreement. If the state declines to pay the amount set by the judge or jury and instead abandons the acquisition, the owner's legal costs are paid by the state. Sometimes where title to the land is clouded, the state will condemn the property simply to obtain a clear title.

The procedural safeguards of appraisal and condemnation are intended, of course, to provide a neutral determination of fair market value. For some properties, however, a price may be *fair* but nonetheless *inadequate*. For example, if forced to sell for fair market value, the owner of an unusually small house or a dilapidated or substandard house may not be able to buy another home in his community for what his own is worth. The result is a dilemma that, for a period, was an impasse in the acquisition of some such properties for Gunpowder Falls State Park. In 1979, however, when the Gunpowder project began to receive federal funds, the payment of relocation assistance became mandatory under federal law to help displaced residents find decent homes. Also, state aid has long been available to cover actual moving costs.

For some owners, however, the problem has not been price but preference: a simple desire to stay where they are. These cases have dragged on for years until only the most difficult are left, often involving holdings entirely surrounded by park property or wedges of private ownership penetrating deep into the park. In some cases the state has not pressed the issue, partly because requiring people to sell their houses generates bad public relations, and also because condemnation typically results in above-average prices. In a few cases the Department of General Services has tried to reach a variety of arrangements with people who do not want to move from their homes or established businesses. Elderly owners have been offered a life license under which the state acquires the property outright for its full value while the former owners retain the privilege to occupy the house for the rest of their lives. They maintain and insure the property but pay no taxes or rent. Another option is a life estate, which requires that the purchase price be reduced by the value of the sellers' right of continued occupancy, as estimated by their life expectancy. If they live longer, they in effect get a windfall; if they die early, the state gets a windfall. Owners of the life estate continue to pay property taxes. Finally, in some cases the state has bought houses or farms and then leased them back to the former owners. This is an arrangement that has been attractive to owners who are approaching retirement but want to continue to farm their land for a few more years. The state, too, finds purchase-and-leaseback to be attractive because the arrangement enables park authorities to have a large measure of control over how the property is used.

Around the perimeter of the park, the state has had trouble buying parts of individual holdings needed to form a readily identifiable boundary that bears an intelligent relationship to the topography of the area and to local roads. Owners have sometimes complained that their "back yards" are being taken—that is, tracts stretching hundreds of feet into the woods behind their houses. With these owners, the Department of General Services has increasingly made use of a variety of affirmative and negative easements. The former allows certain public uses of the land and the latter prohibits development or logging. All of these techniques not only ease the acquisition process but also reduce the state's purchase expenses and maintenance costs. Also, as time passes, landowners discover that having a state park for a neighbor is not the nuisance they initially feared but rather increases their property values substantially.

Finally, there is the issue of funding for the acquisition and development of Maryland's state parks. The principal source is Program Open Space, enacted in 1969 and funded by the state tax of 0.5 percent on the transfer of title to real estate. However, over the years the state legislature has often diverted a large part of this revenue to the general fund. At the same time, various new initiatives, also funded by Program Open Space, have been established to preserve agricultural land, historic sites, and natural areas, often through the purchase of restrictive easements. These are all worthy programs, but they are no substitute for state parks, which are open for use by the public. Presently, all transfer tax revenue goes to one or another land preservation program, but less than 20 percent is allocated to the acquisition of land for state parks. All too often tracts of land that would make valuable additions to these parks have come on the market and been lost permanently to residential or commercial development because the public money to buy them was not available. When this sort of thing happens, it is a double misfortune. Not only is the land in question lost to the park, but its development for other purposes often renders the remaining park—on which the state has already spent tens of millions of dollars—less coherent, less usable, less manageable, and less attractive. As has been done on a few occasions in the past, it would make good sense to issue bonds to purchase land now before parcels that have been identified for inclusion in state parks are lost to development or before the price soars as suburbia spreads.

≈   ≈   ≈   ≈

AUTOMOBILE DIRECTIONS: The Hereford Area of **Gunpowder Falls State Park** is located about 20 miles north of Baltimore. (See •1 on **Map 1** on page 5.) The following directions lead to the large parking lot at Bunker Hill Road.

To the Hereford Area of Gunpowder Falls State Park from Interstate 695 (the Baltimore Beltway): Leave I-695 at Exit 24 for Interstate 83 north toward Timonium and York, PA. Go 12.3 miles, then follow the directions in the next paragraph.

To the Hereford Area of Gunpowder Falls State Park from Interstate 83 (the Harrisburg Expressway): Leave I-83 at Exit 27 for Route 137 (Mt. Carmel Road) and Hereford, shown at the bottom-center of **Map 2** at right. From the top of the exit ramp, follow Route 137 east 0.4 mile to a T-intersection with Route 45 (York Road). Turn left onto Route 45 and go north 0.9 mile to an intersection with Bunker Hill Road on the left. Turn left onto Bunker Hill Road and follow it 1 mile to the parking lot next to Big Gunpowder Falls.

If the parking lot at Bunker Hill Road is full, you can try other lots located where roads cross the river. Each is a fine place to join the circuit outlined on the map.

≈   ≈   ≈   ≈

WALKING: Map 2 at right shows a strenuous 10.5-mile circuit through nearly the entire length of the **Hereford Area of Gunpowder Falls State Park**.

Start by locating the **Gunpowder South Trail**. It is marked with white blazes and crosses Bunker Hill Road a few yards uphill from the parking lot. With your back to the river and the parking lot, bear right onto the white-blazed Gunpowder South Trail. Follow it obliquely uphill and straight through a stand of pines at the top of the slope. Pass a junction with the Bunker Hill Trail (blue blazes) and continue straight downhill on the white-blazed Gunpowder South Trail. Cross a stream (Mingo Branch) and turn left. Zigzag uphill, then continue along the top of a broad ridge between the valley of Mingo Branch on the left and the valley of Big Gunpowder Falls on the right. At an inter-

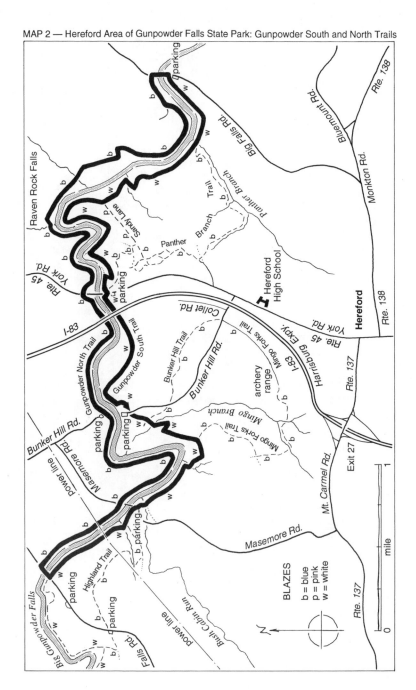

21

section with the Mingo Forks Trail (blue blazes), bear right and go downhill on the white-blazed Gunpowder South Trail. Descend along a ravine, then cross a stream and continue to the bank of Big Gunpowder Falls. With the river on your right, follow the white-blazed path upstream to Masemore Road. Be alert for places where the path is being undermined by erosion.

From the south (or near) end of the Masemore Road bridge, head upstream with the river on your right. At a junction with the Highland Trail (blue blazes), fork right to continue along the river on the white-blazed Gunpowder South Trail to Falls Road.

Cross the bridge at Falls Road and turn downstream on the blue-blazed **Gunpowder North Trail**. Pick you way across a slope of jumbled boulders, where the path is somewhat obscure. With the river on your right, continue for nearly 3 miles downstream past Masemore Road and Bunker Hill Road and under the Interstate 83 bridges. At York Road turn away from the river and climb obliquely up the road embankment. With caution, cross the road.

Continue downstream from York Road on the blue-blazed Gunpowder North Trail, which for the first two hundred yards is difficult and obscure, but then descends to the river's edge. After nearly a mile, the trail passes the foot of a long cascade called Raven Rock Falls, shown in the photograph at left. As the blue-blazed trail continues downstream, it is sometimes distant from the river. For example, after crossing a stream at the bottom of a wide ravine, the trail climbs steeply up a slope covered with mountain laurel, then descends, climbs again, and zigzags down to the river's edge. Continue downstream. Eventually, the blue-blazed trail joins a gravel road. With the river on your right, follow the gravel road to Big Falls Road.

With caution, cross the bridge at Big Falls Road, then turn right upstream on the white-blazed **Gunpowder South Trail**. At times the trail climbs away from the river in order to avoid difficult or even impassable terrain next to the stream, so stick to the white-blazed path, which winds its way for 2 miles to York Road. Along the way, you will pass junctions with the Panther Branch Trail (blue blazes), Sandy Lane (pink blazes), and again (just before York Road), the Panther Branch Trail.

With caution, cross York Road and continue upstream next to the river on the white-blazed Gunpowder South Trail. After passing under the Interstate 83 bridges, the trail climbs obliquely high up the side of the valley, then descends to the meadow and parking lot at Bunker Hill Road.

2

GUNPOWDER FALLS STATE PARK

West Hereford: Gunpowder South Trail, Highland Trail, and Mingo Forks Trail

Map 3 on page 29 shows a walk of 5 miles (8 kilometers) at the Hereford Area of Gunpowder Falls State Park north of Baltimore. Starting at Bunker Hill Road, the route explores the rocky gorge upstream, where well-marked footpaths wind along the valley slopes, ridge tops, and river bank. For half a mile above Falls Road, the trail is fairly rugged as it passes through an area of large, jumbled rocks.

If you want a somewhat longer walk, the dotted line on Map 3 shows an alternative route that adds about 2 miles as you return to Bunker Hill Road. For a still longer walk in the Hereford Area, see Chapter 1.

The Hereford Area is open daily from sunrise to sunset. Dogs must be leashed. The park is managed by the Department of Natural Resources, Maryland Forest, Park and Wildlife Service; telephone (410) 592-2897.

For automobile directions, please turn to page 28. Walking directions start on page 30.

IN COMMON PARLANCE in these parts, Baltimore is "Bawlamer." A brief lexicon of other Bawlamer locutions, such as "Merlin" for Maryland, "Naplis" for our state capital, "Anna Runnel" and "Harrid" for two of our nearby counties, and "Droodle" for Druid Hill, is contained in the urban guidebook *Bawlamer*, published by the Citizens Planning and Housing Association. Less well-known, however, is that our Baltimore dialect is marked by other geographic expressions that are peculiar not for pronunciation but for usage.

Heading the list is *falls,* as in Big Gunpowder Falls. The focus of the present chapter, of course, is not a local cataract. According to William B. Mayre, a Maryland historian who made a specialty of place-names, court records, and old documents of every variety, Baltimore City and Baltimore County are the only area in the United States where there are whole freshwater rivers and streams termed *falls.* Apparently early settlers along the tidal shores of the Gunpowder River and the Patapsco River (or rather "Patapsico," in our local patois) called the streams above tidewater the falls of those rivers. And, of course, compared to tidewater, they do fall and were often dammed and harnessed for waterpower. Hence Big Gunpowder Falls and, for the smaller stream to the north, Little Gunpowder Falls, both of which empty into the tidal Gunpowder River. In Baltimore City, Jones Falls and Gwynns Falls flow into the tidal Patapsco River. Similarly, old maps and other documents call the Patapsco's freshwater section Patapsco *Falls.* For example, an early nineteenth-century print in the possession of the Maryland Historical Society depicts the original mill at Oella opposite Ellicott City and states on its face: "Union Manufactories of Maryland on Patapsco Falls, Baltimore County."

While major freshwater rivers in Baltimore City and Baltimore County are *falls,* the word *run* is used for smaller streams and *branch* for minor ones. Baltimore City has Stony Run, Chinquapin Run, Herring Run, and other runs. As noted in the walking directions at the end of this chapter, two of the tributary streams feeding Big Gunpowder Falls in the Hereford Area are Bush Cabin Run and Mingo Branch, and the walk in the next chapter passes Panther Branch.

Then there is the word *creek,* which is reserved for small tidal rivers. Thus, off the Patapsco River there are Curtis Creek and Bear Creek, among others. And off the creeks branch still smaller creeks, *coves,* and *guts*—this last for especially narrow, serpentine appendages. There is, however, in Baltimore County the anomaly of one *freshwater* stream termed a *creek.* Can you identify it? For the answer, turn to page 31.

Finally, consider the absence of the word *brook,* which has no historical standing here. Mr. Mayre dismisses the term as "literary" and utterly foreign to our area. It is virtually never

seen in old deeds or other documents and appears only in the contrived names given in recent years to housing subdivisions and suburban cul-de-sacs.

So much for *falls* and other riverine terms, but what about "Gunpowder"? The name occurs not only in Big and Little Gunpowder Falls but also in Gunpowder Neck. Although most accounts assume that the name originated with mills where charcoal, sulfur, and saltpeter were ground and mixed to make gunpowder, *The Traveller's Directory, or A Pocket Companion to the Philadelphia-Baltimore Road*, published in 1802, gives a more entertaining even if legendary explanation:

> Great Gunpowder River—Between this and Bush River is Gunpowder Neck, so named from a tradition that the Indians, who formerly lived in this tract, when first acquainted with the use of gunpowder, supposed it to be a vegetable seed; they purchased a quantity and sowed it on this neck, expecting it to produce a good crop.

≈   ≈   ≈   ≈

AUTOMOBILE DIRECTIONS: The Hereford Area of Gunpowder Falls State Park is located about 20 miles north of Baltimore. (See •2 on **Map 1** on page 5. For greater detail, refer to the small corner panel of **Map 3** at right.) The following directions lead to the large parking lot at Bunker Hill Road.

To the Hereford Area of Gunpowder Falls State Park from Interstate 695 (the Baltimore Beltway): Leave I-695 at Exit 24 for Interstate 83 north toward Timonium and York, PA. Go 12.3 miles, then follow the directions in the next paragraph.

To the Hereford Area of Gunpowder Falls State Park from Interstate 83 (the Harrisburg Expressway): Leave I-83 at Exit 27 for Route 137 (Mt. Carmel Road) and Hereford. From the top of the exit ramp, follow Route 137 east 0.4 mile to a T-intersection with Route 45 (York Road). Turn left onto Route 45 and go north 0.9 mile to an intersection with Bunker Hill Road on the left. Turn left onto Bunker Hill Road and follow it 1 mile to the large parking lot next to Big Gunpowder

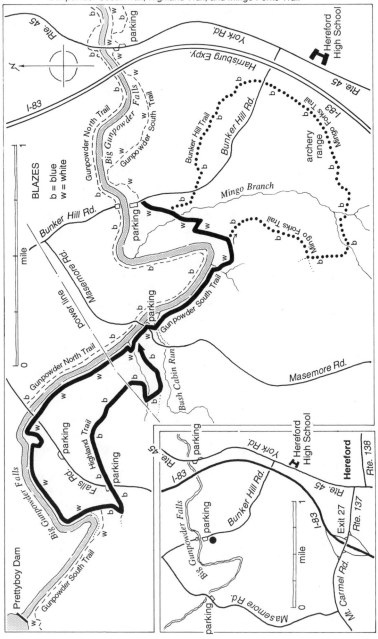

Falls. If the parking lot is full, you can try the lot where Masemore Road crosses the river, as shown on Map 3.

≈   ≈   ≈   ≈

WALKING: Map 3 on page 29 shows a 5-mile route in the western half of the **Hereford Area of Gunpowder Falls State Park**.

Start by locating the **Gunpowder South Trail**. It is marked with white blazes and crosses Bunker Hill Road a few yards uphill from the parking lot. With your back to the river and the parking lot, bear right onto the white-blazed Gunpowder South Trail. Follow it obliquely uphill and straight through a stand of pines at the top of the slope. Pass a junction with the Bunker Hill Trail (blue blazes) and continue straight downhill on the white-blazed Gunpowder South Trail. Cross a stream (Mingo Branch) and turn left. Zigzag uphill, then continue along the top of a broad ridge between the valley of Mingo Branch on the left and the valley of Big Gunpowder Falls on the right. At an intersection with the Mingo Forks Trail (blue blazes), bear right and go downhill on the white-blazed Gunpowder South Trail. Descend along a ravine, then cross a stream and continue to the bank of Big Gunpowder Falls. With the river on your right, follow the white-blazed path upstream to Masemore Road, just beyond a footbridge over Bush Cabin Run. Be alert for places where the path is being undermined by erosion.

From the south (or near) end of the Masemore Road bridge, head upstream with the river on your right. At a junction with the Highland Trail (blue blazes), fork right to continue along the river on the white-blazed Gunpowder South Trail, which leads eventually to Falls Road.

Cross Falls Road and continue upstream with the river on your right. After just 90 yards, watch for a somewhat obscure junction where the white-blazed trail turns left and climbs high up the side of the valley, then descends to the river's edge. (This detour bypasses a large rock formation where the riverside path is precarious.) Farther upstream, follow the white blazes through a long area of jumbled rocks. Eventually, the riverside path becomes smoother as the valley bends left sharply. Then, as the valley begins to turn right, fork left uphill on the white-blazed trail. Follow the white blazes obliquely uphill 150 yards to the intersection with the **Highland Trail** (blue blazes).

Leave the white-blazed Gunpowder South Trail and continue uphill on the blue-blazed Highland Trail. (Or, if you want, you can follow the white-blazed trail to the base of Prettyboy Dam, shown on page 27, then retrace your steps to the Highland Trail. The distance to the dam and back to the Highland Trail is 1.5 miles.)

Follow the blue-blazed Highland Trail uphill, at one point turning left where another trail intersects from the right. Cross Falls Road and pursue the blue blazes past a steel gate and into the woods. Eventually, cross a right-of-way under high electric transmission lines and re-enter the woods. Descend to a stream, then follow it uphill. Cross the stream just short of the power line right-of-way. Turn left and climb to an intersection with another path. Bear left and follow the blue-blazed Highland Trail gradually downhill to the white-blazed **Gunpowder South Trail** next to the river. With the river on your left, bear right downstream and continue to Masemore Road.

From Masemore Road, follow the white-blazed Gunpowder South Trail back to Bunker Hill Road by the way you came at the outset. Or, for variety, you can take the detour indicated by the dotted line on Map 3, which adds about 2 miles. For this longer route, leave the white-blazed trail in order to follow the blue-blazed **Mingo Forks Trail**. Eventually, descend from the upland into the wooded ravine at the head of Mingo Branch, then pursue the blue blazes uphill past an archery range and along a gravel road. Cross Bunker Hill Road near Interstate 83. Descend straight into the woods and follow the blue-blazed **Bunker Hill Trail** gradually downhill through ravines. Again, cross Bunker Hill Road and continue to an intersection with the white-blazed **Gunpowder South Trail**. Turn right and follow the white blazes to the parking lot where you started.

Answer from page 26: Deer Creek, most of which flows through Harford County, extends into northern Baltimore County.

3

GUNPOWDER FALLS STATE PARK

East Hereford: Gunpowder South Trail and Panther Branch Trail

Map 4 on page 37 shows a walk of 4.5 miles (7.2 kilometers) in the Hereford Area of Gunpowder Falls State Park north of Baltimore. Starting at York Road, the route follows a well-marked footpath downstream along a wild and winding stretch of river to Panther Branch, then returns through woods and former farmland above the valley.

The Hereford Area is open daily from sunrise to sunset. Dogs must be leashed. The park is managed by the Department of Natural Resources, Maryland Forest, Park and Wildlife Service; telephone (410) 592-2897.

For automobile directions, please turn to page 36. Walking directions are on pages 36-39.

IN WHAT SORT OF SETTING would you expect to find a beech tree? Sycamore? Virginia pine? Elm? Field guides contain this sort of information, but far more fun is simply to see for yourself. Every outing is an opportunity to practice the visual habit of relating different species of trees to the settings where they typically grow.

Some species are so tolerant in their moisture, soil, and sunlight requirements that they are very broadly distributed. Examples are red, black, and white oak and several species of hickory (shagbark, mockernut, pignut, and bitternut). Together with yellow-poplar (also called tuliptree), these are the main forest trees in the mid-Atlantic region. Sometimes termed sprout hardwoods, they often occur with two, three, or even four trunks, indicating that they grew from suckers emerging from the stumps

What is this? Answer on page 34.   33

or roots of older trees that were cut down or burned. Also common in upland areas are sweet birch, black cherry, and blue ash. Where conditions are moderately wet, red maple, boxelder, American basswood, black tupelo (or blackgum), devils-walk-ingstick, green ash, and slippery elm join the mix. Beech, which has a very shallow root system, favors moist, rich soils of uplands and well-drained lowlands, where it often forms pure stands. Somewhat drier conditions are good for chestnut oak, post oak, blackjack oak, and scarlet oak. All these species can occupy both the canopy and the understory in different combinations or associations.

Some small trees, including witch-hazel, redbud, dogwood, and holly, rarely escape the understory. Allegheny service-berry (or shadbush) occurs in forest borders, where its five-petaled flowers are conspicuous early in spring.

Sometimes forming pure stands in areas of sandy loam, several species of pine—mainly shortleaf, longleaf, loblolly, white, and Virginia pines—occur naturally in eastern Maryland, but often too they are seen in plantations for timber, pulpwood, or watershed protection. White pines, of course, are also a popular ornamental tree and visual buffer. Sun-loving and fast-growing, pines may occur in stands where farm fields have been abandoned and colonized by seedlings. Pine forests, however, are not self-sustaining; the canopy of full-grown pines prevents light from reaching the shade-intolerant pine seedlings. Instead, it is hardwood saplings that establish themselves in the understory, then make a spurt of growth in the sun when the mature pines die or are cut or blown down.

Formerly, the dominance of oaks, hickories, and yellow-poplar in the mid-Atlantic region was shared by American chestnut, but early in the twentieth century all mature American chestnut trees were killed by chestnut blight, a fungus that affects the bark. The disease continues to kill chestnut saplings as they sprout from old root systems, but only after the new growth reaches a height of ten or twenty feet and an inch or two in diameter.

Some species of trees are especially opportunistic. Shortleaf and largeleaf pines, quaking aspen, and pin cherry quickly re-seed burned areas. Eastern redcedar, chokecherry, staghorn sumac, common persimmon, sassafras, black locust, and sweetgum

On page 32: Tree trunk stripped of its bark by beavers.

are among the first trees, along with pines, to grow in abandoned fields. Later, after these areas are taken over by large deciduous trees, some mature pines may remain scattered through the woods. The understory may include a few scraggly redcedars struggling to survive in the dim light, perhaps marking where once there were fence rows separating fields.

Some trees find a niche in extreme conditions. Virginia pine, redcedar, scrub (or bear) oak, and gray birch are among the few species that can tolerate the meager soil and rocky hilltops of our region's serpentine barrens, as described in Chapter 13. Actually, these trees can grow almost anywhere, but they survive over the long run only in areas inhospitable to other trees.

Excessively wet conditions favor certain species of trees, including Atlantic white-cedar, red maple, swamp white oak, water tupelo, and black ash—although all grow in drier settings also. Red maple, in fact, is among the most ubiquitous of trees. Baldcypress, with a fluted, swollen base to its trunk and peculiar "knees" protruding from the water or soil, grows in the Pokomoke River swamps of Maryland's Eastern Shore.

Moist, rich floodplains support many species of trees, including American elm, sweetgum, sycamore, pawpaw, honeylocust, silver maple, white and green ash, holly, and Eastern hophornbeam (or ironwood, which has a fluted, muscular-looking trunk and smooth gray bark). From a hilltop or highway in winter, you can sometimes trace a nearby watercourse simply by the broad swath of white-branched sycamores occupying the floodplain. Such areas also favor a variety of oaks, including overcup oak, water oak, and willow oak. Banks of streams and lakes are often the setting for yet other species, including cottonwood, black willow, American hornbeam, witch-hazel, boxelder, river birch, and smooth alder (usually a shrub with little cones). Cool, shady ravines and moist, north-facing slopes provide a suitable environment for hemlock, often in pure stands with no understory.

Acting over long periods of time, the tendency of each species to thrive in certain settings and to fail or lag in others gives rise to more or less stable associations of trees. The associations blend into one another where the terrain changes gradually, but show sharp demarcations where conditions change abruptly.

However, even as the forest organizes itself along broadly predictable lines, it is often visited with reversals. At any time hurricanes, ice storms, insect infestations, blights, floods, fires, and other such events can undo many decades of maturation and provide the opportunity, here and there, for a new mix of trees and shrubs to establish themselves. These then begin again the process of natural succession that leads eventually to stable plant associations adapted to local conditions and the prevailing climate.

≈   ≈   ≈   ≈

AUTOMOBILE DIRECTIONS: The Hereford Area of Gunpowder Falls State Park is located about 20 miles north of Baltimore. (See •3 on **Map 1** on page 5. For greater detail, refer to the upper panel of **Map 4** at right.) The following directions lead to parking lots where York Road crosses the river.

To the Hereford Area of Gunpowder Falls State Park from Interstate 695 (the Baltimore Beltway): Leave I-695 at Exit 24 for Interstate 83 north toward Timonium and York, PA. Go 12.3 miles, then follow the directions in the next paragraph.

To the Hereford Area of Gunpowder Falls State Park from Interstate 83 (the Harrisburg Expressway): Leave I-83 at Exit 27 for Route 137 (Mt. Carmel Road) and Hereford. From the top of the exit ramp, follow Route 137 east 0.4 mile to a T-intersection with Route 45 (York Road). Turn left onto Route 45 and go north 1.7 miles. Just before the road crosses the bridge over Big Gunpowder Falls, park in one of the small lots on either side of the road.

If the parking areas are full, you may want to try the larger lot at Bunker Hill Road, then walk 0.9 mile downstream on the white-blazed Gunpowder South Trail to York Road. (See Map 2 on page 21.)

≈   ≈   ≈   ≈

WALKING: The lower panel of **Map 4** at right shows a 4.5-mile route in the eastern half of the **Hereford Area of Gunpowder Falls State Park**.

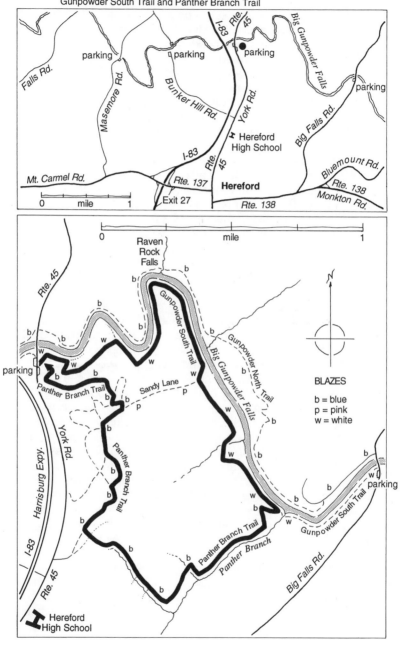

MAP 4 — East Hereford at Gunpowder Falls State Park:
Gunpowder South Trail and Panther Branch Trail

Start at the grassy area that lies east (or downstream) from York Road. The grassy area is reached by wooden steps from the smaller of the two roadside parking lots.

Pick up the white-blazed **Gunpowder South Trail** where it crosses a small stream about 40 yards from the river's edge. Nearby is a stone fireplace. Immediately, fork left at an intersection with Panther Branch Trail (blue blazes), by which you will return at the end of the walk. After about 140 yards, fork right uphill away from the river on the white-blazed trail. Zigzag uphill along the side of the valley. Continue along the crest of the slope, then descend to the bottom of the valley.

With the river on your left, pursue the white blazes downstream, usually near the water but sometimes farther up the side of the valley. Be alert for places where the path is being undermined by erosion. After about a mile, you will pass an intersection with Sandy Lane (pink blazes).

Continue on the white-blazed Gunpowder South Trail through the woods and along the foot of the bluff at a distance from the river. Eventually, follow the path to the right up a ravine, across a stream, then up a smaller ravine and to the left. Continue high above the river, then gradually descend.

Twenty yards before a stream (Panther Branch) joins the river, turn very sharply right onto the **Panther Branch Trail**, which is marked with blue blazes. The trail zigzags uphill over a shoulder and down to the right. For the rest of the walk, follow the blue blazes of the Panther Branch Trail. As you will see if you have sharp eyes, the valley at Panther Branch contains some old stone foundations that may be the ruins of a gristmill and its companion gunpowder mill that blew up on July 7, 1874.

With Panther Branch on your left, follow the blue-blazed path up the valley. Eventually, climb to the right (look for traces of an old millrace on the right) and follow a tributary ravine uphill for 80 yards before turning left to cross a rivulet. Continue above Panther Branch, then curve right up another side ravine. With a very small stream on your left, follow the blue blazes up the ravine and past several paths intersecting from the left. At the head of the ravine, pass through an area that shows the kinds of trees that are the first to grow in former farmland. Continue across a weedy field, more recently abandoned than the area through which you just passed. Cross a rutted track, then (after just a few yards) turn right along the edge of a pine plantation.

Follow the blue-blazed path, which eventually jogs left, then right. Sixty yards after the wide path turns downhill to the left, bear right onto a narrow footpath and pursue the blue blazes downhill through the woods, then up to a path in front of another pine plantation. Follow the path right, then turn right at another trail intersection. Follow the blue blazes as the trail veers left at the next intersection (instead of proceeding straight downhill on pink-blazed Sandy Lane). Turn left again immediately on a narrow footpath through the woods (instead of proceeding straight downhill on the fire lane around the edge of the pines). Follow the footpath for 50 yards, then turn right. Go 30 yards, then bear left onto a narrow footpath. Follow the blazes down a ravine, across a gully, then uphill and along the contour near the rim of the valley. Eventually, descend (with a zig and a zag) to the grassy area by York Road and Big Gunpowder Falls.

4

GUNPOWDER FALLS STATE PARK

Sweet Air Area

The Sweet Air Area is located north of Baltimore City on Little Gunpowder Falls, which forms the boundary between Baltimore County and Harford County. One attraction of the Sweet Air Area is the fact that it includes many large cultivated fields, showing the Piedmont's rolling agricultural landscape at its best. Passing through woods and along farm lanes—and for period following the deep valley of Little Gunpowder Falls—the circuit outlined on **Map 5** on page 49 is 5 miles long (8 kilometers).

The Sweet Air Area is open daily from sunrise to sunset. Dogs must be leashed. The park is managed by the Department of Natural Resources, Maryland Forest, Park and Wildlife Service; telephone (410) 592-2897

For automobile directions, please turn to page 48. Walking directions start on page 50.

WHAT ORNITHOLOGICAL DISTINCTION is shared by Philadelphia, Nashville, Savannah, and Ipswich, Massachusetts? They are the only U.S. municipalities whose names have been given to birds: the Philadelphia vireo, the Nashville warbler, and the Savannah and "Ipswich" sparrows. Perhaps Ipswich should be ousted from this select set, inasmuch as the American Ornithologists' Union has determined that the Ipswich bird is merely a pale race of the Savannah breed. And what about the Baltimore oriole? It was named not for a place but for a family: the Lords Baltimore, colonial proprietors of Maryland. Mark Catesby, an eighteenth-century naturalist, called the oriole the "Baltimore-Bird" because its colors were the same as those of the Baltimores' heraldic flag.

Bird identification is the subject of Chapter 22. This chapter too is wholly bird talk, focusing on the rainy-day pastime of bird names. For example, as a word, *titmouse* is worth a little curiosity. Although a titmouse is easy to identify, how many birders know what the word means? Why is a petrel so called? And what about *killdeer, turnstone, nuthatch, knot,* and other peculiar bird names?

Although many American Indian place names were adopted by the Europeans, the settlers and early ornithologists made a clean sweep when it came to naming—or rather renaming—North American birds. In a few cases where the same species (brant, for instance) were found on both sides of the Atlantic, use of the English name was a matter of course. More often, however, the settlers simply reused the names of Old World birds for similar-looking—but actually different—New World species. The English, for example, have given the name *robin* to various red-breasted birds in India, Australia, and North America. More often still, the use of general names like *wren* was extended to American birds, with the addition of qualifying words to identify individual species (house wren, Carolina wren, and so forth). However, scientific classification has sometimes placed whole categories of American birds in entirely different families than their European namesakes, as in the case of American warblers. The only North American birds in the same family as the European warblers are the gnatcatcher and kinglets—not at all what are called warblers here. Finally, in relatively rare instances, American birds have been given unique and colorful new names based on their behavior, appearance, and songs, as, for instance, the yellow-bellied sapsucker, canvasback, and whip-poor-will.

Early American ornithologists seem to have been quite casual about naming birds. Alexander Wilson (1766-1813), author of the nine-volume *American Ornithology,* once shot a bird in a magnolia tree; hence, *magnolia warbler* for a bird whose preferred habitat is low, moist conifers. After Wilson's death his work was overshadowed by Audubon's superior, life-sized drawings, but Wilson was in many ways the greater pioneer, depicting 264 species of birds, of which 39 were not previously known. Usually Wilson named birds according to the locality where his specimens were collected. He named the Nashville warbler and the Savannah sparrow, but not the Philadelphia vireo. (It was named by naturalist Charles Lucien Jules Laurent Bonaparte, Prince of Canino and Musignano, a nephew of Napoleon Bonaparte and presumably an authority on names.)

Not surprisingly, many of the geographic names given to birds by early ornithologists bear no precise relation to the species' breeding territory or winter range. The Savannah sparrow, for example, is found throughout North America and might just as well have been named for Chicago or Seattle or even Anchorage. Among the Tennessee, Connecticut, and Kentucky warblers (all named by Wilson), only the last is at all likely to be found in its nominal state during the breeding season, and none winter north of Mexico. But probably the greatest geographical misnomer among bird names is our native turkey, after the supposed region of its origin. The name was first applied to the guinea cock, which was imported from Africa through Turkey into Europe and with which the American bird was for a time identified when it was first introduced to Europe in about 1530.

Some bird names, although seeming to refer to specific geographic areas, are actually far broader in their historical meaning. *Louisiana* in Louisiana heron refers to the vast territory of the Louisiana Purchase, even though the bird is usually found only in coastal areas. The species was first collected on the Louis and Clark expedition and was named by Wilson. *Arcadia*, as in Arcadian flycatcher, is an old French name for Nova Scotia, but the term was used generally to suggest a northern clime, as was also *boreal* in boreal chickadee, from the Greek god of the north wind, Boreas.

In addition to birds named *by* early ornithologists and explorers, there are birds named *for* them by contemporary and later admirers of their work. Wilson, for example, is memorialized in the name of a petrel, a phalarope, a plover, a warbler, and also a genus of warblers. Audubon is honored by Audubon's shearwater and "Audubon's" warbler, a form of the yellow-rumped warbler. There was a measure of reciprocity about this last bird name: In 1837 John Kirk Townsend, a Philadelphia ornithologist and bird collector, named "Audubon's" warbler, and a year or two later Audubon returned the favor with Townsend's solitaire. Then there are species named for ornithologists' wives, daughters, and relatives, as in Anna's hummingbird and

Virginia's, Lucy's, and Grace's warblers. Some birds bear human names connected to no one in particular. Guillemot (French for "little William"), magpie (in part based on Margaret), martin ("little Mars"), and parakeet ("little Peter") are thought to be pet names or affectionate tags that have become attached to various species.

Color is probably the dominant theme in bird names. Plumages cover the spectrum, ranging from the red phalarope through the orange-crowned warbler, yellow rail, green heron, blue goose, indigo bunting, and violet-crowned hummingbird. For stripped-down straightforwardness there are names like blue-bird and blackbird. For vividness there are color designations like scarlet tanager, vermilion flycatcher, lazuli bunting, and cerulean warbler. To improve our dictionary skills, there are color-based names like fulvous tree duck, ferruginous hawk, flammulated owl, and parula warbler. For unpoetry, there is hepatic tanager, so called because of the liver-colored, liver-shaped patch on each cheek. For meaninglessness there is the clay-colored sparrow. (What color is that? Answer: buffy brown, at least on the rump.) Some bird names less obviously denote basic hues: vireo (green), oriole (golden), dunlin ("little dull-brown one"), canvasback (for its speckled gray and white back), brant (thought by some to mean "burnt," referring to its black head and neck), and waxwing (whose red-tipped secondary wing feathers recalled to someone the color and substance of sealing wax). A great many bird names pair color with some specific body part, as in redhead, goldeneye, yellowlegs, and so forth.

Shape or other distinctive features often are reflected in bird names. The profile of the bufflehead suggests an American buffalo or bison. The loggerhead shrike has a disproportionately large head. Shovelers have long, broad bills. The word *falcon* is derived from a Latin term for "sickle," suggesting the bird's curved talons. From head to toe, there is a body part that is some bird's nominal identity: tufted titmouse, horned lark, eared grebe (*grebe* itself may come from a Breton word for "crest"), ruffed grouse, pectoral sandpiper (for the air sack under its breast feathers), short-tailed hawk, stilt sandpiper (for its comparatively long legs), rough-legged hawk (for its feathered tarsi), sharp-shinned hawk (it has), semipalmated sandpiper (for its partially webbed feet), and Lapland longspur (for the elongated claw on the hind toe).

Some names indicate size, from *great* and *greater* to *little, lesser,* and *least.* Symmetry would seem to demand a *greatest,* but perhaps that need is filled by *king,* which occasionally refers to stature. The king rail, for example, is the largest of the rails. But sometimes *king* is simply a compliment to a bird's raiment or a reference to distinguishing plumage on its crown, as in the ruby-crowned and golden-crowned kinglets ("little kings"). *Gallinule* itself suggests size, being derived from Latin for "little hen." *Starling* is from the Anglo-Saxon word for bird; with the addition of the diminutive suffix *-ling,* it simply means "little bird." *Titmouse* similarly is a combination of Icelandic and Anglo-Saxon meaning "small bird." The base word *tit* for *bird* also appears in bushtit and wrentit.

A few names, like that of the gull-billed tern, make explicit comparisons with other birds. The hawk owl has a long slender tail that gives this bird a falcon-like appearance. The lark bunting sings on the wing like a skylark, the curlew sandpiper has a downwardly curved, curlew-like bill. The swallow-tailed kite has a deeply forked tail like a barn swallow. The turkey vulture has a head that somewhat resembles that of a turkey. And *cormorant* is derived from French for "sea crow."

Many bird names refer to distinctive behavior. Woodpeckers, sapsuckers, creepers, and wagtails all do what their names suggest. Turnstones do indeed turn over small stones and shells while searching for food. *Black skimmer* describes the bird's technique of sticking its lower bill into the water while flying just above the surface. *Shearwater* similarly suggests the bird's skimming flight. Frigatebirds (also called man-o'-war-birds) were named by sailors for the birds' piratical habit of pursuing and robbing other birds, as do also parasitic jaegers. *Duck* is derived from Anglo-Saxon for "diver." *Nuthatch* is from "nut hack," referring to the bird's technique of wedging a nut into a crevice and then hacking it into small pieces. *Vulture* is akin to Latin *vellere,* "to pluck or tear." The folk name *shitepoke* for various herons is based on these birds' habit of defecating when flushed. Although many people associate *loon* with the bird's lunatic laugh, as in "crazy as a loon," more likely the word is derived from a Norse term for "lame," describing the bird's awkwardness on land—a result of its legs being very near its tail, so that when nesting the loon has to push itself on its stomach. There is, however, at least one North American bird that is named for its mental capacity: the booby. Seamen who raided the isolated colonies thought the birds stupid because they were unaccustomed to predators and inept at protecting themselves. The dotterel (whose name is related to "dolt" and "dotage") is another nominally foolish bird, as is the extinct dodo from Mauritius. Ernest A. Choate, in his fascinating *Dictionary of American Bird Names*, and Edward S. Gruson, in *Words for Birds*, discuss these and other names.

Some birds, such as the whooping crane, clapper rail, piping plover, laughing gull, mourning dove, warbling vireo, and chipping sparrow, are named for how they sound. Similarly, the comparative volume of their vocalizations is the theme that distinguishes between mute, whistling, and trumpeter swans. *Oldsquaw* suggests this duck's noisy, garrulous voice. The catbird mews and the grasshopper sparrow trills and buzzes like the insect. Gruson, however, says that the grasshopper sparrow is named for its diet, as are the goshawk (literally, "goosehawk") and oystercatchers, flycatchers, and gnatcatchers. The saw-whet owl is named for the bird's endlessly repeated note, which suggests a saw being sharpened with a whetstone—a sound now lost to history. The bittern, whose name ultimately is traceable to its call, has a colorful assortment of descriptive folk names, including "bog-bumper," "stake driver," "thunder pumper," and "water belcher." The evening grosbeak and vesper sparrow both tend to sing at dusk. Finally, of course, many birds' songs or calls are also the basis for their names, including the bobolink, bobwhite, bulbul, chachalaca, chickadee, chuckwill's-widow, chukar, crow, cuckoo, curlew, dickcissel, godwit, killdeer, kittiwake, owl, pewee, phoebe, pipits, towhee, veery, whip-poor-will, and willet. *Quail* (like "quack") and *raven* are thought originally to have been imitative of bird calls.

Habitat is a major theme of bird names, as with the surf scoter, sandpiper, seaside sparrow, waterthrush, marsh hawk, meadowlark, wood duck, mountain chickadee, and field, swamp, and tree sparrows. Then there is the *kind* of tree or shrub, as in spruce and sage grouse, willow ptarmigan, pinyon jay, cedar waxwing, myrtle warbler, pine siskin, and orchard

oriole. The barn, cliff, cave, tree, and bank swallows are named for their preferred nesting sites. As noted in Chapter 22, however, *prairie warbler* is a misnomer; the bird is common east of the Mississippi and usually is found in brushy, scrubby areas.

Several bird names are associated with human figures. Knots, which frequent shores and tidal flats, are said to be named for Canute (or Cnut), King of the Danes. To demonstrate to the sycophants of his court that he was not omnipotent, Canute vainly ordered the tide to stop rising. Petrels are thought to be named for Saint Peter, who walked on the water at Lake Gennesaret. When landing in the water, petrels dangle their feet and hesitate for an instant, thus appearing to stand on the waves. Cardinals, of course, are named for the red robes and hats of the churchmen. Similarly, prothonotory warblers have the golden raiment of ecclesiastical prothonotories. The bizarre and contrasting pattern of the harlequin duck suggests the traditional costume of Italian pantomime.

Finally, there is the ovenbird, almost unique among North American birds for being named after the appearance of its nest, which is built on the forest floor and resembles a miniature, domed brick oven. "Basketbird" and "hangnest" are folk names referring to the pendulous nests of orioles.

≈   ≈   ≈   ≈

AUTOMOBILE DIRECTIONS: The Sweet Air Area of Gunpowder Falls State Park is located about 16 miles north of Baltimore. (See •4 on **Map 1** on page 5. For greater detail, refer to the upper panel of **Map 5** at right.) Three approaches—from Interstate 83, Interstate 695 (the Baltimore Beltway), and Interstate 95—are described below.

To the Sweet Air Area from Interstate 83: Leave I-83 at Exit 20A for Shawan Road east toward Cockeysville. Go 0.9 mile to Route 45 (York Road). If the proposed link with Route 145 (Papermill Road) has been constructed, continue straight— but if not, go right 0.3 mile, then turn left onto Ashland Road toward Papermill Road. Continue 5.4 miles, then turn left onto Route 146 (Jarrettsville Pike).

Follow Route 146 north for 3.2 miles, then turn right at a traffic light onto Hess Road. After 1.1 miles, turn sharply right onto

MAP 5 — Sweet Air Area of Gunpowder Falls State Park

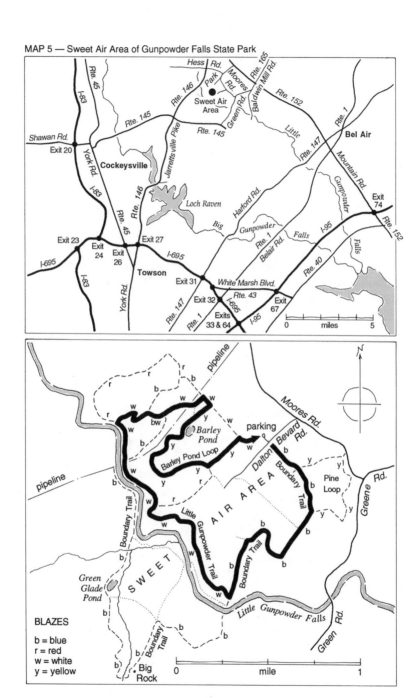

Park Road. Go 0.2 mile, then curve left onto Moores Road. After 0.9 mile, turn sharply right onto Dalton Bevard Road, which leads into the Sweet Air Area of Gunpowder Falls State Park. Go 0.2 mile and then turn right to the parking area—opposite the blue-blazed trailhead on the left.

To the Sweet Air Area from Interstate 695 (the Baltimore Beltway): Leave I-695 at Exit 27A-B for Route 146 northbound. (At first Route 146 is Dulaney Valley Road, but it becomes Jarrettsville Pike after crossing Loch Raven.) Follow Route 146 north for 11.5 miles, then turn right at a traffic light onto Hess Road. After 1.1 miles, turn sharply right onto Park Road. Go 0.2 mile, then curve left onto Moores Road. After 0.9 mile, turn sharply right onto Dalton Bevard Road, which leads into the Sweet Air Area of Gunpowder Falls State Park. Go 0.2 mile and then turn right to the parking area, opposite the blue-blazed trailhead on the left.

To the Sweet Air Area from Interstate 95: Leave I-95 at Exit 74 for Route 152 (Mountain Road). Follow Route 152 north nearly 10 miles to the intersection with Route 165 (Baldwin Mill Road). Turn left and follow Route 165 south just 0.2 mile, then turn right onto Greene Road. After 1.2 miles, turn right onto Moores Road. Go 0.5 mile, then turn left onto Dalton Bevard Road, which leads into the Sweet Air Area of Gunpowder Falls State Park. Go 0.2 mile and then turn right to the parking area, opposite the blue-blazed trailhead on the left.

≈   ≈   ≈   ≈

WALKING: The lower panel of **Map 5** on page 49 shows a circuit of 5 miles via blazed trails through the **Sweet Air Area of Gunpowder Falls State Park**.

Start at the trailhead for the blue-blazed **Boundary Trail**, located on Dalton Bevard Road opposite the entrance to the parking area. Follow the blue blazes up and down through the woods, passing intersections with the yellow-blazed Pine Loop on the left. Pass large fields on the right and houses on the left. Pursue the blue-blazes down to the right, around to the left below a weedy field, and then left into the woods and gradually downhill. Eventually, the blue-blazed trail reaches an intersection with the white-blazed **Little Gunpowder Trail**.

Turn right and follow the narrow, white-blazed trail up and down—and up and down again and again—along the side and rim of the valley, with Little Gunpowder Falls downhill on the left. Continue in and out of several ravines. At one point, pass an intersection with a red-blazed trail. Eventually, descend to the river and follow it upstream. At a pipeline right-of-way, cross the blue-blazed trail and continue upstream on the white-blazed Little Gunpowder Trail.

At an intersection with a trail blazed with red dots, bear right to follow the white blazes up a broad ravine away from the river. At the top of the slope, continue more or less straight as the white-blazed trail is congruent (for awhile) with the blue-blazed path. When the blue-blazed path turns sharply right, stay on the white-blazed trail as it leads left uphill. Pursue the white blazes across a rivulet, again across the pipeline right-of-way, and through scrubby growth to an intersection in front of a house.

Turn right to follow the white blazes toward the parking lot, but after 150 yards, turn sharply right again at the corner of a field in order to follow the yellow-blazed **Barley Pond Loop**. Follow the yellow blazes downhill past the pond, through groves of laurel, and eventually uphill and alongside a field. Bear left where red blazes intersect from the right. Follow the yellow blazes along a row of pines. At a T-intersection, turn right to pursue the white blazes to the parking lot.

5

GUNPOWDER FALLS STATE PARK

Little Gunpowder Trail and Ma & Pa Trail between Bottom Road and Pleasantville Road

Map 6 on page 57 shows a circuit of 4.5 miles (7.2 kilometers) through the remote wooded gorge of Little Gunpowder Falls northeast of Baltimore. Starting at the bridge on aptly named Bottom Road, the route goes upstream on the south side of the river, crosses the bridge at Pleasantville Road, and returns downstream along the north side of the valley before re-crossing the river at Bottom Road. For much of the way, the blazed trails follow the valley's steep slopes, sometimes on footpaths that dip and climb through tributary ravines, and in other sections via the level bed of an old railroad. At the start and end, the route follows local roads for short distances.

The trails are open daily from sunrise to sunset. Dogs must be leashed. The park is managed by the Department of Natural Resources, Maryland Forest, Park and Wildlife Service; telephone (410) 592-2897.

For automobile directions to the starting point at Bottom Road, please turn to page 56. Walking directions start on page 58.

THE TRAILS discussed in this chapter follow, for part of the route, the former railbed of the Maryland & Pennsylvania Railroad, affectionately remembered as the poky but picturesque Ma & Pa. From the passenger station located under the North Avenue bridge at Jones Falls, the line followed the valley of Stony Run gradually uphill through Wyman Park and Roland Park to Towson. From there the Ma & Pa continued to Bel Air in Harford County, then north to Delta in Pennsylvania. From

Delta the railroad ran northwest through Red Lion to York, Pennsylvania. The crescent-shaped route totaled 77 miles, substantially exceeding the more direct 49-mile route of the Northern Central Railroad (featured in Chapter 11). At each end of the line, the Ma & Pa made connections with other railroads—with the Baltimore & Ohio and the Pennsylvania Railroad in Baltimore and again with the Pennsylvania Railroad and the Western Maryland Railroad in York, thus providing dozens of communities and industries along the line with long haul freight service to and from anywhere in the country.

Originally the Ma & Pa was conceived as two entirely separate and unrelated ventures. The first was the Pennsylvania section, chartered in 1868 as the Peach Bottom Railway Company to carry coal from the center of the state to Philadelphia. By 1878 the line's Middle Division operated over narrow-gauge tracks from York to the west bank of the Susquehanna, and on the other side of the river the Eastern Division continued toward Philadelphia, but only as far as Oxford. Except on paper, there never was a Western Division, nor was a bridge built over the Susquehanna. Instead, freight cars were ferried across the river on a flat boat. Financial difficulties in 1881 brought the project to an end. The Middle and Eastern divisions were purchased by separate interests; then the Middle Division was reorganized as the York & Peach Bottom Railway Company.

Meanwhile, a corporation called the Maryland Central Railroad was chartered in 1867 to connect Baltimore and Philadelphia via Bel Air. No construction, however, was undertaken. The company existed only as a speculation until it was rechartered fifteen years later for the purpose of acquiring another Maryland corporation—the Baltimore & Delta Railway Company, which had started building its line in 1880. By 1885 the Maryland Central was operating a narrow-gauge line to Delta, but costs and debt service exceeded income and so the railroad went bankrupt in 1888. After reorganization, the company abandoned the goal of reaching Philadelphia and instead acquired a lease on the York & Peach Bottom Railway, thus combining routes that eventually became the Ma & Pa. Despite formal merger of the lines in 1891, bankruptcy forced their separation two years later. Reorganized and renamed yet again, the roads were operated independently of one another. It was not until 1901, after each part had replaced its narrow-gauge tracks with standard gauge, that they were finally consolidated as the Maryland & Pennsylvania Railroad.

Despite its meandering course that precluded competing successfully for through traffic between Baltimore and York, the Ma & Pa became a modest—a very modest—financial success. It carried farm products from throughout the region, including so much milk that for awhile it was nicknamed the "Milky Way." It also provided mail, freight, and passenger service to 54 communities, including some of middling industrial importance. Spawned by the railroad, there were scores of enterprises, many with their own sidings and a volume of business that justified shipping by the carload. There were also small mineral deposits along the line, plus major quarries at Cardiff, Maryland and Slate Hill, Pennsylvania, to which a spur ran from Delta. In 1926 freight exceeded 400,000 tons, then declined to half that level in the early years of the Great Depression, which the Ma & Pa survived with the help of a loan from the federal government's Reconstruction Finance Corporation. A gradual increase after 1933 became a torrent of traffic during World War II, when gasoline was rationed and industries boomed.

In the decade after the war, tonnage declined as industries turned increasingly to truck transport. Passenger ridership also fell with the declining price of gasoline and the construction of better roads. In 1953 the Ma & Pa began running a deficit. A year later public authorities in Maryland and Pennsylvania and the federal Interstate Commerce Commission approved termination of passenger service. In 1958 the regulatory agencies granted permission for the Ma & Pa to end freight service over half its route, from Baltimore nearly to the boundary with Pennsylvania. After waiting a specified period to see if anyone offered to buy the abandoned line and continue operations, the railroad company sold the track and bridges for salvage. It also sold what land it could, a task made difficult by complicated titles and by clauses in the deeds that restricted uses and even stipulated reversion to prior owners if railroad use stopped. In Pennsylvania the Ma & Pa continued in business and still has some track in operation.

Independently owned and operated, the Ma & Pa was somewhat of an anachronism by the 1940s and '50s. Newspaper articles perennially recounted the pleasures of an outing on the railroad. Reporters on a junket described the old-fashioned friendliness of the staff and the unusually sharp turns, steep grades, spidery wooden trestles, and beautiful river valleys and farmscapes along the line. As compared with the hour-long ride between Baltimore and York on the Northern Central, the Ma & Pa took four hours and its speed rarely exceeded 20 miles per hour. George W. Hilton, author of a history of the Maryland & Pennsylvania Railroad, wrote that "the Ma & Pa was a model railroad at the scale of 12 inches to the foot."

In addition to the sections of railbed followed by this chapter's walk, other remnants of the Ma & Pa are still evident throughout the Baltimore region. The line's demi-roundhouse is located on Falls Road near the Trolley Museum. It is now used by the city's Department of Public Works to hold road salt and to repair vehicles. Nearby is the freight terminal, on which MARYLAND PENNSYLVANIA RAILROAD is painted in large letters. A few hundred yards down Falls Road under the Howard Street bridge, the Ma & Pa connected with other railroads. Homeland Station, now a small residence, stands on Lake Avenue alongside the former railroad bed that still cuts southward through Roland Park and northward past the Elkridge Country Club. Glen Arm Station also survives. And in Towson the line's stone bridge abutments rise on either side of York Road south of the business district.

≈   ≈   ≈   ≈

AUTOMOBILE DIRECTIONS: The trails that border **Little Gunpowder Falls between Bottom Road and Pleasantville Road** are located about 16 miles northeast of Baltimore. (See •5 on **Map 1** on page 5. For greater detail, refer to the corner panel of **Map 6** at right.)

The walk starts at Bottom Road. Two approaches to this spot, one from Interstate 695 (the Baltimore Beltway) and the other from Interstate 95, are described below.

To Bottom Road from Interstate 695 (the Baltimore Beltway): Leave I-695 at Exit 31B for Route 147 (Harford Road) north toward Carney. Go 7.8 miles, then turn left at a

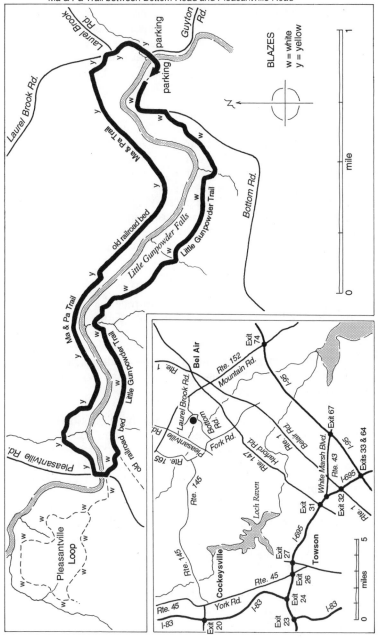

traffic light onto Fork Road. After 1.7 miles, turn right onto Bottom Road and go 2.1 miles, descending steeply toward the end. At the bottom of the valley, there are several small parking areas on the right side of the road. If they are full, cross the bridge and immediately turn right onto Guyton Road, where there are some more parking areas by the river.

To Bottom Road from Interstate 95: Leave I-95 at Exit 74 for Route 152 (Mountain Road). Follow Route 152 north 4.7 miles to the intersection with Route 147 (Harford Road). Turn left and follow Route 147 south 3.3 miles, then turn right onto Fork Road. After 1.7 miles, turn right onto Bottom Road and go 2.1 miles, descending steeply toward the end. At the bottom of the valley, there are several small parking areas on the right side of the road. If they are full, cross the bridge and immediately turn right onto Guyton Road, where there are some more parking areas by the river.

≈ ≈ ≈ ≈

WALKING: Map 6 on page 57 shows a circuit of 4.5 miles along both sides of **Little Gunpowder Falls between the bridges at Bottom Road and Pleasantville Road.** The path along the south side of the valley is the white-blazed Little Gunpowder Trail, and the path along the north side is the yellow-blazed Ma & Pa Trail—so named for the old railroad discussed beginning on page 53.

The first thing to do is to make sure that the bridge at Bottom Road is intact. (For several years it was closed, but should be open again by the time this book goes to press.) It would be a tiresome thing to complete 99 percent of the circuit only to discover at the end that you could not cross the Bottom Road bridge.

Start at the Bottom Road bridge. With the river on the right, follow **Bottom Road** upstream and then steeply uphill. Notice the white blazes by the side of the road. About 130 yards after the road curves left, the white-blazed trail veers right into the woods and along the side of the valley.

With the river toward the right, follow the white-blazed **Little Gunpowder Trail** up and down through tributary ravines and valleys. After a mile, the path joins an old railroad bed, which leads left through a cut. Follow the old railbed, now and again detouring to bypass missing trestles or sodden cuts. Eventually, descend to the right to Pleasantville Road.

Cross the river at Pleasantville Road and turn right to follow the yellow-blazed **Ma & Pa Trail** downstream. Soon, climb steeply left, then descend and climb again through a tributary ravine and along the side of the main valley. Descend gradually to the river's edge and continue downstream. Thirty yards after passing an old trestle footing, climb steeply left to join the railroad bed. Again, the path sometimes makes detours around soggy cuts.

Follow the railbed downstream high above the river. Eventually, where the railroad formerly crossed a tributary valley on a high trestle, descend to the right. With caution, follow a road right a few dozen yards to an intersection, and from there continue straight on **Bottom Road**, as indicated by occasional yellow blazes. Follow Bottom Road downhill to the bridge over Little Gunpowder Falls.

6

GUNPOWDER FALLS STATE PARK

Little Gunpowder Trail between Route 1 (Belair Road) and Interstate 95, including Jerusalem Mill, Jericho Covered Bridge, and Franklinville

Little Gunpowder Falls forms the boundary between Baltimore County and Harford County northeast of Baltimore City. As shown on **Map 7** on page 66, a footpath extends from Route 1 downstream along the river to Jerusalem Mill, pictured at left. From there the trail continues to the covered bridge at Jericho Road and then on past the manufacturing hamlet of Franklinville. The southern trailhead is at the Kingsville Athletic Fields near Interstate 95. The total distance one way is 5 miles (8 kilometers).

The easiest way to see the entire trail is to divide it in two. On separate days, start at either end and walk to Jerusalem Mill near the midpoint, then turn around and go back by the way you came. Most of the trail is well maintained and clearly marked—although there is a rough section opposite Franklinville.

The trail is open daily from sunrise to sunset. Dogs must be leashed. The park is managed by the Department of Natural Resources, Maryland Forest, Park and Wildlife Service; telephone (410) 592-2897. **At Jerusalem Mill, there is a small museum**, open Saturday and Sunday afternoons from 1:00 to 4:00.

For automobile directions to the trail's two end points, and also to Jerusalem Mill, please turn to page 63. Walking directions start on page 65.

MAKE A PILGRIMAGE to Jerusalem along Little Gunpowder Falls. A predilection for alliterative biblical place-names is also evident in nearby Jericho and Joppa (a variant of Jaffa).

Like the Big Gunpowder Falls, the Little Gunpowder formerly powered a succession of mills, including the eighteenth-century Jerusalem Mill, shown on page 60. Although the machinery is gone, the structural frame and exterior have been restored, and the mill now serves as the headquarters of Gunpowder Falls State Park. There is also a small museum.

Jerusalem Mill was founded in 1772 by David Lee, a Quaker who—like the Ellicotts described in Chapter 15—moved here from Bucks County, Pennsylvania. Lee bought Jerusalem from Isaiah Linton, who already operated a sawmill and perhaps also a gristmill at the site. For its day the new structure erected by Lee was a large mill, which Lee ran on a merchant basis, buying wheat outright in large quantities from farmers and selling the flour on his own account, rather than merely grinding grain for a share of the product, as was done at smaller country mills. Lee also ran a farm, and during the Revolution he manufactured gunstocks and (according to some accounts) assembled flintlock guns. For this less-than-pacifistic enterprise, the Fallston Friends Meeting reprimanded him in 1776.

Lee's son Ralph and grandson David (he built the large house that still stands near the mill) carried on the milling business. Ralph Lee's customers included Baltimore's Jewish community, which annually sent a representative to the mill to oversee the grinding of wheat and to certify, by stamping the barrels, that the flour was fit for use at Passover. One object of this inspection was to make sure that the flour had minimal moisture content (moisture causes flour to ferment slightly) and was therefore suitable for making unleavened bread.

Owned by the Lee family for at least 125 years, the mill continued in operation under other owners until the death of the last miller in 1961, when it was bought by the state. During the middle third of this century, the mill ground feed for farmers in Baltimore and Harford Counties and produced buckwheat flour and cornmeal. The miller also sold gasoline, beer, soft drinks, cigarettes and candy. Even as late as mid-century, the works were powered by an overshot waterwheel, but in the final years of operation, the mill ran on electricity after a flood breached the dam.

Isaiah Linton (who had sold the Jerusalem tract to David Lee) also sold a millsite downstream in 1772 to Elisha Tyson, another

Quaker miller. Tyson operated Jericho Lower Gristmill before moving to Baltimore, where he became a locally prominent abolitionist. In 1827 Dean Walker and members of the Shaw and Tiffany families established the manufacturing hamlet of Franklinville at the site of Tyson's mill and set about making cotton goods. The first cotton mill burned in 1881. The second cotton mill opened in 1884 and is now occupied by the Belko Corporation, makers of rubber belting and other rubber products. Upton Reed's shovel foundry downstream started in 1808, evolved into the Franklinville Ironworks, and closed about 1860. With its still-operating plant and neatly arranged houses for workers, Franklinville is one of the region's best examples of a small mill village. Also still standing is the former company store and a large storage barn for cotton bales. The factory is visible from the trail across the river, but to see the town you should drive there before or after your walk.

Located between Jerusalem Mill and Franklinville is Jericho covered bridge, built in 1865 and shown on page 6. Its present structure includes concealed steel reinforcement installed in 1983. Such bridges were covered to prevent the wood trusses from rot.

≈   ≈   ≈   ≈

AUTOMOBILE DIRECTIONS: The trail that borders **Little Gunpowder Falls between Route 1 (Belair Road) and Interstate 95** is located about 16 miles northeast of Baltimore. (See •6 on **Map 1** on page 5.)

As shown on **Map 7** on page 66, you can park at Route 1 or at the Kingsville Athletic Fields off Franklinville Road—or in-between at Jerusalem Mill. Directions to each of these three places from Interstate 695 (the Baltimore Beltway) and also from Interstate 95 are given below. For your first visit, I recommend parking at Route 1, as indicated by the bold dot on the two small panels of Map 7.

To the parking lot at Route 1 (Belair Road) from Interstate 695 (the Baltimore Beltway): Leave I-695 at Exit 32B for Route 1 north toward Bel Air. Follow Route 1 for 9.4 miles. Just before crossing the bridge over Little Gunpowder Falls (which forms the boundary between Baltimore County and Harford County), turn left into a roadside parking area paved with gravel.

To the parking lot at Route 1 (Belair Road) from Interstate 95: Leave I-95 at Exit 74 for Route 152 (Mountain Road). Follow Route 152 north 4.2 miles to the intersection with Route 1. Turn left and follow Route 1 south 1.4 miles to the roadside parking area on the right, just beyond the bridge over Little Gunpowder Falls.

To the parking lot at Jerusalem Mill from Interstate 695 (the Baltimore Beltway): Leave I-695 at Exit 32B for Route 1 north toward Bel Air. Follow Route 1 for 7.4 miles. At a traffic light, turn right onto Bradshaw Road, then turn left in a few dozen yards onto Jerusalem Road. Follow Jerusalem Road 1.9 miles, then turn left into the parking lot just beyond Jerusalem Mill, now the park headquarters.

To the parking lot at Jerusalem Mill from Interstate 95: Leave I-95 at Exit 74 for Route 152 (Mountain Road). Follow Route 152 north 2.1 miles, then turn left onto Jerusalem Road. Follow Jerusalem Road 1.1 miles to the parking lot on the right for Jerusalem Mill, now the park headquarters.

To the parking lot at the Kingsville Athletic Fields from Interstate 695 (the Baltimore Beltway): Leave I-695 at Exit 32B for Route 1 north toward Bel Air. Follow Route 1 for 7.4 miles. At a traffic light, turn right onto Bradshaw Road. After 1.2 miles, turn left onto Franklinville Road and go 0.6 mile to the entrance for the Kingsville Athletic Fields on the right, just after an intersection with Sherwood Road. Follow the entrance road 0.3 mile, then note the blue blazes on the left and white blazes on the right, just beyond a large parking lot. Park in the nearest available space.

To the parking lot at the Kingsville Athletic Fields from Interstate 95: Leave I-95 at Exit 74 for Route 152 (Mountain Road). Follow Route 152 north just 0.7 mile, then turn left onto Franklinville Road. After 1 mile, jog left and then right to continue on Franklinville Road for another 1.4 miles, in the process crossing Little Gunpowder Falls and passing the village of Franklinville.* Just before an intersection with Sher-

---

* If you have never seen Franklinville, take the time to detour right onto Jericho Road for a quick look at one of the best surviving examples of a mill hamlet in Baltimore County.

wood Road, turn left toward the Kingsville Athletic Fields. Follow the entrance road 0.3 mile, then note the blue blazes on the left and white blazes on the right, just beyond a large parking lot. Park in the nearest available space.

≈   ≈   ≈   ≈

WALKING: Map 7 on page 66 shows the **Little Gunpowder Trail** between Route 1 (Belair Road) and Interstate 95.   Although it has a few steep climbs, the northern section between Route 1 and the covered bridge at Jericho Road is easy and very attractive. The riverside trail is marked with white blazes, and another trail farther from the river is blazed with blue. The middle section past Franklinville is more difficult and less well maintained. And the southern section near I-95 is marred by noise from the highway, so it is cut short by the route shown on the map. The total distance one way is 5 miles. From Route 1 to Jerusalem Mill and back is 4.5 miles. From the Kingsville Athletic Fields to Jerusalem Mill and back is 5.5 miles.

There are two sets of walking directions. One starts at Route 1 and heads downstream; the other starts at the Kingsville Athletic Fields off Franklinville Road and heads upstream.

To start at Route 1, cross the bridge over Little Gunpowder Falls, and then—using great caution—cross Route 1. At a sign declaring, "Harford County Welcomes You" (located about 10 yards from the end of the guardrail), follow the white-blazed **Little Gunpowder Trail** downstream, with the river on the right. At Wildcat Branch, follow the small tributary upstream about 40 yards before crossing.

After crossing Wildcat Branch, continue on the white-blazed trail uphill to the left along the side of the tributary ravine, then eventually curve right along the rim of the main valley high above Little Gunpowder Falls. Descend to a junction with a blue-blazed trail. You can return later via this trail, but for now turn sharply right downhill to continue on the white-blazed path along the river's edge. Eventually, the trail passes a junction with the other end of the blue-blazed trail, then continues alongside a large meadow. Soon the trail joins a muddy trough, which is actually the old Jerusalem Mill headrace. After a hundred yards, turn right out of the millrace and follow the white blazes to Jerusalem Mill, where you may want to stop in.

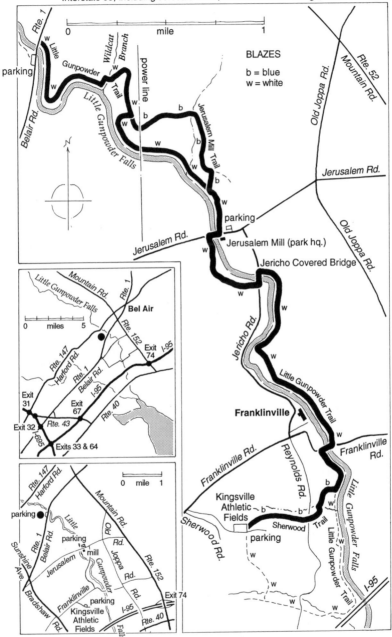

From Jerusalem Mill, cross Little Gunpowder Falls on the road bridge, then turn left downstream on the white-blazed trail. With the river on your left, continue to the covered bridge at Jericho Road.

With caution, cross the covered bridge and turn right downstream. Pass some houses on the opposite bank. As the river curves right, follow the white blazes uphill and along the bluff above the river, then down again to the river's edge. Eventually, climb again past rock outcrops opposite the mill at Franklinville.

At a truss bridge, cross the river and continue downstream on the white-blazed Little Gunpowder Trail. At an intersection with the blue-blazed **Sherwood Trail**, turn right uphill. Follow the blue blazes across Reynolds Road, through the woods, and past playing fields to the parking lots at the Kingsville Athletic Fields.

To start at the Kingsville Athletic Fields off Franklinville Road, follow the blue-blazed **Sherwood Trail** through the woods, across Reynolds Road, and downhill to the junction with the white-blazed **Little Gunpowder Trail**. With the river on the right, head upstream. Cross a truss bridge and continue upstream with the river on the left. In some places the white-blazed trail is fairly rough, but it eventually leads to the covered bridge at Jericho Road.

With caution, cross the covered bridge and pursue the white blazes upstream to Jerusalem Road. Again, cross the river on the road bridge, which leads to Jerusalem Mill, where you may want to stop in.

From the blacksmith shop opposite the mill, follow the white-blazed Little Gunpowder Trail across the grass and into the woods about 50 yards from the river's edge. Climb the berm of the old millrace and then, in front of a field, turn left to follow the white blazes along the wet and muddy millrace itself.

At a fork in the trail, bear right onto the blue-blazed **Jerusalem Mill Trail**. (You can return later via the white-blazed path along the river's edge.) Follow the blue blazes uphill, then left along an old lane where you may find a few white blazes from a prior system of trail markings. Eventually, after crossing a power-line right-of-way, rejoin the white-blazed trail and continue straight. After crossing Wildcat Branch, turn left for 40 yards, then turn right and head upstream to Route 1.

7

GUNPOWDER FALLS STATE PARK

Central Area: Sweathouse Branch Wildlands

Map 8 on page 78 shows a walk of 4.5 miles (7.2 kilometers) at the Central Area of Gunpowder Falls State Park northeast of Baltimore. The route follows well marked trails along the Big Gunpowder, up a tributary ravine, across the upland, and down the remote valley of Sweathouse Branch, with a short spur to Long Green Run, shown at left.

Please note that the route entails fording Sweathouse Branch twice. Although this stream is usually only a few inches deep, wear shoes or boots that you don't mind getting wet.

The Sweathouse Branch Wildlands are open daily from sunrise to sunset. Dogs must be leashed. The park is managed by the Department of Natural Resources, Maryland Forest, Park and Wildlife Service; telephone (410) 592-2897.

For automobile directions, please turn to page 77. Walking directions are on pages 77-79.

THE DOMINANT FORCE shaping the earth's surface is stream erosion, which attacks any elevated region and works to reduce it to a lower plain. It works slowly but relentlessly, achieving effects over eons. And as the process passes through a sequence of stages, it produces characteristic landforms that are seen at the stream-valley parks of the Baltimore region.

Although the process of erosion is ceaseless, it of course speeds up during periods of peak flow. Most erosion in the mid-Atlantic states is attributable to a relatively few heavy rains each year and—even more so—to less frequent but spectacular flood rains. Although these infrequent events may seem freakish, over millions of years they are commonplace and may be said to occur with regularity. In Maryland two inches of rain in 24 hours is termed a "two-year storm." It fills streams to their banks and causes severe erosion. Five inches of rain in 24 hours is a ten-year storm, and seven inches is a hundred-year storm. Running off the upland into a gorge like the Patapsco or Gunpowder valley, such a torrent can in a few hours do what is normally the erosive work of decades, moving tremendous amounts of earth in the turbulent floodwater.

Continental glaciation has also contributed to stream erosion, even in areas like Maryland that were never reached by the ice sheets that advanced from Canada. For instance, the valley of the Susquehanna River (including what is now Chesapeake Bay) was cut mostly by the immense torrent of meltwater that flowed out from the continental glaciers that on four occasions during the last million years covered New York and northern Pennsylvania, receding most recently about 12,000 years ago.

Going hand in hand with erosion—or really as a necessary precursor to it—is the process of weathering, by which a region's rocky foundation is, near the surface, broken down into smaller and smaller pieces that can be carried away by water, which is itself a powerful weathering agent. For example, through *frost action*, water can enter cracks in the rocks and split them apart when the water freezes, eventually reducing rocks near the surface to crumbly fragments. This is the chief form of *physical weathering*, but there are other physical processes, including penetration into rock fissures by roots of trees and other plants, which as they grow pry the rocks apart.

As rocks are reduced to smaller fragments by physical processes, *chemical weathering* becomes increasingly important, and again water is a major agent. Through *hydrolysis*, water reacts with minerals in the rocks, creating clay and freeing some elements which are carried away in solution. Through *carbonation*, carbon dioxide in soil (where it is produced by bacteria) or in the air combines with water to form a weak acid called carbonic acid, which dissolves limestone. Through *oxidation* some minerals, of which iron is the chief, react with oxygen in air and in water, thus contributing to the disintegration of the parent rock of which the oxidized minerals were formerly part. Acting together, physical and chemical weathering convert bedrock to soil or to an intermediate, crumbly substrate called *saprolite*, on which the process of erosion can then work, as discussed below.

Wherever rain falls on land, or whenever snow melts, any downward-pitched depression or swale, even though at first shallow or insignificant, is self-aggrandizing, collecting and channeling the water that flows off a broad area of upland. Even in the absence of such troughs, water flowing in sheets down a "smooth" hillside tends to organize itself into runnels that in turn erode little rills, some of which may develop into gullies and eventually into ravines that carry away the runoff. Initially, many minor watercourses are dry between rains, but some may be fed continuously by springs or the outflow from wetlands where precipitation is stored for a period before continuing its journey to the sea. Gradually, the gullies and ravines deepen with erosion, and once they penetrate the water table, they are fed by a steady seepage of groundwater. Now and again steep slopes may simply slump downhill, or a steep embankment may collapse directly into a stream, where the loosened material is easily carried away.

As a stream extends itself by developing tributaries, its erosive power rapidly increases. The larger drainage area concentrates more water in the main channel downstream, where stream energy is swelled by the greater mass of moving water. The increase in energy is more than directly proportional to stream volume. As the volume increases, an ever-smaller fraction of the river's energy is consumed in overcoming friction with the streambed, and in consequence the speed of the river increases and so does its ability to carry fine clay, silt, and sand in suspension, to abrade and wear down rocks, and to push and role pebbles and cobbles downstream.

Obviously, the ocean constitutes a base level below which a river cannot erode.* Nonetheless, even as a river approaches sea level, the current continues to erode the bank laterally

---

* Submarine canyons, like those along the edge of the Continental Shelf, are not an exception to this principle. Such canyons—and also the valley now occupied by Chesapeake Bay—were carved by rivers during the depths of the Ice Age, when so much water was amassed on land as continental ice that the level of the sea was as much as three hundred feet lower than it is now.

wherever the stream is deflected by each turn. This tendency to carve wider and wider curves is present along the entire river but is accentuated in the lower, older reaches where stream volume is greatest. As the river approaches the ocean, downward cutting is no longer possible, but sideward cutting can continue as long as there is flow. Gradually, a meandering course develops as the river snakes back and forth, eroding first one side of the valley and then the other. When sinuosity becomes so extreme that the curves loop back on themselves, the current will intercept the channel farther downstream, cutting off the looping meander. Thus, as millennia pass, the river migrates in an ever-changing course over a broad floodplain, leaving behind abandoned channels here and there. Where rivers flow out of the Piedmont, the alluvium spreads to form the continuous apron of the Coastal Plain, across which rivers sweep in ever-changing courses.

At the mouth of the river where it empties into an ocean or estuary, a distinctive geologic feature takes shape. As the current dissipates in the standing water, the capacity of the stream to carry material in suspension is reduced and then eliminated, so that the river's load of sand and silt is dropped and forms a delta. Because the current slows gradually, the deposits tend to be sorted, with larger, heavier particles dropped first. After the delta has extended itself a considerable distance in one direction, a flood may cut a new and shorter channel to open water, causing the former course to be abandoned, at least for a period. Large deltas typically have several channels or sets of channels among which the stream shifts as deposits are concentrated first in one and then in another.

Meanwhile, the countless gullies and ravines at the river's headwaters continue to fan outward like the branches of a growing tree. As the tributaries extend themselves, the watershed becomes larger and larger. A growing river may even intercept and divert to itself (or *capture*) streams that previously took a different course to the sea. Material eroded from areas far up a river's many tributaries is redeposited downstream in alluvial floodplains, sandbars, and mudbanks. Such deposits are re-eroded, transported downstream, and redeposited over and over again as the river's capacity to carry sand and silt fluctuates with the volume of runoff.

According to one conceptual model of stream erosion developed in the nineteenth century by William M. Davis, an examination of several variables—including stream gradient, valley depth, valley width, and number of meanders—will indicate the stage of development that has been reached by any stretch of river. In the earliest stage, gullies and ravines eat into the elevated land surface. Because the dominant direction of cutting is downward, the gullies and ravines are steep-sided and V-shaped, and even after they join to form larger valleys, the gradient of the streambed is steep compared to navigable waterways. Rapids are common. There are only minor flats in the valley bottom. The ratio of valley depth relative to width is at its maximum. Such a stream was said by Davis to be in *youth*.

As a stream's elevation approaches base level, the gradient diminishes and downward cutting slows. Bends in the course of the stream become accentuated, meanders start to develop, and the width of the valley increases relative to its depth. Sideward cutting produces a continuous floodplain. Such a stream is said to be in *maturity*.

Finally, when downward cutting has become so slow as virtually to cease and the stream is as close to base level as it can get, sideward cutting may eventually produce a nearly flat and featureless valley, much wider than it is deep, across which the river meanders from side to side. The gradient is low, and the broad bottomland is marked only by the scars, swamps, and lakes left by former channels. Perhaps a few rock hummocks and hills—more resistant to erosion than were their surroundings—are left rising above the low valley floor. This stage of river development is *old age*. The ultimate (and largely theoretical) expression of old age is what Davis called a *peneplain*, meaning "almost a plain" and denoting a surface of regional extent and low elevation, with only small variations in relief, produced by long-continued fluvial erosion. Most geologists today, however, think that even if other geologic events, such as fluctuations in sea level and movements in the earth's crust, were not occurring (and of course they do occur), prolonged erosion would create a landscape in which low, rolling hills occupy far more of the region than Davis postulated, especially where vegetation protects the land surface. For example, the Coastal Plain, exemplified by the Patuxent Research Refuge in Anne Arundel

County (Chapters 22 and 23) is the closest thing our region has to level terrain. And even there the land surface undulates considerably.

Of course, never does all of a river reach old age. The gullies and ravines at the river's headwaters remain youthful as they continue to spread out and consume the upland. The river is also likely to have a mature midsection.

The terms *youth, maturity,* and *old age* can also be applied to an entire region to describe the extent to which it has been acted upon by stream erosion. As an upland region experiences the headward erosion of streams, more and more of the landscape is given over to a branching system of gullies, ravines, and valleys. Eventually, the upland lying between different branches or even different watersheds is cut away until the divide changes from a wide plateau to a narrow ridge, and then to a low, rounded rise. Meanwhile, the valleys slowly widen and develop broad, flat floodplains. For as long as an area is mostly upland, it is said to be in youth. During the period that valley walls and slopes occupy most of the landscape, the region is said to be in maturity. And when most of the landscape is given over to bottomland, the area is said to be in old age. Of course, the terms *youth, maturity,* and *old age* do not describe the actual age of a river or landscape, but only its stage of erosional development—and even so, the terms are not exact or altogether meaningful. For instance, the Coastal Plain would seem to exemplify old age, and yet even there the higher areas within the plain are being dissected and reduced by branching systems of small streams like any other upland, even though the range of relief is not as great as in the Piedmont. Nonetheless, the analogy to a living organism is helpful if the main goal is to understand the general tendency or sequence of stream erosion.

There are, of course, complicating factors and forces at play, including the effect produced by varying degrees of resistance to erosion among the different kinds of rocks that underlie a river's watershed. It is a common thing for rivers to show a profile passing from youth to maturity to old age (at this last stage, complete with a wide valley and meandering course), then to reenter a relatively narrow valley with a steep gradient before once again transitioning to an older landscape. This pattern may occur several times along a single river, and in each case the sections characterized by a wide valley and meandering course are in areas of relatively unresistant rock compared to what is found next downstream. In effect, the more highly resistant bedrock that occurs at intervals along a river forms a sort of dam or base level for the portion of the watershed that is farther upstream. In theory, prolonged erosion should eventually eliminate such anomalies by wearing away even the resistant rocks that cause them.

The varying degrees of resistance to erosion among different kinds of rocks have other effects also. Where differences in resistance are minimal, a river (if viewed from the air) tends to branch out into tributaries like a tree viewed in profile. This pattern is called *dendritic*. But where some rocks are more easily eroded than others, the stream pattern will reflect this fact. For example, a *trellis pattern*—like a grape vine strung on parallel wires or a fruit tree espaliered to a garden wall—is characteristic of areas where alternating hard and soft beds of rock have been tilted or folded by movements in the earth's crust and then partially eroded away. Where the hard layers intersect the land surface, they remain as high parallel ridges. Where the softer layers intersect the surface, they are eroded into parallel valleys by streams that sometimes manage to link from one valley to the next. Such trellis patterns are seen in the Valley and Ridge geologic province of western Maryland. Stream patterns can also reflect the tendency of some rocks to split into rectilinear joints, as does sandstone.

Finally, tectonic movements in the earth's crust can, for protracted periods, cause the land to rise at rates less than, equal to, or greater than the countervailing rate of erosion, thus retarding or even renewing the sequence of erosion outlined in this discussion. Some such movements may be isostatic adjustments by which pieces of the crust, which are "floating" on softer layers below, rise as the surface is worn away, much as an iceberg would rise if only the part above water were subject to melting. Another factor is that crustal plates, spreading from rifts in the ocean basins, sometimes collide with the continental margins, causing the land to bow, buckle, and rise even as it erodes. Careful studies have shown that if present rates of erosion are applied to the past, the Appalachian Mountains should have been worn away long ago, but upward movement has

enabled them to endure despite erosion. One result of uplift is that the general contours of the land surface—especially in areas of middling relief like Maryland's Piedmont province— are far more stable than the ongoing process of fluvial erosion would indicate.

Turning to the landscape at hand, as you walk along any of the stream valleys discussed in this book, study the terrain to determine the degree to which it conforms to the pattern outlined above. And for a discussion of this question as applied to Big Gunpowder Falls, see Chapter 8 starting on page 81.

≈   ≈   ≈   ≈

AUTOMOBILE DIRECTIONS: The Central Area of Gunpowder Falls State Park is located about 12 miles northeast of Baltimore. (See •7 on **Map 1** on page 5. For greater detail, refer to the upper panel of **Map 8** on page 78.) The parking lot is located where Route 1 (Belair Road) crosses Big Gunpowder Falls. Two approaches, one from Interstate 695 (the Baltimore Beltway) and the other from Interstate 95 at White Marsh, are described below.

To the Central Area of Gunpowder Falls State Park from Interstate 695 (the Baltimore Beltway): Leave I-695 at Exit 32B for Route 1 north toward Bel Air. Follow Route 1 (Belair Road) about 5.5 miles to the bridge over Big Gunpowder Falls. Immediately after crossing the bridge, turn right into the parking lot for Gunpowder Falls State Park.

To the Central Area of Gunpowder Falls State Park from Interstate 95 at White Marsh: Leave I-95 at Exit 67B for Route 43 west (White Marsh Boulevard). Go about 2.5 miles, then turn right for Route 1 north (Belair Road) toward Perry Hall. At the top of the ramp, turn right and follow Route 1 for 4.2 miles to the bridge over Big Gunpowder Falls. Immediately after crossing the bridge, turn right into the parking lot for Gunpowder Falls State Park.

≈   ≈   ≈   ≈

WALKING: The lower panel of **Map 8** on page 78 shows a circuit of 4.5 miles in the **Sweathouse Branch Wildlands at Gunpowder Falls State Park**.

MAP 8 — Central Area of Gunpowder Falls State Park: Sweathouse Branch Wildlands

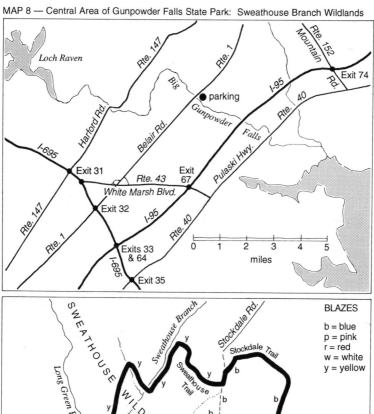

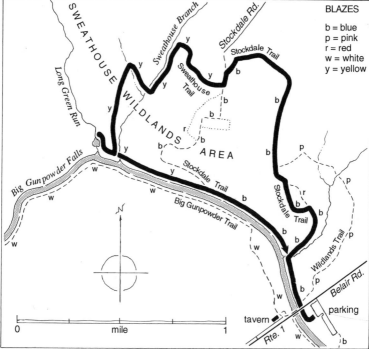

Start by descending from the parking area to the tunnel at the near end of the Belair Road bridge. Go under Belair Road, then continue straight into the Sweathouse Branch Wildlands Area. After just a few dozen yards, pass an intersection with the Wildlands Trail (pink blazes). With the river on your left, follow the blue-blazed **Stockdale Trail**, which at the next trail junction bears right. Turn here and follow the blue blazes across a stream and uphill away from the river. (You will return later toward the parking lot via the main riverside trail.)

At the top of the slope, bear left and follow the blue blazes along the edge of a pine plantation, then curve right and continue uphill. Twice you will pass a red-blazed trail intersecting from the right. Continue through an old farmyard, now overgrown with trees and brush. (The nearby pine plantations occupy former farm fields.) At a fork in the trail, bear left on the blue-blazed path where the pink-blazed Wildlands Trail intersects from the right. Continue through the woods, with the slope falling off to the left.

Eventually, the blue-blazed Stockdale Trail reaches an intersection with the yellow-blazed **Sweathouse Trail**. Turn right and follow the yellow blazes downhill, through old fields (now overgrown with trees), and into the valley of Sweathouse Branch. Follow Sweathouse Branch gradually downhill, at one point crossing the stream. Continue as the trail climbs to the right up a tributary ravine, then turns left across a rivulet. Follow the yellow blazes high above Sweathouse Branch and then gradually downhill.

At the bottom of the slope only a few yards from Sweathouse Branch, a spur trail intersects from the right. To visit a pool and large sloping rocks near the mouth of Long Green Run (see the photograph on page 68), follow the spur trail for 250 yards, then return to the yellow-blazed Sweathouse Trail.

To return to the parking lot at Belair Road, follow the yellow blazes across Sweathouse Branch and along the bottom of the valley. Soon Big Gunpowder Falls appears on the right. At an intersection with the **Stockdale Trail**, follow the blue blazes straight 0.8 mile, with the river on your right.

8

GUNPOWDER FALLS STATE PARK

Central Area: Lost Pond Trail and Sawmill Trail

Map 9 on page 85 shows a walk of 4.5 miles (7.2 kilometers) at the Central Area of Gunpowder Falls State Park northeast of Baltimore. The route follows the river past Pot Rocks to the Long Calm, then explores the upland and several tributary valleys on the way back to the starting point.

Please note that in the vicinity of Pot Rocks, Big Gunpowder Falls can be very turbulent and powerful during periods of high water, so do not wade in the river. Also, the route fords Broad Run. Although this stream is usually shallow, wear shoes or boots that you don't mind getting wet.

The trails are open daily from sunrise to sunset. Dogs must be leashed. The park is managed by the Department of Natural Resources, Maryland Forest, Park and Wildlife Service; telephone (410) 592-2897.

For automobile directions, please turn to page 84. Walking directions start on page 86.

IN TERMS OF THE STAGES of stream development discussed in Chapter 7, the stretch of Big Gunpowder Falls traversed by this walk is still young. The river flows in a steep-sided valley. Only narrow strips of bottomland flats border the river, and there are some places where the sides of the valley slope directly into the water. The channel does not meander but rather is confined by the valley walls. The river flows over and among large rocks, and at intervals there are major rapids.

Three miles below the Route 1 bridge, however, Big Gunpowder Falls leaves its rocky Piedmont valley and flows out over the Coastal Plain, composed of gravel, sand, silt, and clay deposited either as marine or delta sediments during periods when the region was submerged beneath the ocean. Since the beginning of the Pleistocene epoch (or Ice Age) in North America about a million years ago, the sea has advanced and receded across the Coastal Plain many times, depending on how much of the planet's water was amassed in continental glaciers. As would be expected, the relative ease of erosion in the soft marine and deltaic sediments has enabled the rivers that now cross the coastal zone to advance rapidly into maturity and even old age. For example, when Big Gunpowder Falls reaches the Coastal Plain, the valley walls dwindle and disappear. The river flows slowly within mud and gravel banks over a broad lowland marked by former channels that are located far from the present course of the river. The Gunpowder has even had time to develop a large delta where it reaches tidewater at Days Cove.

Although in most respects Big Gunpowder Falls conforms to the pattern of stream development summarized in the preceding chapter, several anomalies exist. One curiosity is that some of the Gunpowder's tributary valleys, such as the Dulaney and Cockeysville Valleys, have gentle stream gradients and smooth, broad (in other words, *old*) profiles compared to the relatively youthful main gorge farther downstream. How can this be? After all, Dulaney Valley Branch and Beaver Dam Run at Cockeysville have far, far lower volumes and less erosive power than the Gunpowder's main course, and in consequence they are supposed to be less advanced towards old age than the section of river below them. The fact is, however, that some of the Gunpowder's tributaries flow through areas underlain by Cockeysville marble, which (because it is limestone) dissolves more easily than the gneiss, serpentine, granite, gabbro, and other hard crystalline rocks that predominate throughout the region. Thus, the terrain along a river and its tributaries can reflect different stages of erosional development in no particular sequence, depending on the underlying rock.

The variety of rock types, their different degrees of resistance to erosion, and complications in their structure may also have contributed to some of the abrupt twists and turns that occur in the valley of Big Gunpowder Falls above Route 1. For the most part, however, the Gunpowder and its many tributaries show

the spreading, branchlike pattern of a dendritic stream system, as is typical in areas where there is no systematic rock structure that dictates the pattern of erosion.

Another anomaly is evident in Maryland's Piedmont upland, which consists of gentle, rounded hills characteristic of a mature stream system. Yet the rolling landscape is further dissected by a youthful system of gorges and ravines. This combination of features suggests that the entire Piedmont, after being shaped by erosion into a region of moderate, rounded ridges and broad valleys, was uplifted. The rise of the land increased stream gradients and renewed the ability of rivers to erode downward. As a result, the streams cut youthful gorges into the old surface, producing the present landscape in which the gentle hills and even the broad bottomlands of the former valleys remain as elevated shoulders above the entrenched gorges. In the terminology of geologists, such a process of regional uplift and renewed erosion is called *rejuvenation*.

There is evidence in Maryland and along the East Coast that the uplift of the Piedmont has not progressed at a steady rate relative to sea level, which itself has fluctuated. After each uplift, the land along the coast was exposed to the horizontal cutting action of waves and meandering rivers. In consequence, on a regional scale the topography of both the Piedmont and the Coastal Plain roughly forms a flight of terrace-like surfaces that parallel the coast and even extend upstream in the major river valleys.

≈   ≈   ≈   ≈

AUTOMOBILE DIRECTIONS: The Central Area of Gunpowder Falls State Park is located about 12 miles northeast of Baltimore. (See •8 on **Map 1** on page 5. For greater detail, refer to the corner panel of **Map 9** at right.) The parking lot is located where Route 1 (Belair Road) crosses Big Gunpowder Falls. Two approaches, one from Interstate 695 (the Baltimore Beltway) and the other from Interstate 95 at White Marsh, are described below.

To the Central Area of Gunpowder Falls State Park from Interstate 695 (the Baltimore Beltway): Leave I-695 at Exit 32B for Route 1 north toward Bel Air. Follow Route

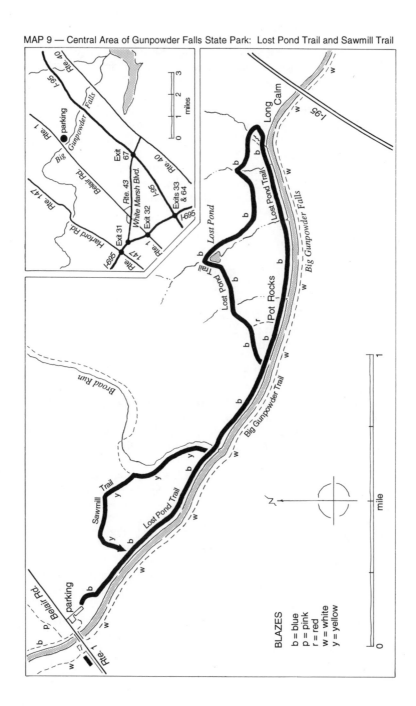

BLAZES

b = blue
p = pink
r = red
w = white
y = yellow

85

1 (Belair Road) about 5.5 miles to the bridge over Big Gunpowder Falls. Immediately after crossing the bridge, turn right
into the parking lot for Gunpowder Falls State Park.

**To the Central Area of Gunpowder Falls State Park
from Interstate 95 at White Marsh:** Leave I-95 at Exit 67B
for Route 43 west (White Marsh Boulevard). Go about 2.5 miles,
then turn right for Route 1 north (Belair Road) toward Perry Hall.
At the top of the ramp, turn right and follow Route 1 for 4.2 miles
to the bridge over Big Gunpowder Falls. Immediately after
crossing the bridge, turn right into the parking lot for Gunpowder Falls State Park.

≈ ≈ ≈ ≈

WALKING: Map 9 on page 85 shows the blue-blazed **Lost
Pond Trail** and yellow-blazed **Sawmill Trail** along the north
bank of Big Gunpowder Falls downstream from Route 1 (Belair
Road). The route is 4.5 miles round-trip and entails fording
Broad Run. Although this stream is usually only a few inches
deep, wear shoes or boots that you don't mind getting wet.

Start at the far end of the parking lot at Route 1. With the river
on the right, follow the blue-blazed **Lost Pond Trail** downstream. Pass an intersection with the yellow-blazed Sawmill
Trail. (As shown on the map, you can return by that trail at the
end, but for now, continue on the blue-blazed Lost Pond Trail.)
After passing another intersection with the yellow-blazed trail,
cross Broad Run.

At a fork in the trail where blue blazes lead both ways, bear
right toward Pot Rocks. (You will return later via the other fork
from Lost Pond.) Pass an intersection with a red-blazed trail.
Eventually, as the noise from Interstate 95 becomes audible,
watch for another fork in the blue-blazed trail. Fork right across a
stream, then follow the blue blazes left uphill toward Lost Pond.
With the noise of I-95 behind you, descend across a stream,
then climb obliquely to the rim of the valley. Continue along the
crest, with the slope falling off to the left. Eventually, follow
another tributary valley to Lost Pond.

After circling counter-clockwise three-quarters of the way
around Lost Pond, bear right on the level, blue-blazed path
away from the pond. Continue through another tributary valley
and then past fields on the right. At an intersection with the red-

blazed trail, continue on the blue-blazed path toward the parking lot. Eventually the trail zigzags downhill to the river's edge.

With the river on the left, return upstream. After re-crossing Broad Run, bear right onto the yellow-blazed **Sawmill Trail**. Follow the yellow blazes up along the side of the tributary valley, across the wooded upland, and back down to the juncture with the blue-blazed **Lost Pond Trail** by Big Gunpowder Falls. With the river on the left, follow the blue blazes to the parking lot.

9

GUNPOWDER FALLS STATE PARK

Central Area: Big Gunpowder Trail between Route 147 (Harford Road) and Route 40 (Pulaski Highway)

Located northeast of Baltimore, the trail shown on **Map 10** on page 93 extends for 8.5 miles (13.6 kilometers) along the south bank of Big Gunpowder Falls. For most of this distance, the river flows through a deep, wooded valley. But as you approach Route 40 at the trail's eastern end, the river leaves the Piedmont and enters the Coastal Plain. The easiest way to see the entire trail is to walk to each end and back from the large parking lot at the midpoint, where Route 1 (Belair Road) crosses the river.

The trail is open daily from sunrise to sunset. Dogs must be leashed. The park is managed by the Department of Natural Resources, Maryland Forest, Park and Wildlife Service; telephone (410) 592-2897.

For automobile directions, please turn to page 92. Walking directions are on pages 92-97.

THIS RIVERSIDE WALK passes the sites—and in a few cases the relics among the woods—of some of the iron furnaces, forges, nail factories, and other industrial operations that were located along Big Gunpowder Falls during the eighteenth and nineteenth centuries. As at any other mill, low rock and wooden dams created a fall of water that turned a water wheel. By means of a series of gears and cams, the wheel operated the bellows for the smelting furnaces and forges, and also the mechanical hammers that beat the white-hot pig iron to remove impurities and to flatten it into plates and bars that later could be worked, rolled, or cast into useful objects.

In 1719 Maryland's colonial legislature established a legal procedure to encourage the development of water power for the production of iron. The law stated in part: ". . . be it Enacted that if any person or persons shall desire to set up a forging mill or other convenience for carrying on Iron Works on land not before cultivated adjoining a stream, he may get a writ *ad quod damnum*"—that is, a writ of land condemnation. If the owner of the land refused to build a forge himself, the petitioner was granted a deed for 100 acres, "the owner being paid for it." The law further provided: "If pig iron is not run in seven years, the grant is void." Not fewer than twenty-three of these writs of private condemnation were granted between 1733 and 1767, most of which resulted in ironworks being built.

One forge site on Big Gunpowder Falls was at the Long Calm, where Philadelphia Road used to ford the stream. (The Long Calm is located upstream from the present-day Interstate 95 bridge.) A forge was built here in 1757 by the Nottingham Company, which acquired the land by condemnation. Because the owners of the Nottingham Company were either British or Loyalists, their property was expropriated during the Revolution by the state Office of Confiscated Effects, whose ledgers show the site to have included "Forges, Sawmill, Gristmill, Forge Dam, Water Courses, and Many Improvements." In 1781 the state auctioned the Nottingham works to Charles Ridgely and Company. Under Ridgely's ownership the forge manufactured a variety of products, as indicated by a newspaper advertisement:

> Cannon (from Nine to Two-pounders), Bar-Iron, pig iron, pots from 15 gallons to three quarts, kettles from 45 to 15 gallons; Dutch-ovens, tea-kettles, skillets, salt-pans, flat irons, mortars and pestles, wagon-boxes, stoves, dripping pans and bakers. . . . N. B. Castings of any sort made on the shortest notice.

In 1795 Ridgely's Nottingham Forge burned to the ground, but was rebuilt. Forty years later, when David Ridgely tried unsuccessfully to sell the property, it was described in the advertisement as including a new dam and two forges, one new and the other built in 1827 for rolling out iron strapping to make barrel hoops. The company also had a wharf 2.5 miles downstream at tidewater.

By 1840 the plant was operated under lease by Horace Abbott and Company, which had a subcontract to make engine parts for the *Kamchatka*, a steam frigate being built in New York for the Russian navy. A reporter for the *American* visited the forges at the Long Calm and wrote:

> I proceeded to the other works on the Falls of the Great Gunpowder River, 14 miles from Baltimore near the Philadelphia Turnpike. This establishment was fitted up by these gentlemen for the purpose of making a heavier kind of work. The hammer which they have erected is driven by a powerful water wheel, 22 feet in diameter, with 14.5-foot buckets, assisted by a fly wheel of 18 tons weight. There are two air furnaces besides several large fires for heating. When I was there, the workmen had just completed the main center shaft for the Russian steam frigate above alluded to. This shaft is the largest ever made in this country, being 14.5 feet in length and 18.5 inches in diameter, and is estimated to weigh *thirteen thousand* pounds.

In 1845 David Ridgely sold the forges at the Long Calm to Robert Howard, who the next year built an iron-smelting furnace just west of Philadelphia Road. In 1856 this furnace produced 1,100 tons of iron during thirty weeks of continuous blast. Two years later, however, Howard's forges and furnace on Big Gunpowder Falls were put out of operation permanently by a flood that destroyed the dam and cracked the furnace.

The walking directions on pages 92-97 point out some specific features of these and other works that are still discernible along the trail. *Not* visible from the trail, however, are the substantial stone structures (most have been converted to private residences) of the Gunpowder Copper Works, located on the far side of the river facing Harford Road near the trail's upstream end. The copper works were constructed in the first decade of the nineteenth century by Levi Hollingsworth, who supplied the United States Navy with copper sheathing for ships during the War of 1812. There was also a mill for manufacturing copper bolts with which to fasten the sheathing, since the use of dissimilar metals would have speeded corrosion. The plant's chief claim to fame was that it rolled the copper for the dome of the national Capitol when it was rebuilt after the original building had been burned by the British in 1814, about two weeks before the attack on Baltimore, as described in Chapter 19. Hollingsworth's dome lasted until the 1860s. The copper works remained in operation until the 1860s or '70s.

≈   ≈   ≈   ≈

AUTOMOBILE DIRECTIONS: The Central Area of Gunpowder Falls State Park is located about 12 miles northeast of Baltimore. (See •9 on **Map 1** on page 5. For greater detail, refer to the small corner panel of **Map 10** at right.) The parking lot is located where Route 1 (Belair Road) crosses Big Gunpowder Falls. Two approaches, one from Interstate 695 (the Baltimore Beltway) and the other from Interstate 95 at White Marsh, are described below.

To the Central Area of Gunpowder Falls State Park from Interstate 695 (the Baltimore Beltway): Leave I-695 at Exit 32B for Route 1 north toward Bel Air. Follow Route 1 (Belair Road) about 5.5 miles to the bridge over Big Gunpowder Falls. Immediately after crossing the bridge, turn right into the parking lot for Gunpowder Falls State Park.

To the Central Area of Gunpowder Falls State Park from Interstate 95 at White Marsh: Leave I-95 at Exit 67B for Route 43 west (White Marsh Boulevard). Go about 2.5 miles, then turn right for Route 1 north (Belair Road) toward Perry Hall. At the top of the ramp, turn right and follow Route 1 for 4.2 miles to the bridge over Big Gunpowder Falls. Immediately after crossing the bridge, turn right into the parking lot for Gunpowder Falls State Park.

≈   ≈   ≈   ≈

WALKING: Map 10 at right show the white-blazed **Big Gunpowder Trail**, which stretches 8.5 miles along the south bank of the river between Route 147 (Harford Road) and Route 40. Approximately at the midpoint is Route 1 (Belair Road).

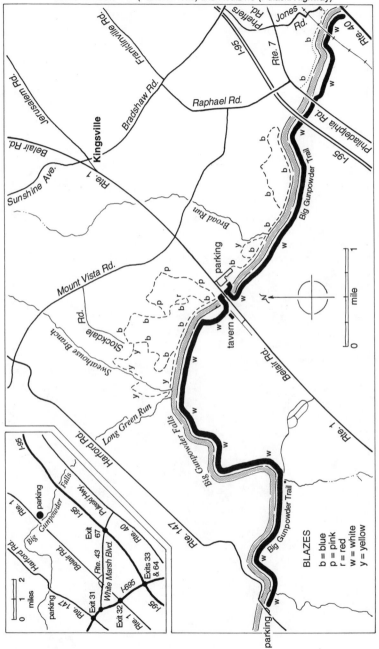

BLAZES

b = blue
p = pink
r = red
w = white
y = yellow

The easiest way to see the whole trail is to divide it in two. On one day start at Route 1 and walk upstream to Route 147 and back. Directions start in the next paragraph. On another day start at Route 1 and walk downstream to Route 40 and back, as described at the bottom of this page.

Walking upstream from Route 1 (Belair Road) to Route 147 (Harford Road) and back: The round-trip distance is 9 miles.

Start by descending from the parking area to the tunnel at the near end of the Route 1 bridge. Go under Route 1, then immediately turn left to follow the trail that crosses the bridge on the upstream side.

At the far end of the bridge, bear right and follow white blazes down a gravel ramp next to a tavern. Continue straight across a grassy area. Cross a stream and continue into the forest on a narrow footpath that winds through the woods and eventually reaches the river's edge.

With the water on your right, follow the riverside footpath for as long as you care to walk, keeping in mind that you will return by the same route. Be alert for places where the trail is being undermined by erosion. After 3 miles, the trail reaches a road and passes to the right of a brick transformer building. This is a good place to turn back if you do not want to hike the full distance.

For the whole trail, continue for 1.5 miles along the river's edge. Near Harford Road the trail fords a stream that during high water can more easily be crossed on the rocks a few dozen yards upstream; do not cross, however, if the water is flowing over the rocks.

Walking downstream from Route 1 (Belair Road) to Route 40 and back: The round-trip distance is 8 miles. Aesthetically, the trail is sub-par where it passes under Interstate 95 and Route 7 (Philadelphia Road), but for most of the way, it is very pleasant. Toward the end the trail makes the interesting transition from the Piedmont to the Coastal Plain.

Start by descending from the parking area to the near end of the Route 1 bridge. Without going through the tunnel under the road, cross the river via the path on the downstream side of the bridge.

With the river on your left, follow the white-blazed Big Gunpowder Trail downstream. Be alert for places where the path is being undermined by erosion. Now and then the trail is obscure, but you cannot get lost; simply keep the river on your left.

Approximately 200 yards upstream from the Interstate 95 bridge, the path abruptly rises a few feet and passes above—and to the right of—the stone abutment of what was once a wooden dam. There is a matching abutment on the opposite bank. The dam supplied water to power Robert Howard's nineteenth-century ironworks at the Long Calm. The low earthen ridge that extends from the abutment away from the river toward higher land was, of course, part of the dam. Presumably Howard's millrace ran along the side of the valley to his forge farther downstream at the Philadelphia Road. The intake for the race appears to have been located about 25 yards from the dam abutment. The land in the vicinity of the I-95 bridge has been completely regraded, but starting about 50 yards downstream from the bridge apron, the path is unusually level for 75 yards, and for part of that distance it is supported by a stone retaining wall, all of which may indicate that the path there follows the former millrace.

Continue under the bridge at Interstate 95 , then follow the path toward another bridge at Philadelphia Road.

A bridge—the Forges Bridge—was first built at Philadelphia Road in 1822, a few years after the road itself was moved from the ford at the Long Calm.

Pass under the bridge at Philadelphia Road, then bear obliquely up the embankment to an old road, now closed to cars. With the river on your left, continue downstream on the old road, which eventually reaches an area now overgrown with weeds and brush.
An expanse of rocks and gravel next to the river (and just upstream from the railroad bridge) is a good place to stop if you do not want to continue downstream 0.2 mile to Route 40—although if you stop here, you will miss the transition to the visibly different terrain and substance of the Coastal Plain. To continue to Route 40, follow the path under the railroad bridge

and along the muddy, sandy plain, then return by the way you came. Because it is subject to flooding, the trail here is sometimes obscure—but that is part of the interest.

As noted above, downstream from the present-day Philadelphia Road bridge, the asphalt path or road leads 0.5 mile to a circular area of weeds and brush. This was the site of the Joppa Iron Works, also known as Big Gunpowder Mills or the Patterson Iron Works. The works were constructed in 1817, and by 1820 fifteen men and six boys were employed producing sheet iron, barrel hoops, spikes, cut nails, and brads. By 1850 the Patterson Iron Works employed 130 hands producing 36,000 kegs of nails annually. The following year the works were rebuilt on a larger scale to include six puddling furnaces, one heating furnace, one water-driven hammer, two trains of rolls to produce sheet iron, and thirty-seven nail machines to cut nails from the sheets. The works continued in operation until the 1860s, after which they were dismantled. In 1913 a distillery was built on the old ironworks foundations. The distillery buildings survived until the property was acquired for park purposes in 1970.

On the opposite bank of the river, a small cut-stone puddling furnace is built into a cleft in the rock back a few dozen yards from the river's edge next to the rapids. These rapids, incidentally, are the last on Big Gunpowder Falls.

10

LOCH RAVEN

Located north of Baltimore, Loch Raven is surrounded by forested land that helps to protect the reservoir's water quality. Running through this buffer zone are many trails that are open to the public for walking. Two routes are described below.

The bold line on **Map 11** on page 103 traces a walk of up to 10 miles (16 kilometers) round-trip. **Please note** that this route is possible only on Saturday and Sunday between 10:00 A.M. and 5:00 P.M., when a portion of Loch Raven Drive is closed to motor vehicles. With its sweeping views over the water, the roadway provides a pleasant promenade. For the full hike shown by the bold line, continue on a dirt fire road that winds around wooded hillsides and ravines. The trail eventually ends at the water's edge. Return by the way you came or via some of the narrow foot trails also shown on the map as finely dotted lines, one of which follows the shore for about a mile.

The boldly dotted line on Map 11 shows a route of up to 5 miles (8 kilometers) round-trip. Fire roads lead up and down through the woods to a remote promontory north of the dams. This area is open daily from dawn to dusk.

The reservoir and watershed areas are managed by the Baltimore City Bureau of Water and Waste Water; telephone (410) 795-6151. Dogs must be leashed. Swimming and wading are prohibited.

For automobile directions, please turn to page 102. Walking directions are on pages 102-105.

LOCH RAVEN IS ONE of three major reservoirs owned and managed by Baltimore City. They serve not just Baltimore itself but also much of the metropolitan region. In fact, most of the water system's 1.8 million users are outside the city. The other two reservoirs are Prettyboy, located upstream from Loch Raven on Big Gunpowder Falls, and Liberty Reservoir on the North Branch of the Patapsco River. Both Loch Raven and Liberty Reservoir are the last impoundments on their rivers before the water is removed and treated for drinking. Prettyboy Reservoir simply provides additional storage within the Gunpowder watershed. Baltimore also has the right to pump water from the Philadelphia Electric Company's Conowingo Dam on the Susquehanna River, but the city does so only during droughts or in other emergencies.

To protect the region's water supply, Baltimore City owns about nine square miles of land surrounding each of its three reservoirs. In managing these buffer areas, the city has adopted a multiple-use policy that allows a wide variety of recreational activities as long as they are compatible with the chief priority of maintaining high water quality. Permitted activities include fishing, hiking, and—on a limited basis—horseback riding and mountain biking. Rowboats can be rented at the Loch Raven Fishing Center off Dulaney Valley Road. Also, permits for private boats are distributed annually, but no gasoline motors or sailboats are allowed on the reservoirs. Moreover, boaters must sign a pledge agreeing not to use their boats elsewhere. In this way the watershed managers hope to prevent the spread to the reservoirs of zebra mussels, which are thought to cling to the hulls of boats and which have become a major problem in some places because they clog waterworks intake pipes. Also, an eighteen-hole golf course has long existed at Pine Ridge on the western shore of Loch Raven. Owned by the city but managed by a private corporation, the golf course is subject to various restrictions limiting the use of lawn chemicals. In the mid-1990s, golf proponents pushed for a second course at Pine Ridge, but the proposal was rejected by Baltimore's Board of Estimates on the grounds that a second golf course might increase chemical pollution in the reservoir.

The range and intensity of recreation allowed on Baltimore's watershed lands is liberal compared to what is permitted at many other municipal reservoirs in the East. Although studies have shown that boating on reservoirs and hiking, riding, and picnicking in adjacent buffer areas do not significantly impair water quality, watershed managers are understandably reluctant to compound their difficulties by running something resembling public parks, especially at a time when water quality in the reservoirs is declining because of ongoing development throughout the watershed. And even setting aside the issue of bacteriological and chemical pollution, there can be no doubt that the presence of people causes tiresome problems for Baltimore's watershed managers. For example, because crowds and drinking got out of hand, Baltimore closed its picnic area at Loch Raven and has curtailed use of the Liberty Dam overlook. Also, litter is pervasive, thrown overboard from boats, scattered at fishing spots along the shore, and heaped at focal points such as the trailhead below Prettyboy Dam. Another bane is off-road motorcycles, and even mountain bikes are perceived to contribute to erosion and sedimentation during wet weather or at wet locations, such as stream crossings. Rather than banning mountain biking outright, guidelines developed jointly by the Department of Public Works and mountain-biking groups restrict riders to designated fire road, but it remains to be seen whether this compromise is successful.

Recreational use of reservoirs and adjacent watershed lands also increases administrative burdens. Areas popular with visitors have to be patrolled more often to enforce regulations. (Incidentally, watershed police have full power to issue citations and to arrest offenders.) Although much of the responsibility for overseeing the wide range of activities at Baltimore's reservoirs has fallen on the city's Watershed Section, some of the administrative duties have been shifted to other agencies with a more immediate interest in public recreation. The Baltimore County Department of Recreation and Parks runs the Loch Raven boat rental and fishing concession; telephone (410) 252-8755. The state's Department of Natural Resources manages the reservoir's fisheries. Mountain-biking clubs participate in trail maintenance and try to inform riders about rules and responsibilities.

In summary, the residents of the Baltimore region are very fortunate that the city's reservoirs and watershed lands are open to the public for a wide variety of recreational activities. The continuation of this policy, however, depends on the cooperation and reasonable behavior of those who use these areas.

≈   ≈   ≈   ≈

AUTOMOBILE DIRECTIONS: Loch Raven is located about 10 miles north of Baltimore. (See •10 on **Map 1** on page 5. For greater detail, refer to the corner panel of **Map 11** at right.)

To Loch Raven from Interstate 695 (the Baltimore Beltway): Leave I-695 at Exit 27 for Route 146 (Dulaney Valley Road) north. Follow Route 146 north 4 miles. Immediately after crossing a bridge over Loch Raven, bear right on Dulaney Valley Road where Jarrettsville Pike heads left. Continue on Dulaney Valley Road 1.7 miles. Where Dulaney Valley Road turns left at Peerce's Plantation Restaurant, go straight on Loch Raven Drive and follow it 1 mile to the intersection of Loch Raven Drive and Morgan Mill Road.

Pay close attention to signs indicating where parking is permitted and where (and when) it is not. Areas for parking are different on weekdays and weekends. On weekdays, park on Loch Raven Drive a few hundred yards beyond the gates. On weekends you must park outside the gates, even if you arrive before they are closed.

≈   ≈   ≈   ≈

WALKING: Two routes at **Loch Raven** are described below. The first is possible only on Saturday and Sunday, when Loch Raven Drive is closed to motor vehicles between 10:00 A.M. and 5:00 P.M. The second route, for which directions start on page 104, is feasible any day of the week.

The bold line on Map 11 at right shows a route of 10 miles round-trip, assuming that you go out and back the same way.

Start at the intersection of Loch Raven Drive and Morgan Mill Road. Pass the orange gates and follow Loch Raven Drive, with the reservoir on your right. Follow the road along the edge of the reservoir, across a bridge, and gradually uphill to another pair of orange gates at the intersection of Providence Road and Loch Raven Drive.

Immediately beyond the orange gates, turn right past a green gate and enter the woods on a fire road. From here to the water's edge, the route shown by the bold line on Map 11 follows fire roads, which are wide enough to accommodate a

MAP 11— Loch Raven

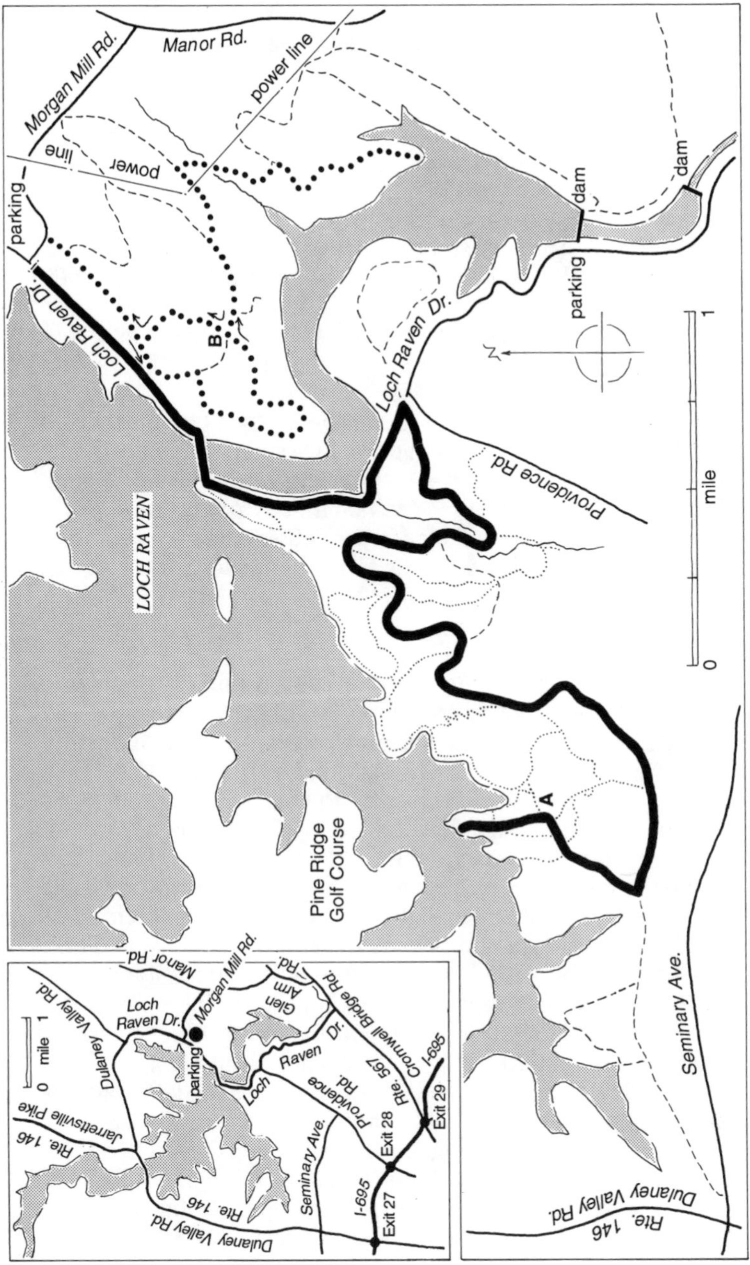

MAP 11— Loch Raven

LOCH RAVEN

Pine Ridge Golf Course

Jeep (although in some places they are overgrown with grass). Ignore narrow side trails—although for variety you may want to use some of them as you return.

Follow the fire road through the woods. Altogether, go about 3 miles as the road winds, dips, climbs, and curves along the hillside, with the slope falling off to the right.

Eventually, the terrain becomes less hilly and the woods less mature—or that is, the trees get somewhat smaller, some pines appear, and the understory becomes choked with vines and scrubby growth. Turn sharply right at a major intersection. (If you cross a stream where a chainlink fence and lawn are only 15 yards to the left, retrace your steps 100 yards to the intersection.) After turning, continue through the woods. Follow the main track to the water's edge.

You can of course return to the starting point by the way you came, but you may prefer to devise your own route via the foot trails that are shown on the map as finely dotted lines. Some follow the shore. To get started on these trails, retrace you steps from the water's edge for about 350 yards. As the main path starts to curve to the right, turn left onto a narrow trail at a junction marked **A** on the map.

The boldly dotted line on Map 11 on page 103 shows a route of 5 miles round-trip.

Start on a fire road that leaves Morgan Mill Road 160 yards uphill from the intersection of Morgan Mill Road and Loch Raven Drive. With the reservoir downhill to your right, enter the woods past a signboard and follow the fire road along the hillside, passing (after only 90 yards) a trail that veers left. Continue along the hillside, where in winter the reservoir may be visible downhill to the right through the trees. Follow the fire road as it gradually descends and passes another trail intersecting from the left—and by which you will return at the end of the walk.

Continue straight on the wide path as it passes within a dozen yards of Loch Raven Drive. Follow the rough, eroded path up a ravine for about 200 yards, then turn right at the first trail junction. Follow this path up and then around to the left, with the land sloping off to the right toward the reservoir.

Eventually the path climbs away from Loch Raven to a four-way trail junction marked **B** on Map 11. Turn right. After only 50 yards, pass a trail intersecting from the right. Continue straight gradually uphill, then along a plateau. At an intersection by a gravelly clearing and log dump, bear right downhill. Pass under high power lines as you descend obliquely along the eroded, gullied path. Near the bottom of the ravine, turn sharply right and continue gradually downhill. Cross a stream under the power lines, then continue along the side of the valley and obliquely uphill. Just as the fire road reaches the top of the slope, fork right, then again bear right in a dozen yards. Follow the trail to the water's edge at the tip of a promontory, where the Loch Raven Dam is visible across the water.

To return to your car, first go back to the four-way trail junction at point **B** on Map 11, and there turn right. Follow the trail through the woods and downhill. At an intersection, turn sharply right and follow the path back to your starting point at Morgan Mill Road.

11

NORTHERN CENTRAL RAILROAD

Located north of Baltimore, an old railroad now forms a hikers' highway through forest and farmland. As shown on **Maps 12-15** on pages 116-119, the trail stretches 40 miles (64 kilometers) between York, Pennsylvania and Ashland, Maryland, which is located near Hunt Valley. The roadbed has been paved with finely crushed rock, making a hard-packed surface that is suitable for bicycling as well as for walking. In addition to the two end points, several other access points are described in the auto-mobile directions, making possible a series of shorter trips.

The trail is open daily from sunrise to sunset. Dogs must be leashed, and bicycles must have bells or horns. Cyclists should yield to other trail users, pass with care, and keep their speed to a moderate, safe pace.

In Pennsylvania, the trail is called the **York County Heritage Rail Trail** and is managed by York County Parks; telephone (717) 840-7440. In Maryland the trail is called the **Northern Central Railroad Trail** and is managed as part of Gunpowder Falls State Park by the Department of Natural Resources, Mary-land Forest, Park and Wildlife Service; telephone (410) 472-3144 or (410) 592-2897.

For automobile directions, please turn to page 114. Walking directions start on page 121.

THIS OUTSTANDING HIKE-BIKE TRAIL follows the old roadbed of the Northern Central Railway. If I may editorialize for a moment, writing my various *Country Walks* books has made me familiar with a number of Rails-to-Trails projects, and this is the best that I have seen. For mile after mile the trail follows the valleys of Big Gunpowder Falls, Little Falls, Beetree Run, and Codorus Creek through the rolling Piedmont landscape of Maryland and Pennsylvania, passing through towns and hamlets that originally were spawned by the rail-road.

The Northern Central Railway was chartered in Maryland as the Baltimore & Susquehanna in 1828, one year after incorporation of the nation's first railroad, the Baltimore & Ohio. Plans for the B&S called for the railway's northern terminus to be located at the Susquehanna riverport of York Haven, which was near the projected route of Pennsylvania's Main Line Canal. The new railroad would thus tap the commerce of the entire Susquehanna basin and bring to Baltimore trade that might otherwise go to Philadelphia. Not surprisingly, enthusiasm for the venture was high in Baltimore (sales of stock were oversubscribed within the first few days), but for three years legislators in Harrisburg refused to grant authority for the line to enter Pennsylvania.

Construction of the railroad began anyway at Baltimore in 1829. Progress was slow and more costly than anticipated, partly because there was no American railroad expertise on which the B&S could draw. Just building the first few miles up the Jones Falls Valley to what is now Lake Roland (the reservoir did not then exist) took until 1831. Using horse-drawn cars, the railroad earned what income it could by hauling chromite and copper ore from Isaac Tyson's mines at the Bare Hills. Textile mills in the lower Jones Falls Valley also provided traffic. From Lake Roland the B&S extended its line northwest through the Greenspring Valley to Owings Mills, which was reached in 1832. That same year the company imported a small steam locomotive from England, and the railroad started hauling flour from Owings Mills and Rockland Mills.

The Greenspring line, however, was not profitable. Even before it was finished, it was relegated to branch status when Pennsylvania finally accepted the Baltimore & Susquehanna. (This was done by authorizing a Pennsylvania company called the York & Maryland Line Railroad that was to be operated by the B&S. As a *quid pro quo*, Maryland allowed the southward extension of Pennsylvania's Tidewater Canal along the Susquehanna.) From a junction with the Greenspring tracks at Lake Roland, the B&S resumed building northward, reaching the limestone and marble quarries at Texas and Cockeysville in 1834 and '35 and John Weise's White Hall paper mill in 1836. The spread of industrial development up the Jones Falls Valley as far as Mt. Washington also gave business to the B&S. Even so, huge loans, a moratorium on interest payments, and increased subscriptions of stock by Maryland and Baltimore were necessary to keep construction of the railroad going.

In 1838 the B&S reached York. Abandoning for the time being its original plan to go to York Haven, the company financed construction through York of an east-west subsidiary railroad linking Wrightsville on the Susquehanna with Gettysburg. After 1840, coal, lumber, and pig iron that were transshipped from the Susquehanna at Wrightsville greatly increased tonnage carried by the B&S to Baltimore.

For about a dozen years Wrightsville was the northern terminus of the B&S, but in 1850 the company began construction of a subsidiary railroad to York Haven, and from there on to Harrisburg. B&S trains started serving Harrisburg in 1851—the same year that the B&O completed its line to the Ohio River at Wheeling. Also in 1851, the B&S created yet another subsidiary to build a railroad still farther north along the Susquehanna to the anthracite fields in the vicinity of Sunbury, Pennsylvania.

Before the line to Sunbury was completed, however, the Baltimore & Susquehanna and its associated railroads in Pennsylvania were insolvent. By the standards of the day, these companies had developed an extensive regional system, but in doing so they had taken on more debt and more construction expense than they could handle. In 1854 the Baltimore & Susquehanna merged with its Pennsylvania subsidiaries and was rechartered as the Northern Central Railway. The new company was still saddled with all the old debts but was granted authority to issue more stock and to borrow more money from Maryland and Pennsylvania in order to finish the line to Sunbury. Even before the Sunbury extension was completed in 1858, the company's precarious financial condition improved as it entered coal country and started hauling anthracite south to Baltimore. From then on the railroad prospered.

The Northern Central Railway figured tangentially in a curious incident in February 1861, when President-elect Abraham Lincoln traveled in a zigzag route from Illinois to New York, then south to Washington. In the presidential election, Lincoln had carried every free state and no slave states (of which Maryland was one). By mid-February seven states in the deep South had already seceded from the Union and formed the Confederate States of America. In Baltimore Lincoln had received only about a thousand votes from the minuscule Republican faction, some of whose leaders—highly unpopular in the city—thought it would be a fine thing to have a parade or at least a small procession when Lincoln arrived. The city government itself declined to plan an official reception or to send a delegation to meet Lincoln ahead of time in Harrisburg, to which he had gone from Philadelphia in order to address the Pennsylvania legislature. Lincoln's itinerary called for him to take the Northern Central Railway from Harrisburg to Baltimore on February 23, then proceed to Washington the same day.

For the trip down from Harrisburg, the Northern Central supplied a special express train, pulled by one of its best locomotives and equipped with spare pieces of machinery in case of a breakdown. According to the *Baltimore Exchange*, flagmen were posted every half-mile along the line, and watchmen guarded every bridge. On the morning of the 23rd, Mrs. Lincoln and her two children took this train—but President-elect Lincoln did not. Warned by detective Allan Pinkerton, Senator William Seward, and General Winfield Scott that there was a conspiracy to kill him in Baltimore, Lincoln had left Harrisburg for Philadelphia secretly the prior evening. From Philadelphia he took a sleeping car to Baltimore, through which he passed in the middle of the night, and in this way arrived unannounced in Washington at 6 o'clock in the morning. When the story got out, newspapers hostile to Lincoln heaped ridicule on the president-elect, depicting him in cartoons as a quaking figure in a nightcap or even disguised in a Scotch-plaid cap and a long cloak, which according to some stories he had borrowed from his wife. Newspapers and magazines sympathetic to Lincoln took a different line, and it was not long before they were trumpeting sensational and contradictory accounts of the Baltimore assassination conspiracy that had been cleverly foiled. However, no evidence of a plot to kill Lincoln in Baltimore ever turned up, and no one was ever arrested in connection with the matter.

As for Mrs. Lincoln, convinced that her husband had been given bad advice, she reached Baltimore without incident. Her travel arrangements, however, included the precaution of getting off the Northern Central train a stop before it pulled into the Calvert Street station, where it was met by nearly the entire Baltimore City police force and an immense crowd that groaned and hooted.

During the Civil War the Northern Central Railway was repeatedly a target of saboteurs and Confederate raiders. After Virginia seceded from the Union on April 17, 1861, Southern sympathizers in Maryland vehemently objected to the transit across their state of Northern troops rushing to secure Washington, D.C. Following the confrontation of April 19 between a Baltimore mob and the Sixth Massachusetts Regiment on its way to Washington, Mayor Brown and the Baltimore board of police commissioners (and possibly also Governor Hicks) authorized destroying the railroad bridges leading from the north into Baltimore in order to prevent the arrival of more troops and the outbreak of more rioting. Over a period of four days, parties of police and militiamen burned the Northern Central's bridges all the way to the border with Pennsylvania. Telegraph lines were cut and some bridges of the Philadelphia, Wilmington & Baltimore Railway were also destroyed.

The officer in charge of wrecking the Northern Central was Lieutenant John Merryman of the Baltimore County Horse Guards. A prominent landowner residing at Hayfields (now a golf community on Shawan Road), Merryman more than once waved his sword in front of crowds of cheering onlookers and shouted something to the effect that "We'll stop them from stealing our slaves." After federal troops gained control of Baltimore in May, Merryman was imprisoned in Fort McHenry and charged with treason—but not tried. In *Ex-Parte Merryman*, his appeal for judicial help became the subject of the ruling by Roger B. Taney, Chief Justice of the Supreme Court of the United States, that President Lincoln's suspension of the writ of *habeas corpus* was unconstitutional—a decision that Lincoln and the military authorities simply ignored until they were confident that danger had passed.

The railroad spans into Baltimore were rebuilt over a period of a month, but in 1863, nearly three dozen Northern Central bridges in York County, Pennsylvania, were wrecked during Robert E. Lee's invasion culminating at Gettysburg in the first three days of July. The damage was repaired at government expense by four hundred laborers from the United States Military Railroad Corps. Working day and night and using prefabricated wooden trusses, these men rebuilt the bridges and put the line back in service in just two weeks. Four months later Lincoln took a Northern Central train for part of his journey to Gettysburg to deliver his address dedicating the battlefield cemetery.

In 1864 the Northern Central bridge over the Gunpowder Falls north of Cockeysville and ten bridges south of the town were burned by a detachment of Confederate raiders during Jubal Early's march through Maryland to the outskirts of Washington. From Cockeysville Confederate cavalry led by Colonel Harry Gilmor were sent still farther east to destroy the railroad bridge of the Philadelphia, Wilmington & Baltimore Railway over the Gunpowder. Gilmor succeeded in damaging the bridge and in burning two trains—acts which did not prevent him from becoming police commissioner of Baltimore in 1877.

Finally, the Northern Central Railway saw the Civil War close when, twelve days after Lee's surrender at Appomattox and a week after Lincoln's assassination, the president's body was transported by train to Illinois for burial. According to *The Sun* for April 22, 1865, "The front of the Calvert Station of the Northern Central Railway was very beautifully trimmed with mourning, as were also the windows communicating with the ticket office. The funeral train provided by this company consisted of eight first-class passenger cars and a baggage car, all appropriately decked in the habiliments of mourning." At small stations and road crossings along the Northern Central line, silent crowds gathered to see the train pass.

Although the Northern Central repeatedly suffered damage during the Civil War, the conflict nonetheless brought prosperity to the railroad. One large Northern Central shareholder was Simon Cameron, briefly Lincoln's Secretary of War in 1861. Described by one historian as "a man who always stood ready to combine his personal business with the public's," Cameron gave military traffic to the Northern Central in the opening months of the war before his scandalous conduct caused Lincoln to send him out of the way as ambassador to Russia. More significantly, over the long course of the war, the Northern Central was strategically located between the industrial cities of the North and what came to be the main theater of action in Virginia. Hauling war material helped the railroad to boost its revenue by 186 percent during the war and to pay its old debts.

Following the Civil War, the Northern Central gradually became an adjunct of the Pennsylvania Railroad, which had started to acquire Northern Central stock in 1861. From its junction at Harrisburg with the Pennsylvania Railroad's main line between Pittsburgh and Philadelphia, the Northern Central provided the shortest route to tidewater. By 1863 the Pennsylvania Railroad had purchased nearly 34 percent of the Northern Central's shares, which was enough to exercise working control. Starting in 1874 the president of the Pennsylvania Railroad also served as president of the Northern Central, and finally in 1914 the Northern Central executed a 999-year lease and became an integral part of the vast Pennsylvania Railroad system.

The late nineteenth and early twentieth centuries were the glory years of the Northern Central. From the 1870s to 1913, annual revenue increased by more than 400 percent, chiefly from traffic in coal, lumber, and grain. Passenger traffic also boomed, and by 1893 the Northern Central had thirty-two weekday trains out of Baltimore, including seven non-stop runs to Harrisburg, one local to York, five locals to Parkton, eleven locals to Cockeysville, and eight trains on the Greenspring Branch. The railroad spurred the development of Lutherville, Mt. Washington, Ruxton, Riderwood, and other suburban communities.

By the late 1920s, however, the Pennsylvania Railroad was in decline. Coal provided less and less traffic as industries switched to petroleum and natural gas. Obsolete factories in Pennsylvania began to close and to relocate in the South and in other low-wage regions. Business shrank further during the Great Depression. Although World War II provided a temporary surge in rail traffic, the postwar boom in automobile and truck transport left the railroad weaker than ever. In the 1950s the Pennsylvania Railroad began to abandon unprofitable branches and segments.

Marylanders who knew the Northern Central as a working railroad remember it chiefly as a commuter line from Parkton southward into Baltimore's old Calvert Street station, a site now occupied by the Sunpapers building. Next to the station was the railroad's freight warehouse, which has become the Downtown Athletic Club. From Parkton to Baltimore the railroad had two sets of tracks. Termed collectively the Parkton Local, commuter trains in the 1950s arrived downtown at 7:30, 8:30, and 10:00 A.M. Ralph Reppert of the Sunpapers commented that the schedule accommodated "the workers, the clerkers, and the shirkers." After complaining for years of its financial losses from operating commuter trains on the Northern Central, the Pennsylvania Railroad was allowed to terminate local passenger service in 1959. Long-distance passenger service over the Northern Central line ended in 1971. Finally, freight service was halted abruptly when the railroad was severely damaged by flooding from three days of rain during Tropical Storm Agnes in 1972. Having declared bankruptcy in 1970, the Penn Central Corporation (created in 1968 by the merger of the Pennsylvania Railroad and the equally-shaky New York Central) refused to repair the Northern Central north of Cockeysville. In Maryland the state purchased the abandoned line in 1980, two years after the U.S. Department of Interior had approved a Rails-to-Trails grant of $450,000. In Pennsylvania, York County undertook to extend the trail northward along the still extant tracks. Now the Northern Central from Ashland (near Cockeysville) to York, Pennsylvania is an immensely successful hike-bike trail, and the line from Hunt Valley southward to Baltimore is used by the Mass Transit Administration's light-rail commuter trains.

≈   ≈   ≈   ≈

AUTOMOBILE DIRECTIONS: The railroad trail that in Pennsylvania is called the **York County Heritage Rail Trail** and in Maryland the **Northern Central Railroad Trail** stretches 40 miles. At the trail's northern end is York, Pennsylvania, and at the trail's southern end is Ashland near Hunt Valley. (See •11 for Ashland on **Map 1** on page 5.) **Maps 12-15** on pages 116-119 show the trail in four overlapping sections arranged in sequence from north to south, as indicated by the diagram on each map.

The following directions are to several parking lots located at intervals along the trail. There are also many other parking lots indicated on the maps, as you will see for yourself when you go.

The automobile directions start on **Interstate 83 (the Harrisburg Expressway)**, which can be reached via Exit 24 off **Interstate 695 (the Baltimore Beltway)**.

York is located at the northern end of the railroad trail and is shown at the top of **Map 12** on page 116. To reach the York trailhead, leave I-83 at Exit 8 for Route 462 (Market Street), about 41 miles north of the Baltimore Beltway. At the bottom of the exit ramp, turn left and follow Route 462 west toward York. Go 0.5 mile, then stay on Route 462 as it turns right onto North Harrison Street and left onto East Philadelphia Street. Continue 1.7 miles and then—after crossing Beaver Street and Pershing Avenue—turn left into a parking lot next to Codorus Creek.

This is the northern trailhead, and now that you have found it the next task is to find a place to park. On weekends, you can park here if there is room, but on weekdays you must park elsewhere. Your best option is to use one of the nearby parking garages. To do so, turn right out the lot onto Pershing Avenue, left onto Market, left again after three blocks onto Duke, then left yet again onto Philadelphia. This maneuver will take you past several parking garages.

Glen Rock in Pennsylvania is shown at the center of **Map 13** on page 117. This town is located 14.5 miles south of York on the railroad trail. A few miles below Glen Rock is the Borough of **Railroad** and a few miles above Glen Rock is the unincorporated hamlet of **Hanover Junction**.

To reach these places, leave I-83 at Exit 1 for Route 851. (This exit is nearly 26 miles north of the Baltimore Beltway.) Follow Route 851—**not** *truck* 851—west for 2 miles. After passing uphill through Shrewsbury, the road descends into the valley of Codorus Creek, where the railroad trail is located. Near the bottom of the slope, there is a parking lot on the right next to the trail as it passes through the Borough of Railroad.

To continue to Glen Rock or Hanover Junction, turn right at a T-intersection and follow Route 616 north, which you can only do by pursuing the route signs religiously. After going 3.3 miles (which brings you to the middle of Glen Rock), turn left downhill onto Water Street, then turn right almost immediately, just beyond the railroad. The Rail Trail parking lot is at the end.

To continue to Hanover Junction, follow Route 616 north 4.6 miles from Water Street in Glen Rock. The parking lot for the Rail Trail County Park is on the right.

MAP 12 — York County Heritage Rail Trail (i.e, the Pennsylvania portion of the Northern Central Railroad Trail) between York and Hanover Junction

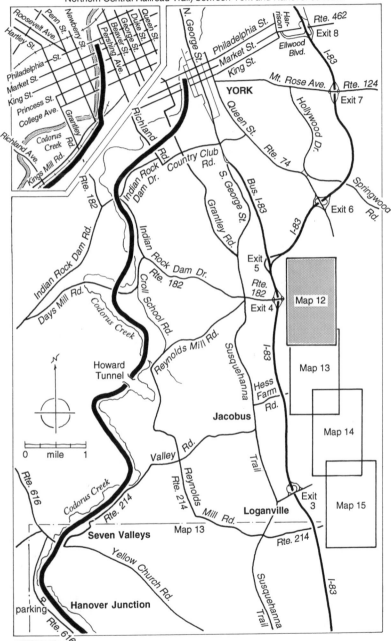

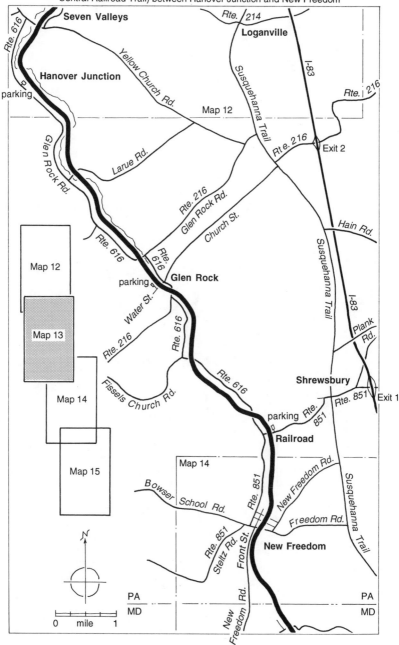

117

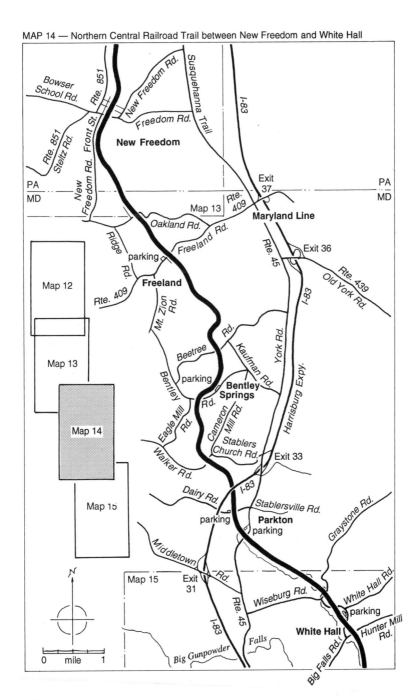

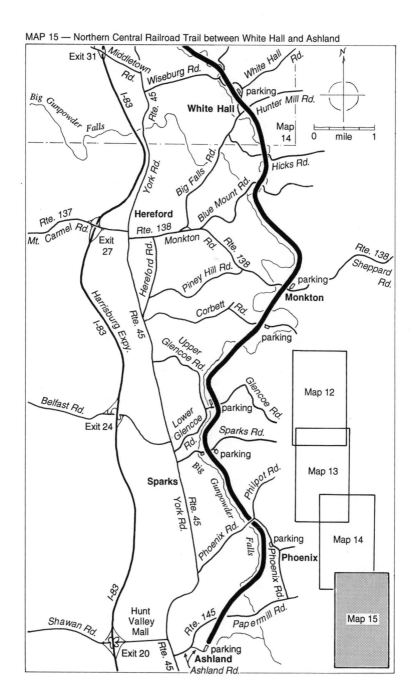

119

Freeland in Maryland is shown about a third of the way down **Map 14** on page 118. The large parking lot here is located 7.7 miles south of Glen Rock.

To reach Freeland from the south—i.e., from the vicinity of Baltimore—leave I-83 at Exit 36 for Route 439, Maryland Line, and Bel Air. (This exit is 21.3 miles north of the Baltimore Beltway.) Turn right at the top of the ramp to follow Route 439 west toward Maryland Line. Go 0.3 mile, then turn right (north) onto Route 45 (York Road). Follow Route 45 north 1 mile to a crossroads with Route 409 (Freeland Road). Turn left (west) onto Route 409 and go 1.7 miles to the parking lot on the right for the Northern Central Railroad Trail.

To reach Freeland from the north—i.e., from Pennsylvania—leave I-83 at Exit 37 for Freeland Road. From the crossroads at the top of the ramp, go straight 1.7 miles to the parking lot on the right for the Northern Central Railroad Trail.

If there is no room to park at Freeland, you probably can find room in the large lot at Bentley Springs, located 2.8 miles south along the trail.

White Hall in Maryland is shown in the area of overlap at the bottom of **Map 14** and top of **Map 15** on pages 118 and 119. This town is located 7.5 miles south of Freeland. To reach White Hall, leave I-83 at Exit 31 for Middletown Road and Parkton. (This exit is 15.6 miles north of the Baltimore Beltway.) Follow Middletown Road east toward Parkton 0.7 mile, then turn right (south) at a T-intersection with Route 45 (York Road). After just 0.3 mile, turn left onto Wiseburg Road. Go 1.4 miles, then turn right to continue on Wiseburg Road 0.3 mile to the parking lot on the right.

If there is no room at White Hall, there are small lots in Parkton, about 2 miles up York Road. One lot is on Frederick Road and the other on Dairy Road, both of which intersect with York Road.

Ashland* is located at the southern end of the railroad trail and is shown at the bottom of **Map 15** on page 119, about 10.5 miles below White Hall. To get to Ashland, leave I-83 at Exit 20A for Shawan Road east toward Cockeysville. (This exit is located

---

* Ashland was an iron-making town founded next to the railroad in 1844. By 1867 the company had three furnaces that used a pre-heated blast of air to smelt iron with Pennsylvania anthracite. In 1870 the work force numbered about a hundred men. The long stone building next to the parking lot formerly housed workers. Some of the brick houses at Ash-

5.3 miles north of the Baltimore Beltway.) Follow Shawan Road 0.8 mile, then turn right (south) at an intersection with Route 45 (York Road). After just 0.3 mile, turn left onto Ashland Road. Go 0.4 mile, then head half-right on Ashland Road into a housing development called Ashland at Hunt Valley. Continue straight on Ashland Road for a quarter of a mile to a parking lot for the Northern Central Railroad Trail.

If there is no room to park at Ashland, you can try parking 2 miles up the trail at a lot located on Phoenix Road. Many people also park where Papermill Road crosses the trail. (Papermill Road, incidentally, may someday be linked directly westward to the intersection of Shawan Road and York Road.)

≈   ≈   ≈   ≈

WALKING and BICYCLING: The bold line on **Maps 12-15** on pages 116-119 shows the railroad trail. The route is unmistakable throughout its entire length, with the possible exception of the first half-mile at York, which is described below. Occasionally, you must cross roads and parking lots, so use caution at all places where cars may be present.

To start at York, which is the northern terminus, see the corner panel on **Map 12** on page 116. From the riverside parking lot at the intersection of Philadelphia Street and Pershing Avenue, follow the paved path that borders Codorus Creek upstream (i.e., south). Notice the orange posts and gates and the signs for the Heritage Rail Trail County Park. These are the "blazes" that will guide you out of town. Soon the river curves right, but you should continue straight next to the railroad. The trail borders the railroad nearly all the way to Maryland.

To start at Ashland, which is the southern terminus, the trail leads straight out the end of the parking lot.

To start at other points along the trail, you can of course head north or south. Typically, the trail is located immediately adjacent to the parking lots.

---

land also were part of the company village. The furnaces, formerly located east of the railroad, operated until 1884, then again briefly in 1887. The works were torn down in 1893 and most of the houses were demolished in 1984, when the village was redeveloped.

12

OREGON RIDGE PARK

Map 16 on page 127 shows a figure-eight route of 4 miles (6.4 kilometers) at Oregon Ridge north of Baltimore. From the visitor center, the trail climbs the wooded ridge, then descends to Ivy Hill Pond and follows Baisman Run through a deep ravine. Several times the trail fords the shallow stream, so wear appropriate shoes or boots. Again the trail climbs the ridge and follows the broad crest back toward the starting point.

Oregon Ridge Park is open daily from sunrise to sunset while daylight saving time is in effect (i.e., from early April to late October). The rest of the year, it is open from 9:00 A. M. to 5 P.M. Dogs must be leashed. The park is managed by the Baltimore County Department of Recreation and Parks; telephone the Nature Center at (410) 887-1815.

For automobile directions, please turn to page 126. Walking directions are on pages 126-129.

ENTERING OREGON RIDGE PARK, visitors pass several structures that are remnants of the company town of Oregon Furnace. A handsome stone building now occupied by the Oregon Grille at Shawan and Beaverdam road was formerly the company store, patronized not only by employees but also by farmers and residents from the surrounding area. Farther along on the right side of the entrance road is the dilapidated frame manager's house. It is followed by a small springhouse and a derelict boarding house for unmarried laborers. Below the boarding house is a grassy path that once was the village's main street—the "Avenue"—that ran along the foot of the slope. A duplex tenant house stands at the far end of the Avenue, and near the Oregon Ridge Nature Center is a small reconstructed tenant house. These dwellings are all that is left of the 20 houses listed on the tax ledger for 1876. Another vestige of the ironworks is Oregon Lake swimming pond, which is an old ore pit or *bank* that has become filled with groundwater. Another ore bank, now resembling a ravine, is crossed by the pedestrian bridge at the end of the Nature Center. And nearby are more big holes in the hillside where ore was dug and limestone quarried. As for the furnace itself, it stood on the south side of the Avenue about 60 yards from the boarding house, but nothing substantial remains.

Oregon Furnace operated during the middle of the nineteenth century. If it was typical for the period, the furnace was a fat, tapering stone stack with a hollow core lined with fire brick. Like the stack itself, the core become progressively bigger in diameter toward the bottom or *bosh*. And below the bosh was a small sump called the *crucible*. As was usual, the furnace was located at the foot of a slope so that the top of the stack could be reached by a wooden trestlework ramp or bridge extending more or less horizontally from the top of the bluff. The furnace was 36 feet tall and 11 feet across at the bottom. The bellows were powered by a steam boiler and piston, to which water ran through a flume from Oregon Branch a quarter-mile upstream.

When the furnace was in operation, iron ore, anthracite fuel, and limestone flux were carted across the bridge and dumped into the top of the stack, which also served as the chimney. The purpose of the flux was to react with impurities in the ore to isolate pure iron, which melted and sank to the crucible. Occasionally the furnace belched streams of sparks, and at night a red glow illuminated the sky and village. To intensify combustion, the bellows pumped in air that had been preheated by passing through iron pipes and masonry chambers built into the furnace. This *hot blast*, as it was called, increased the furnace temperature and speeded the rate of smelting as compared to earlier cold-blast furnaces.

Once fired, the furnace was kept in continuous blast for many months at a time, until supplies were used up or the furnace lining deteriorated to the point where it had to be replaced. Men know as fillers labored around the clock, feeding the furnace at regular intervals as the ore, fuel, and flux were consumed. Working in a recessed casting arch at the bottom of the stack, the founder—a man of experience and judgment—occasionally opened the higher of two taps by removing its plug of baked mud in order to draw off, or rake out, the molten slag that floated on the heavier molten iron. And by opening a lower tap, the founder could sample the iron itself and to some extent control its quality by calling for an adjustment in the proportion of ingredients. Then, two or three times a day, the founder released the molten iron into molds dug in the sandy floor of the casting house, which was a barnlike structure built next to the stack. Typically, the molds consisted of nothing more that short, parallel troughs branching at right angles from a main channel. In the early days of iron making, the main channel and the smaller molds were noted to resemble a sow with suckling pigs; hence the term *pig iron* for crude iron. After the iron cooled, the pigs were snapped off with sledge hammers and the sow broken into convenient lengths for sale to foundries, rolling and slitting mills, and other manufacturers of iron products.

Never incorporated, the Oregon Company was originally a partnership of Richard Green, an experienced ironmaster, and Walter Farnandis, a director of Green Mount Cemetery in Baltimore City. Green and Farnandis start buying land and mineral rights at Oregon Ridge in 1846. In 1849 the assessor added to the account of Richard Green a "new furnace" worth $35,000. It probably went into blast for the first time that year. Apparently the furnace was not altogether satisfactory, for it was substantially redesigned and rebuilt in 1853 by Artemas Wilhelm, "whose fame as a builder of furnaces has extended far and wide," according to the *Baltimore County Advocate* for May 28. The new design greatly improved the arrangement of pipes and chambers for the hot blast. On January 14, 1854, the *Advocate* reported that the Oregon iron furnace "ran out in one week over one hundred and ten tons of no. 1 iron. This is considered by persons acquainted with these matters to be the largest yield ever given by any one furnace in the United States in the same period of time."

Although some of the Oregon Company's cart drivers appear to have been slaves hired out by their owners, most of the laborers were Irish. At that time, tens of thousands of men and women each month were emigrating from Ireland to the United States to escape the Potato Famine that had started in the mid-1840s. The Irish who worked for the Oregon Company regularly had brawls with other Irishmen from rival Ashland Furnace, which also mined ore at Oregon Ridge. (Ashland Furnace itself was located three miles away on the Northern Central Railroad at what is now the southern end of the hike-bike trail featured in Chapter 11.) According to one memoir, the two groups of Irish miners at Oregon Ridge each built a blockhouse for defense. In 1852 the Oregon Company and the Ashland Iron Company merged their businesses, with Richard Green as manager. Oregon Furnace remained in operation until 1857, and after that the site served only as one of many sources of ore for Ashland Furnace.

Mining at the Oregon site continued until Ashland Furnace closed in 1884. Thomas Kurtz, the last foreman at the Oregon pits, bought the 457-acre tract and carried on the general store. Kurtz may have used the old furnace as a source of ready-cut rock when he expanded the store in 1879. His family held the property until 1969, when Baltimore County bought it for inclusion in Oregon Ridge Park.

≈ ≈ ≈ ≈

AUTOMOBILE DIRECTIONS: Oregon Ridge Park is located 12 miles north of Baltimore near the Hunt Valley Business Community. (See •12 on **Map 1** on page 5. For greater detail, refer to the upper panel of **Map 16** at right.)

To Oregon Ridge Park from Interstate 695 (the Baltimore Beltway): Leave I-695 at Exit 24 for Interstate 83 north toward Timonium and York, PA. Go 5.5 miles, then follow the directions in the next paragraph.

To Oregon Ridge Park from Interstate 83: Leave I-83 at Exit 20B for Shawan Road west toward Oregon Ridge Park. Follow Shawan Road west about 1 mile, then turn left at a traffic light onto Beaver Dam Road. Go only 20 yards, then fork right toward the nature center and beach. Follow the park road 0.4 mile to the nature center parking lot.

≈ ≈ ≈ ≈

WALKING: The lower panel of **Map 16** at right shows a 4-mile figure-eight route at **Oregon Ridge Park**, where the trails are marked by colored blazes.

MAP 16 — Oregon Ridge Park

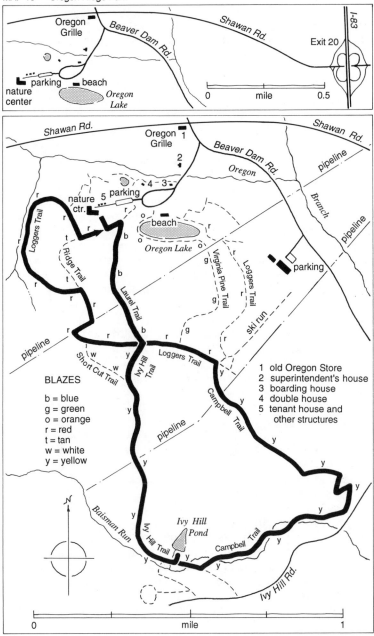

BLAZES

b = blue
g = green
o = orange
r = red
t = tan
w = white
y = yellow

1 old Oregon Store
2 superintendent's house
3 boarding house
4 double house
5 tenant house and
   other structures

127

Start at the end of the parking lot. From there follow the asphalt road to the Oregon Ridge Nature Center, which has exhibits on the history, wildlife, and vegetation of Oregon Ridge.

After visiting the nature center, locate a pedestrian bridge leading from the end of the building across an old ore pit to an intersection with the red-blazed **Loggers Trail**. Turn left onto the red-blazed trail and go 150 yards, then turn very sharply right uphill onto the blue-blazed **Laurel Trail**. Follow the blue blazes uphill. Cross the wide swath of a gas pipeline right-of-way and continue uphill on the blue-blazed trail. The blue trail ends at a skewed four-way intersection.

From the end of the blue trail, cross the red-blazed Loggers Trail and follow the yellow-blazed **Ivy Hill Trail** through the woods, across another gas pipeline right-of-way, and downhill to the spillway from Ivy Hill Pond on the left (next to Baisman Run on the right).

You can return from the pond by the way you came, or you can continue on the figure-eight route shown on Map 16. To complete the figure-eight, descend from the dam at Ivy Hill Pond and turn left onto the yellow-blazed **S. James Campbell Trail**. (Campbell played a leading roll in raising money from local corporations and foundations to buy this part of the park.) With Baisman Run toward your right, follow the yellow blazes 170 yards to where the path fords the stream. Usually Baisman Run is easily crossed, but you will have to assess conditions for yourself when you are there.

After crossing the stream, go 75 yards, then turn left to continue on the yellow-blazed trail. After only 25 yards, ford back across Baisman Run, then continue on the yellow-blazed trail along the foot of the slope, with the stream toward your right. Before long, ford Baisman Run again and yet again. Eventually, as the yellow-blazed trail approaches Ivy Hill Road, the path curves left and climbs away from Baisman Run. Continue as the trail curves still father left and climbs away from the road, then zigzags to reach the top of the slope.

Follow the yellow-blazed trail along the broad crest of a ridge, rising very gradually as you go. Eventually, the trail cuts diagonally across a pipeline right-of-way, then continues for 140 yards through the woods to a junction with the red-blazed **Loggers Trail**. Here you should turn left, but first you may want to take in the view from the head of the ski slope, which can be reached by following the red blazes half-right.

As noted above, turn sharply left from the yellow-blazed Campbell Trail onto the red-blazed Loggers Trail. Follow the red blazes along the broad crest of Oregon Ridge and past intersections with the green-blazed Virginia Pine Trail, the blue-blazed Laurel Trail, the yellow-blazed Ivy Hill Trail, and the white-blazed Short Cut Trail. Follow the red blazes all the way to a gas pipeline right-of-way, and there turn right to follow the right-of-way 150 yards before veering half-left at the top of the hill. Re-enter the woods on the red-blazed Loggers Trail and go 190 yards, then turn left (where the tan-blazed Ridge Trail continues straight). Follow the red-blazed path downhill and along the side of a ravine, then eventually to the right. Continue more or less straight on the wide, red-blazed trail where the tan-blazed path intersects from the rear-right. Continue to the bridge leading left to the starting point at the nature center.

13

SOLDIERS DELIGHT NATURAL ENVIRONMENT AREA

Located northwest of Baltimore near Owings Mills, Soldiers Delights is an unusual landscape of rocky meadows and stunted, piney woods. The figure-eight route outlined on **Map 17** on page 137 is 3.5 miles long (5.6 kilometers).

Soldiers Delight is open daily from 8:00 A.M. to sunset. Dogs must be leashed. The visitor center is open Wednesday through Sunday from 9:00 to 4:00. The area is managed by the Department of Natural Resources, Maryland Forest, Park and Wildlife Service; telephone (410) 922-3044. If there is no answer, call (410) 461-5005 for the Patapsco Valley State Park, through which Soldiers Delight is administrated.

For automobile directions, please turn to page 136. Walking directions start on page 138.

THERE'S CHROME IN THEM THAR HILLS at Soldiers Delight.

Perhaps this news lacks the galvanic impact of a gold strike, but the fact remains that during the second quarter of the nineteenth century, ownership of chromite mines in the Soldiers Delight district and at other outcroppings of serpentine rock in Maryland and southeastern Pennsylvania enabled Isaac Tyson, Jr., founder of the Baltimore Chrome Works, to control the world chromium market and to become a very wealthy man.

The serpentine formations that break the surface in a few locations north and west of Baltimore are like nothing else in the region. They are commonly called serpentine *barrens*, and appropriately so. Large meadows of yellow and red-tinted grass cover the hills. Blackjack oak, post oak, and Virginia pine (all small, drought-tolerant species of trees) also grow from the meager soil. The shallow, stony earth not only lacks organic matter but also contains heavy concentrations of magnesium, which inhibits the ability of plants to absorb nutrients. The savannahs and stunted forest offer hikers a refreshing change from the farmland, river gorges, and tall deciduous woods so typical of Maryland's Piedmont region. Even if you have no background in botany, you can enjoy the look of the Indian grass, little bluestem, purplish three-awn, beardgrass, turkeyfoot, broomsedge and other grasses typical of midwestern prairies. Depending on the season, visitors can also find birdsfoot violets, fame-flowers, blazing stars, sandplain gerardias, sundrops, asters, knotweed, goldenrod, fringed gentians, and other wildflowers. At least 34 rare or endangered species of plants are found here, many of them showing special adaptations (such as hairy surfaces or leaves that curl up at midday) in order to cope with the drought and heat of summer. The best way to learn more about these plants is to join a walk led by a qualified naturalist. Call or stop by the visitor center for information on flower walks and other programs at Soldiers Delight.

Serpentine is a greenish metamorphic rock found near Baltimore not only at Soldiers Delight but also in the Bare Hills west of Lake Roland. The exterior of Baltimore's Mount Vernon Place Methodist Church, which has a distinctly greenish hue, is serpentine from the Bare Hills. Perhaps, too, you are familiar with the old greenish stone school on Falls Road in the Bare Hills just uphill from Princeton Sports. As a structural stone, however, serpentine is not altogether satisfactory because it has random soft spots which cause the surface of some stone blocks to flake off from exposure to the weather. Varieties of serpentine have also been used for decorative interior trim in banks, hotels, and office buildings. For about a hundred years until the early 1980s, a greenish agglomerate of serpentine and calcite was quarried at Cardiff in Harford County and sold under the trade name of Maryland Green Marble, although it is not a limestone, as are true marbles.

More significantly, the occurrence of serpentine in Maryland is associated with the presence of chromium. In 1808 or 1810 chromium ore was discovered in the serpentine outcroppings at the Bare Hills estate of Jesse Tyson, a wealthy flour and grain merchant. The Tysons' gardener showed some black rocks to

Tyson's son, Isaac, who was a student of geology, mineralogy, and chemistry. He identified the rocks as chromite, and analysis established that the ore was of a salable grade.

With financial assistance from his father, the young Tyson started mining the ore on a small scale. Ore was extracted at the Bare Hills as early as 1811, and by 1817 Tyson was also mining chromite from stream deposits (called placers) in the serpentine barrens at Soldiers Delight. As with gold mining, the stream sands were washed in a sluice (called a buddle) to concentrate the heavy chromite. The ore was then shipped to paint and ceramic factories in England, for at that time chromium was used chiefly to make brilliant pigments, dyes, and glazes (hence chrome-yellow, chrome-orange, chrome-green, and other chrome hues).

Chromite mining was only a small part of Isaac Tyson's business as a manufacturer of chemicals, but in 1827 he hit pay dirt. He noticed that a cider barrel that had been brought in a wagon to Belair Market in Baltimore was steadied by rocks that he recognized as chromite. He traced the stone to the Reed farm near Jarrettsville in Harford County, obtained mineral rights to the property, and there, at what came to be called Chrome Hill, found a massive deposit of ore only eight feet below the surface. The Reed Mine was developed quickly and became so profitable that Tyson temporarily suspended his mining operations at other sites.

Tyson continued, however, to search out serpentine formations in Maryland and Pennsylvania, and he bought or leased property wherever there were indications of chromium. Not long after the Reed discovery, Tyson opened the Wood Mine in the State Line district of Lancaster County, Pennsylvania. This operation was another bonanza, eventually proving to be the richest chromium mine in the United States. Isaac Tyson's mines were far more productive and economical than other sources, with the result that between 1828 and 1850 virtually all of the chromium used in the world came from his mines.

Tyson's search for chromite also led to his involvement in the mining and smelting of iron and copper. He had a copper works at the Bare Hills, faintly recalled nowadays by Copper Hill Road and Coppermine Terrace off Falls Road. In league with his partners, he eventually owned most of the copper deposits in

Maryland. He visited pits, smelting plants, and ironworks up and down the East Coast. He was a leader in the use of new and more efficient methods of refining ore, such as smelting with hard coal and pre-heating air to create a hot blast. Engrossed with mining and minerals and intent on holding down competition, he or his agents sedulously investigated deposits and mining claims from Maine to Virginia, west to Arkansas and Missouri, and even in Cuba and Spain. "I am now going to Stafford in Vermont and for what purpose?" he wrote in his journal on December 1, 1833:

> All for the sake of gain and how great the sacrifice. My beloved wife not yet out of her bed and requiring the sympathy and solace of her husband. My little children requiring the care and attention of their father & and my business neglected. . . . I am able to talk philosophically on these subjects and show the unreasonableness of avarice and the folly of accumulating wealth for children and yet I find myself pursuing the beaten track.

In 1845 Tyson and his associates established the Baltimore Chrome Works for the manufacture of chromium compounds from raw ore. The plant was located on the western arm of Fells Point at the entrance to the Inner Harbor. Tyson's timing in this venture was fortunate because the export market for unprocessed ore began to decline after the discovery of high-grade chromite in Turkey in 1848 by a geologist who had gained some of his experience working for Tyson. Although the export of chrome ore from the United States had practically ceased by 1860, the manufacture of chromium compounds at Baltimore continued and was carried on by Tyson's sons after his death in 1861. Local mines were eventually closed as the Baltimore Chrome Works obtained ore more cheaply from company-owned mines in California and later in New Caledonia. Until a rival plant was established in Philadelphia in 1882, the Baltimore Chrome Works supplied virtually all the chromium chemicals used by American industry.

Tyson's principal operation at Soldiers Delight was the Choate Mine. It was opened before 1839 and was worked intermittently until about 1886. It consisted of an inclined shaft sloping to the southwest for as much as 200 feet and fanning out to a mine face 160 feet wide. During World War I, when chromium was needed to make high-grade steel for armaments, the Choate Mine was reopened for a brief period. The ore was washed and concentrated in a local buddle operated by the Triplett family, who in 1893 had bought mineral rights to six acres from the Tysons. The entrance to the Choate Mine is still visible, but the sloping shaft should not be entered. Visitors should also be cautious around other old shafts in the area, where a variety of minerals were mined at one time or another. For example, talc was mined at Soldiers Delight and ground at local mills to make talcum powder.

Soldiers Delight is now a state "natural environment area," meaning that aside from the visitor center and trails, no recreational development is planned. The state first began to purchase land here in 1970 after ten years of lobbying and fundraising by local conservation groups, including the Citizens Committee for Soldiers Delight and Soldiers Delight Conservation, Inc. Money has been supplied by private donations and by the county, state, and federal governments. About 2,000 acres has been purchased as of the year 2001.

To reverse the gradual disappearance of grasslands at Soldiers Delight, the state has initiated a program to cut down encroaching species of trees—chiefly Virginia pine—and to burn the underbrush, briars, and meadows periodically, as Native Americans did for centuries before the arrival of Europeans. Used by the Indians as a tool for flushing out deer and other game during hunts, fire is a triggering mechanism for many species of prairie plants. Early accounts by settlers remark on the large grasslands, far greater than today, that existed at Soldiers Delight and other areas northward to Pennsylvania. Used for grazing livestock, Soldiers Delight was still mostly grassland well into the twentieth century. Aerial photographs from the 1930s show how much has been lost since then. To restore the grasslands, the program of fire calls for burning about 100 acres each year for ten years.

The site of the old Baltimore Chrome Works has also seen major changes. In 1908 the company combined with two rival firms to form the Mutual Chemical Company of America. During the next half-century, Mutual greatly expanded its Inner

Harbor plant for processing chromium compounds, and in the early 1950s the facility was the world's largest chromium chemical plant. In 1954 Mutual was acquired by the Allied Chemical Corporation (now Allied-Signal, Inc.), which in 1984 ceased operations at the Inner Harbor's gateway. After the production there of toxic chromium compounds for more than 140 years, the soil was found to be impregnated with cancer-causing chromium chemicals that leaked into the Patapsco River at a rate of about 60 pounds per day. During the early 1990s, the site underwent decontamination. The cleanup effort included sealing the chromium in the soil under a seven-foot cap of clay, gravel, and heavy plastic sheeting. An impermeable barrier was installed around the shoreline. The cleanup cost Allied-Signal about $100 million. The site is now awaiting redevelopment.

≈　　　≈　　　≈　　　≈

AUTOMOBILE DIRECTIONS: Soldiers Delight Natural Environment Area is located about 12 miles northwest of Baltimore. (See •13 on **Map 1** on page 5. For greater detail, refer to the small corner panel of **Map 17** at right.)

To Soldiers Delight from Interstate 695 (the Baltimore Beltway): Leave I-695 at Exit 19 for Interstate 795 (the Northwest Expressway) toward Owings Mills and Reisterstown. Go 6.3 miles, then follow the directions in the next paragraph.

To Soldiers Delight from Interstate 795 (the Northwest Expressway): Leave I-795 at Exit 7B for Franklin Boulevard westbound. (If you are coming from the north, take Exit 7, then turn left onto Nicodemus Road and right onto Franklin Boulevard.)
　　Follow Franklin Boulevard west 0.4 mile, then bear right onto Church Road. After 0.8 mile, turn left at a T-intersection with Berrymans Lane. Go 0.4 mile, then turn sharply left onto Deer Park Road. Follow Deer Park Road 1.2 miles, then turn right into the entrance for the Soldiers Delight Visitor Center. As you enter the parking lot, notice the white-blazed trail on the right, where the walk described below starts.

To Soldiers Delight from Route 26 (Liberty Road): Route 26 runs through Randallstown northwest of Exit 18B off

MAP 17 — Soldiers Delight Natural Environment Area

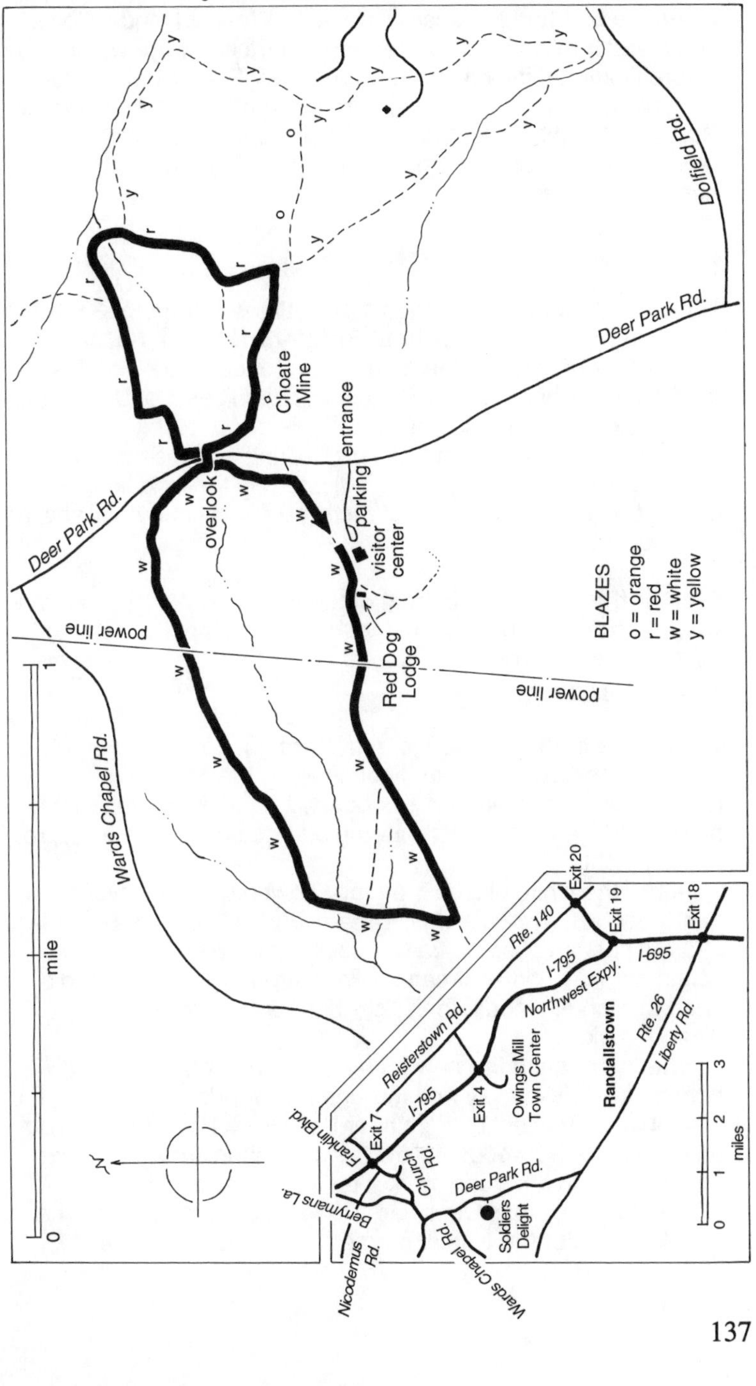

BLAZES

o = orange
r = red
w = white
y = yellow

Choate Mine

entrance

parking

visitor center

overlook

Deer Park Rd.

Deer Park Rd.

Dolfield Rd.

Red Dog Lodge

power line

power line

Wards Chapel Rd.

mile

N

Exit 20

Exit 19

Exit 18

Rte. 140

I-795

Northwest Expy.

I-695

Rte. 26

Liberty Rd.

Randallstown

Reisterstown Rd.

I-795

Owings Mill Town Center

Exit 4

Exit 7

Franklin Blvd.

Church Rd.

Deer Park Rd.

Soldiers Delight

Berrymans La.

Nicodemus Rd.

Wards Chapel Rd.

miles

0 1 2 3

137

Interstate 695 (the Baltimore Beltway). West of Randallstown—and about 5 miles from the Beltway—there is a large water tower where Route 26 intersects with Deer Park Road. Follow Deer Park Road north 2 miles, then turn left into the entrance for the Soldiers Delight Visitor Center. As you enter the parking lot, notice the white-blazed trail on the right, where the walk described below starts.

≈ ≈ ≈ ≈

WALKING: **Map 17** on page 137 outlines a route of 3.5 miles in the form of a figure-eight at **Soldiers Delight Natural Environment Area.** The loop west of Deer Park Road is marked with white blazes. The smaller circuit east of Deer Park Road is marked with red blazes.

There are other trails at Soldiers Delight, and they too are shown on the map. The route indicated by the bold line, however, provides the best look at the area's serpentine barrens, as described below.

Start at the parking lot in front of the visitor center. Locate the white-blazed trail that runs along the right side of the parking lot as you face the building. Follow this trail past the visitor center. After 150 yards, veer right past the chimney-end of Red Dog Lodge.

From the front of the lodge, head straight downhill. Pass under some power lines and continue on the white-blazed trail through clearings and piney woods. At a fork in the rutted trail, bear left. Eventually, after passing a large field on the left, turn sharply right.

Follow the white blazes gradually downhill through woods and past clearings, across a small stream, and uphill. Go more or less straight past an obscure trail intersecting from the right. Descend across another stream. Climb through a clearing and a short stretch of woods, then bear right uphill on the white-blazed track.

When you reach the power lines, continue obliquely uphill across the right-of-way and through the woods. Eventually, the white-blazed trail bends right near Deer Park Road. When you emerge from the woods, follow the road shoulder right a few dozen yards to a historic marker for Soldiers Delight.

With caution, cross Deer Park Road and turn right along the shoulder. Enter the woods on the red-blazed trail. After 170 yards, the trail bends left near the entrance to Isaac Tyson's Choate Mine. Follow the red-blazes through the woods to a T-intersection, and there turn left to continue on the red-blazed loop.

Follow the trail through the woods, right at a trail junction, and gradually downhill. Pass a trail intersecting from the right at the center of a small clearing. Re-enter the woods on the red-blazed trail and cross a small stream, then turn left and continue straight uphill through more clearings. Eventually, turn left, then right to follow the red blazes uphill to Deer Park Road, with the historic marker to the left as you emerge from the woods.

With caution, cross Deer Park Road at the historic marker. With the road on the left, re-join the white-blazed loop as the trail follows the shoulder south 50 yards, then veers half-right into the woods. Continue as the white-blazed footpath runs parallel with Deer Park Road, then turns right onto a gravel road that leads to the visitor center.

14

PATAPSCO VALLEY STATE PARK

McKeldin Area

The route outlined on **Map 18** on page 147 follows deep, wooded valleys at the confluence of the Patapsco River's North and South Branches, located near Marriottsville west of Baltimore. A spur trail leads to McKeldin Falls, among the largest of our local cascades. Altogether, the circuit and spur total 4 miles (6.4 kilometers). As described in Chapter 15, the McKeldin trailhead is also a good place to start for a long walk down the Patapsco Valley through a section never seen by most park visitors.

The McKeldin Area opens daily at 8:00 A.M. during the period from Memorial Day to Labor Day. It opens at 10:00 A.M. during the rest of the year. And it closes at sunset, year-round. It is also closed on Thanksgiving and Christmas. An admission fee is charged on weekends and holidays during April through October. Pets are prohibited. The park is managed by the Department of Natural Resources, Maryland Forest, Park and Wildlife Service; telephone (410) 461-5005.

For automobile directions to the McKeldin Area, please turn to page 145. Walking directions start on page 146.

"FRANKLY, I LIKE THE SOUND of the Governor Theodore R. McKeldin Recreation Area," said Governor Theodore R. McKeldin at the dedication ceremony for this section of Patapsco Valley State Park in 1957. For more than a decade McKeldin had been one of the leading advocates for the expansion of the park to include the entire Patapsco Valley downstream from Sykesville as well as the North Branch below Liberty Reservoir. As governor, McKeldin was in the enviable position of being able to implement what he described as a "brilliant plan" that he had come across after taking office—a plan developed earlier at his recommendation while mayor of Baltimore but shelved by the previous governor. The plan called for the extension into the greater Baltimore area of the system of stream-valley parks first proposed in the Olmsted Brothers report fifty years earlier (as discussed in Chapter 17).

Prior to the 1950s, Patapsco Valley State Park included less than 1,500 acres in a patchwork between Route 40 (Hollofield) and Route 1 (Avalon). The park—or Patapsco River Forest Reserve, as it was at first called—had started with a gift to the state of 434 acres in 1907, at a time when President Theodore Roosevelt (for whom McKeldin was named) and his chief forester, Gifford Pinchot, were popularizing the philosophy of conservation, withdrawing immense public tracts from sale to the private sector, and establishing federal forest reserves. In 1912 the state legislature for the first time appropriated funds for the purchase of forest lands to be managed by the Maryland State Board of Forestry.

By the time of the Great Depression during the 1930s, the Patapsco River Forest Reserve had about 1,300 acres. During this period the area was improved with trails, picnic grounds, shelters, and campsites constructed by workers of the federally sponsored Civilian Conservation Corps, which had a camp at the Avalon area (Chapter 16). The CCC provided useful work, income, and vocational training for unemployed single men. The organization was run on a semi-military basis by the War Department and assigned projects selected and supervised by the Department of Agriculture. Living in barracks, the workers comprised companies of about two hundred men. Base pay was $30 per month, and if a man's family at home was on relief, most of his wages were sent there. At its peak in 1935, the CCC had more than a half-million men in over 2,600 camps working on forest and wildlife protection, flood control, soil conservation, and the development of federal, state, and local parks.

As the primary use of the Patapsco River Forest Reserve shifted from forest preservation to recreation, the name was changed to Patapsco Valley State Park under the newly consolidated Department of State Forests and Parks (now the Department of Natural Resources). The federal government's construction of the George Washington Memorial Parkway and the Blue

Ridge Parkway during the 1930s, plus the immense popularity of weekend driving and picnicking, influenced plans for the new park. In 1946, the Patapsco River Valley Commission, appointed by then-Mayor McKeldin, drew up a plan for enlarging the state park to 15,000 acres connected by a riverside parkway for cars. The road was never built but other aspects of the plan reappeared in a study prepared by private consultants for the Maryland State Planning Commission in 1950. The new plan called for a linear park of 8,500 acres averaging half a mile in width and extending 37 miles along the river from the Hanover Street Bridge in Baltimore to Sykesville. Improvements were to include not only the usual hiking and riding trails and picnicking and camping facilities, but also golf courses (even miniature golf), swimming pools, a miniature railroad, a carousel, dance pavilions, restaurants, cabins, and lodges. The total cost was estimated at $6 million and a period of twelve years was thought sufficient to complete the project.

During the next twenty-five years the park grew in fits and starts. For a period, land acquisition stalled at about 4,500 acres as funds were exhausted and state and local officials and a citizen advisory committee debated which land should be given priority for purchase. A major area of contention was the marsh and floodplain along the lower Patapsco, where gravel mining had left a series of small lakes in the flats beside the river. This area has since been acquired at the urging of officials of Anne Arundel County and serves chiefly as a wildlife sanctuary. It has not been developed for recreation because of periodic flooding. By 1972, when even areas of the Patapsco Valley that are only rarely flooded were devastated by Tropical Storm Agnes, the park had about 7,000 acres spread among Carroll, Howard, Baltimore, and Anne Arundel counties and was visited yearly by an estimated 4.5 million people.

Yet at the same time that millions of dollars were being spent to expand the park, industrial pollution and suburban growth were turning the Patapsco River into a regional sewer. At first the problem was not without a sort of perverse drollery. Children who swam at Ellicott City in the early 1900s had to post a lookout on the rocks upstream to warn companions to get out of the water whenever the Dickey Mill at Oella released dye into the river. But by mid-century swimming was unthinkable.

Sykesville, Ellicott City, and other communities and institutional facilities dumped their untreated waste into the river. Industries added oil, solvents, and other chemicals, and canneries and distilleries poured in slurries of food scraps, pulp, and grain. The river stank. Newspaper accounts during the 1960s reported floating islands of bubbling sludge and a river bottom coated with decomposing matter. Detergents produced a frothy surface that gave the appearance of snow and ice year-round. Massive fish kills occurred annually during periods of particularly toxic discharges. By 1967 a study by the Maryland Department of Water Resources classified the Patapsco River below Ilchester, where effluent from the paperboard mill used to be discharged into the river, as "grossly polluted."

Since then, however, water quality in the Patapsco has improved significantly. Industries and communities along the river have been required to connect into the large Patapsco interceptor sewer line that during the late 1960s was run up the valley from the Patapsco Wastewater Treatment Plant at Wagners Point. Also, the torrent caused by Tropical Storm Agnes flushed the accumulated filth from the riverbed (and dumped it in the tidal portion of the Patapsco at Baltimore City). Still, however, incidents of industrial pollution and sewage overflows occur occasionally, and sediments from erosion and stormwater runoff give the water its characteristic murky appearance.

After the 1972 Agnes flood, the Maryland Department of Natural Resources undertook to re-evaluate previous park plans for the Patapsco. The job was assigned to the Department's own staff of professional land planners. Working with members of the Maryland Park Service and a newly appointed citizen advisory committee, the state's design team developed a revised master plan that was adopted in 1979 and on the basis of which the General Assembly authorized a park totaling 15,200 acres. This figure has since been increased to 16,082 acres, of which nearly 15,000 had been acquired as of the year 2001. Previously, the state had concentrated on buying only the valley bottom and slopes because they were visually and environmentally sensitive (and in most cases cheap as well), but much of the acreage bought since 1979 is outside—though still adjacent to—the immediate valley. In these areas, the plan called for development of extensive campgrounds and picnic areas set back from the valley rim, where the pavilions, toilets, and offices would be beyond the reach of flood, easily accessible from nearby roads, and yet visually isolated in the woods. The valley slopes and bottomland were reserved for low-cost improvements and low-key uses, such as riding and walking trails.

Aside from calling for a larger park, the 1979 Patapsco master plan was generally more austere than earlier plans. The Department of Natural Resources adopted the policy that the chief purpose of state parks is to promote the enjoyment and protection of natural, historic, and scenic features rather than to provide tennis courts, skating rinks, swimming pools, golf courses, and other recreational facilities that are more appropriately the responsibility of local governments—and this has been the prevailing philosophy ever since. Many of the big picnic areas and campgrounds contemplated for Patapsco Valley State Park have never been built and probably will be postponed indefinitely—or at least be scaled down—in recognition of the fact that Patapsco visitors no longer use these types of facilities as much as they once did, preferring instead to walk, bicycle, or ride horses for the day in a natural setting. The main project now receiving consideration is the development of a continuous trail through the entire length of the park to link eventually with the Gwynns Falls Trail and BWI Trail.

≈   ≈   ≈   ≈

AUTOMOBILE DIRECTIONS: The McKeldin Area of Patapsco Valley State Park is located about 13 miles west of Baltimore. (See •14 on **Map 1** on page 5. For greater detail, refer to the upper panel of **Map 18** on page 147.) The entrance is on Marriottsville Road north of Marriottsville. Several approaches are described below.

To the McKeldin Area from Interstate 695 (the Baltimore Beltway): Leave I-695 at Exit 16 for Interstate 70 west toward Frederick. Go about 8 miles, then follow the directions in the next paragraph.

To the McKeldin Area from Interstate 70 *westbound***:** Leave I-70 at Exit 83 for Marriottsville Road. (This exit is located 3.7 miles west of the juncture with **Route 29**.) Turn right at the

top of the ramp and follow Marriottsville Road north through Marriottsville 4 miles to the park entrance on the right. Park your car
in the lot just beyond the small ranger station at the top of the
entrance road.

To the McKeldin Area from Interstate 70 *eastbound*:
Leave I-70 at Exit 82 for Route 40 east. At the first traffic light,
turn left and follow Marriottsville Road north through Marriottsville 4.7 miles to the park entrance on the right. Park your car in
the lot just beyond the small ranger station at the top of the entrance road.

To the McKeldin Area from Route 26 (Liberty Road):
Route 26 runs through Randallstown northwest of Exit 18B off
Interstate 695 (the Baltimore Beltway). From the intersection of
Route 26 and Marriottsville Road west of Randallstown—nearly
5 miles from the Beltway—follow Marriottsville Road southwest
4.7 miles to the park entrance on the left. Park your car in the lot
just beyond the small ranger station at the top of the entrance
road.

≈ ≈ ≈ ≈

WALKING: The lower panel of **Map 18** at right shows a 4-mile
circuit at the **McKeldin Area of Patapsco Valley State
Park**. Directions start in the next paragraph. For a 9-mile hike
down the Patapsco Valley to Dogwood Road, see Chapter 15.

Start at the tiny ranger station at the top of the entrance road.
From there, follow the entrance road back downhill toward
Marriottsville Road for 70 yards. At the first bend, head straight
off the road onto a wide path entering the woods. This is the
Switchback Trail, and it is marked with white paint blazes.
Except for one deviation noted below, the route described here
follows this trail.
Follow the path through the woods, then gradually downhill
and around to the left by Marriottsville Road. Continue along
the bottom of the slope. Pass a trail intersecting from the left in
order to continue straight downhill to the floodplain bordering
the South Branch of the Patapsco River.
Turn left along the valley bottom and continue with the river
on your right. Eventually, turn right at an intersection and follow
the white-blazed path along the river bank, then up and straight

Map 18 — McKeldin Area of Patapsco Valley State Park

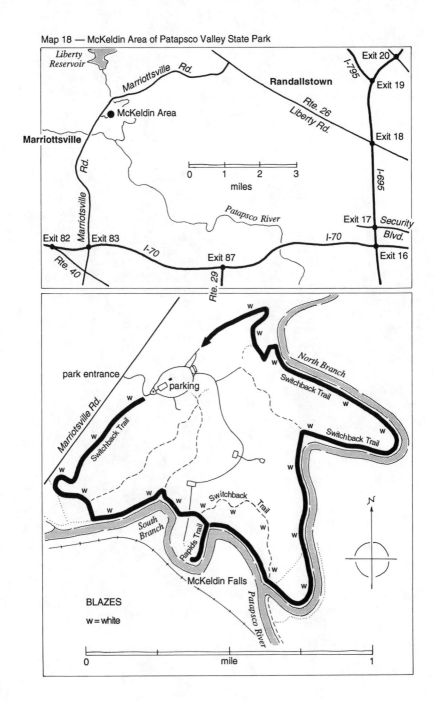

across an asphalt road. At the next trail junction, ignore for now the white blazes leading left; instead, fork right downhill on the **McKeldin Rapids Trail**, which is more scenic.

At the river's edge, where the Patapsco bends sharply, follow a trail upstream several hundred yards to McKeldin Falls, as shown on the map, then return downstream to the sharp bend in the river. From there, continue downstream on the riverside path to the confluence of the North and South Branches of the Patapsco River. At one point the trail leads over jumbled rocks and across a large, bare rock surface sloping into the river. **If you prefer not to cross the rock slope**, which can be slippery when it is wet or icy, retrace your steps to the white-blazed trail and follow it right gradually uphill to the rim of the valley and then down again to the confluence of the North and South Branches of the Patapsco River.

Because of the dam at Liberty Reservoir, the North Branch usually has little water. With the river on your right, follow the white-blazed **Switchback Trail** upstream along the North Branch. After about 0.7 mile, turn right at a T-intersection and continue on the white-blazed trail, still with the river on your right, although it is often out of sight. Follow the path along the valley bottom, around to the left, and along the river. Eventually, the trail crosses a jumble of rocks shortly before the river bends slightly to the right. After about 220 yards, turn left to climb very steeply away from the river on the white-blazed path. (If you run into a cliff blocking further progress along the river's edge, you will know that you have gone too far and should retrace your steps 70 yards.)

Follow the white-blazed footpath as it zigzags steeply away from the river. At a trail junction near the crest of the slope, turn right. Follow the white-blazed path along the top of the slope, then gradually downhill and to the right along the side of the valley. Continue as the trail gradually climbs, then curves sharply left. Follow the path to a picnic area and then along an asphalt road that at one point provides a view of Liberty Dam to the north. Continue straight to the parking lot by the ranger station. Be alert for cars.

15

PATAPSCO VALLEY STATE PARK

between the McKeldin Area and Dogwood Road

Located west of Baltimore, this remote section of Patapsco Valley State Park provides the opportunity to walk all day in nearly complete solitude. The route shown on **Maps 19 and 20** on pages 166 and 167 stretches for 9 miles (14.4 kilometers) along the wooded valley. Hard-core hikers may enjoy the opportunity for a long walk round-trip; however, the easiest way to see the entire trail is to walk from each end to the middle and back on two separate days.

Please note that if you start at the McKeldin Area, one of the first things to do is to ford the North Branch of the Patapsco River. Because Liberty Dam is located only a mile upstream, the North Branch usually has little water (as shown on page 169), but you cannot know for sure until you get there. **Do not cross** unless you can clearly see that the water is not too deep. (At the ford discussed in the walking directions, there is rarely more than a foot of water, but sometimes there can be much more.) If you plan to hike the entire trail one way—i.e., without retracing your steps to return to your car— start at the McKeldin Area so that you will know at the outset whether or not you can safely ford the North Branch. For comfort, you may even want to carry in your daypack a pair of old sneakers and change into them while you ford the river so that the rest of the time you can walk with dry feet.

The McKeldin Area opens daily at 8:00 A.M. during the period from Memorial Day to Labor Day. It opens at 10:00 A.M. during the rest of the year. And it closes at sunset, year-round. It is also closed on Thanksgiving and Christmas. An admission fee is charged on weekends and holidays during April through October. Dogs—in fact all pets—are prohibited.

At Dogwood Road you can enter the park starting at 8:00 A.M. year-round. You must leave by sunset. Dogs are permitted on a leash.

Patapsco Valley State Park is managed by the Department of Natural Resources, Maryland Forest, Park and Wildlife Service; telephone (410) 461-5005.

For automobile directions, please turn to page 164. Walking directions start on page 165.

DANIELS, formerly a large mill village but now mostly ruins, is one of the chief landmarks located along the Patapsco River in the stretch of valley covered by this chapter. As recently as the mid-1900s, there was a functioning three-story stone mill, 48 by 230 feet, and various brick and cement-block structures for the manufacture of heavy canvas, denim, industrial belting, and hose. A concrete dam furnished 400 horsepower and generated surplus electricity that was sold to the Baltimore Gas and Electric Company. Located on a big bend in the river, the 550-acre property included a post office, a community hall, a general store, and 118 single-family, two-family, and rowhouse dwellings, most of them brick, averaging five rooms each, many without interior plumbing. In 1940, this was Alberton. Before that, the town was called Elysville. For three generations it had been a company town owned by James S. Gary & Sons. But on November 23, 1940, the entire town—houses, factory, and machinery—was sold for $65,000 to the C. R. Daniels Company of Newark, New Jersey, at an auction held in front of the general store to foreclose Gary & Sons defaulted mortgage. The company simply had been unable to survive the Great Depression.

A few years later, however, stimulated by the immense demand for canvas and cotton duck during World War II, the factory was again humming. Operations continued until the rain-generated floodwaters of Tropical Storm Agnes churned through the mill in 1972, but not before the Daniels Company itself, in a remarkable exercise of milltown proprietorship, had razed all the houses in 1968, destroying a town since named to the Register of Historic Places, evicting about a quarter of the mill's employees and many of its pensioners, but perhaps saving their lives and certainly their property from the subsequent devastation of Agnes.

Elysville got its start in the 1840s when the Elysville Manufacturing Company, consisting of Thomas Ely, his three brothers, and Hugh Balderson, started building the original stone mill, now almost completely demolished. The Baltimore & Ohio Railroad already passed through the stretch of curving valley bottom. Constructing, equipping, and operating the mill were more costly than anticipated, and in 1845 the Ely brothers decided to convey it to a new corporation called the Okisko Company, funded with more capital from additional shareholders. The Elys' company was paid with a large block of Okisko stock, but still the enterprise foundered despite improvements to the mill. Eventually, after protracted litigation that reached the state's highest court three times, the property was sold for the benefit of unpaid contractors and other creditors.

During the 1850s, the mill was bought and sold by a succession of corporations, some of them simply reorganizations of prior owners. For a time, the property was owned by the Alberton Manufacturing Company, one of whose principals was Jacob Albert, an Okisko creditor whose name stuck to the community. In 1861 the mill and town came under the firm control of James S. Gary, a self-made man whose fortune propelled his son, James A. Gary of Baltimore, to the position of Postmaster General for President McKinley and to leadership of the Maryland Republican party until his death in 1920.

Under Gary ownership, the mill at Alberton became a solid financial success for the first time, helped by large contracts for canvas tents and wagon covers during the Civil War. In 1860 the mill employed 50 men and 120 women running 120 looms. An oakum factory was also in operation making caulking from cotton waste. By 1895 the mill had grown to 340 looms. Many employees were children. (During the 1890s, Maryland's cotton factories employed more children under age sixteen than any other type of manufacturing enterprise, with an average starting age of twelve.) By 1915 about 400 hands were employed at Alberton.

During most of the period between the Civil War and World War I, the mill and the surrounding town were managed by Samuel F. Cobb, remembered by his former workers and subordinates as an Old Testament-like figure with a long white beard who was not only boss but *de facto* mayor as well, summoning outside authority only as need arose. Cobb's diaries describe the practice of sending recruiters to Virginia and West Virginia to attract employees—especially families with many girls, since inexpensive female labor was preferred. One recruiter supposedly enticed a family to move to Alberton to work in the mill by telling them that bananas, free for the picking, grew in the surrounding woods. When the new employees complained to Mr. Cobb that there were no bananas, he replied that the monkeys had eaten them all. Although almost certainly apocryphal, the story may nonetheless accurately reflect the tenor of Mr. Cobb's regime.

The company policy for management of the mill was a combination of long hours and low wages matched by equally low rents for comfortable houses, according to the standards of the times. Even as late as 1968, the C. R. Daniels Company was charging a top rent of $4.50 per week for a seven-room house, provided that the head of the family worked in the mill. The company also provided free firewood, Christmas gifts for children, support for a growing variety of community activities, and charity for those of its "family" who suffered misfortunes. One building was a general store and restaurant, with a bowling alley in the basement and a library on the second floor where movies were shown weekly. This insular and paternalistic system was the norm at company towns, nor was it resented by most employees. At Oella, for example, unemployed workers were allowed to remain in their company-owned homes free of rent during the Great Depression, and in return the workers repeatedly voted not to unionize.

Aside from the mill, the center of town life at Alberton was the churches. James A. Gary built the Gary United Methodist Church on the hill south of the mill in 1879 as a memorial to his father. This handsome structure is the only building in the community undamaged by flood or fire. Other churches were encouraged, including the Catholic chapel of St. Stanislaus Kostka, whose priest in winter sometimes skated down the frozen river from Woodstock College of the Sacred Heart to conduct Sunday service. In the 1920s the chapel was struck by lightning and burned. Its ruins, pictured on page 150, are located on the hillside across the river and slightly downstream from the mill. An Episcopal congregation existed until World War I. Subsequently, its stone church with a squat, square tower and cupola was incorporated into the mill complex, as still seen today. In 1940 a small Pentecostal church was built near the railroad bridge across the river from the mill. At one point during the 1972 flood, only the roof and tower of the church were visible. (Although the church still stands in part, it is not safe to enter.) Dozens of company houses used to front Alberton Road above and below the Pentecostal church. The residents crossed to the mill on a pedestrian suspension bridge like the one at Orange Grove, featured in Chapter 16. Other houses—Upper and Lower Brick Row—stood along the hillside across the railroad from the mill.

Following World War I, the company's business began to decline as the owners failed to modernize the mill. During the Great Depression, operations nearly stopped altogether. Many employees worked only one or two days a week in order to spread wages among as many people as possible. Gary & Sons obtained a loan from the federal government's Reconstruction Finance Corporation, but when the firm was unable to keep up its payments, the entire enterprise was sold to the C. R. Daniels Company. Daniels renovated the mill and much of the housing but eventually announced that it was going to demolish the dwellings because it could not afford the cost of still further repairs and improvements—estimated at $750,000—in order to bring the residences up to housing code standards. Despite an outcry from local housing-assistance agencies and historic preservation groups, the town (with a population then of about 500 people) ceased to exist in 1968, although the mill continued in business.

In 1972 Agnes struck. The water rose so fast that five people were caught in the mill building and had to be evacuated from the roof by helicopter. The former town store was pushed off its foundation and swept away. When the flood receded, cars, trucks, flotsam, and wreckage were left heaped against the buildings, which were coated inside and out with mud. Snarls of nylon yarn trailed from windows and the tops of telephone poles. The C. R. Daniels Company suffered a very large uninsured loss—as high as $2.7 million, according to some newspaper accounts—and pulled out of the valley. (The company now has a plant near Ellicott City.) Then in 1978, the mill, while being used as a warehouse, was gutted by fire. One stair tower remains. There is also a tall square chimney and a few other structures, including the former stone Episcopal church. Now the property, which combines the visual attractions of a war zone and dump, is used by a mulching operation, a firewood supplier, and a welding company. Across the river, where much of Elysville-Alberton-Daniels once stood, the land has been incorporated into Patapsco Valley State Park.

ELLICOTTS UPPER MILLS, located near this chapter's Dogwood Road trailhead, has suffered an even greater eclipse than Daniels. If you approach Dogwood Road in accordance with the automobile directions on page 164, you will descend steeply into the Patapsco Valley on Old Frederick Road and then cross the railroad and the river. This site was purchased by the Ellicott family in 1774 from James Hood, who in 1768 had built a dam and mill here for grinding corn. Four years earlier the Ellicotts had bought undeveloped land farther downstream at what became the Lower Mills and later Ellicott City. At that time the Upper Mills was more valuable than the Lower Mills because it was located where the main road linking Baltimore and Frederick forded the river. When the Ellicott property was divided, the Upper Mills was assigned to Joseph Ellicott, the oldest of the three Ellicott brothers. Ironically, nothing now remains at the Upper Mills.

When Joseph Ellicott moved his family from Pennsylvania to Maryland in 1775, he tore down the mill built by James Hood and constructed another for milling wheat using the latest inventions and improvements, many of his own design. On the shelf of land at the west end of the present-day bridge, he also built a large house and an ornamental garden with a fish pond and fountain spouting water ten feet high. When the Upper Mills tract was resurveyed in 1797, it was called "Fountainville."

Like his brothers at the Lower Mills, Joseph also built a general store that sold groceries and dry goods. Although the store reportedly did a good business, society must have been limited. Four of Joseph's nine children married the orphaned brothers and sisters of the Evans family, whom the Ellicotts had brought with them from Pennsylvania.

When Joseph Ellicott settled at the Upper Mills, he was already wealthy, having traveled to England ten years before to claim and liquidate his great-grandfather's estate to which he was heir. In Pennsylvania he had been high sheriff of Bucks County and a member of the provincial assembly. His preoccupation with mathematics, clockmaking, mill works, and mechanics had also earned him prominence in scientific circles, and it is said that as he got older, these interests almost completely precluded social intercourse even with his own family. One of his projects was a four-faced musical grandfather clock that played twenty-four tunes and marked seconds, minutes, hours, days, months, years, phases of the moon, and motions of the planets.

Joseph died in 1780 but his widow, Judith, maintained her household at the Upper Mills until her death in 1809. By then the mill and store had greatly declined in value. The Frederick Turnpike had been relocated through the Lower Mills, which in time utterly supplanted the small settlement farther upstream.

ELLICOTTS LOWER MILLS (now Ellicott City) is not included here as a "country walk," but no discussion of major industrial sites along the Patapsco River is complete without mentioning it. The energy, perseverance, and success of the Ellicotts led others to follow their example.

In 1772 Joseph, John, and Andrew Ellicott, Quaker brothers who milled flour in Bucks County, Pennsylvania, bought land on both sides of the Patapsco River above and below the future site of Ellicott City. Their newly-acquired stretch of valley was uninhabited, uncultivated, and inaccessible except by footpath, although most of the surrounding upland had long been farmed by tobacco planters. The attraction of the valley site lay in the steep gradient of the river, for the Ellicotts' purchase included exclusive water and power rights for two miles above and below the dam and mill that they proposed to build. Most of their 700-acre purchase was bought cheaply from an Englishman who may have feared the approaching Revolution, but another 20 acres were obtained under a 1669 law that allowed entrepreneurs to gain control over riverside land for fifty years if they built and operated a gristmill. In 1774 the Ellicott brothers also purchased an existing dam and mill for grinding corn four miles upstream, where the then-Frederick Road (now *Old* Frederick Road) crossed the river.

Prior to their purchases in the Patapsco Valley, Andrew and John Ellicott had traveled on horseback over the middle counties of Maryland between the Patapsco and the Blue Ridge. They concluded from their tour of inspection that the region was suited for growing wheat and had ample water power for grinding grain. Tobacco was then the main cash crop near Baltimore, but the European demand for American tobacco had slumped, payment from European dealers was slow, and yields were declining as the soil became depleted. Wheat was the rising crop, demanded by the expanding cities of the Eastern seaboard and exportable also to southern Europe and the Caribbean. Maryland's upper Eastern Shore was prospering as a region that grew wheat shipped out through the port of Chestertown. Baltimore, which had access to a vast western and northern hinterland, offered still greater possibilities, and the Ellicotts were determined to be part of the region's burgeoning grain market. Already, as a matter of agricultural heritage, the new German settlers in central Maryland (where Frederick had been named for the kings of Prussia) preferred to grow wheat. Between 1749 and 1774 the export of wheat and flour from Annapolis had increased by nearly 600 percent, and the growth of wheat exports from Baltimore had been even more dramatic.

From the outset Joseph Ellicott concentrated his attention on the improvement of the upstream site where Frederick Road crossed the Patapsco; this became known as the Upper Mills. John, Andrew, and Andrew's sons undertook development of the lower stretch of river. They brought their household goods, tools, and farm implements by boat from Philadelphia to Elkridge Landing, which at that time was an important tobacco port at the head of navigation on the Patapsco River. From Elkridge, the Ellicotts' possessions—and those of their workmen whom they had persuaded to come with them—were carried by wagon along a riverside road that the party had to hack and build as they went. For the final mile, everything was carried by hand on a footpath along the river to the new settlement. Even the wagons themselves had to be disassembled and carried in.

By 1774 the Ellicotts had supervised the clearing of land and the construction of a low dam, a sawmill, a gristmill, a log boarding house, and a number of wooden houses. At first the brothers grew and milled their own wheat in order to demonstrate to the nearby tobacco planters that wheat could be cultivated and sold profitably. Charles Carroll of Carrollton, one of the largest and most forward-looking planters in Maryland, became a financial backer of the Ellicotts. After the brothers built a road extending five miles west from their mill to Carroll's vast plantation at Doughoregan Manor, Carroll converted much of his land from tobacco to wheat.

Towards the end of the American Revolution, the flow of wheat from nearby plantations to Ellicotts Lower Mills had increased to the point where the Ellicotts decided to enter the export trade as soon as peaceful conditions returned. In 1783 the Ellicotts built a wharf at the corner of Light and Pratt streets in Baltimore. They not only exported flour but also imported ironware, tea, mirrors, dinner sets, glassware, linen, silks, satins, brocades, liquors, wines, and other goods, which they sold to the planters through their new store (erected in 1790) of Ellicott & Company at the Lower Mills. Planters from throughout the region congregated at the store and post office, bringing their wheat in exchange for credit at the store. The Ellicotts also built and operated a school at the Lower Mills.

In 1791 Ferdinand M. Bayard, a member of the French Academy of Arts and Sciences, recorded his impression of a visit to the Lower Mills:

> The river, upon the borders of which Mr. Ellicott has built his mill, is enclosed by two chains of uncultivated hills. . . . The bottom of the river, whose channel can hardly be decried, is full of broken rocks which the waters have not yet worked smooth. Some masses are raised above the surface of the river, whose waters, dashing against them, keep up continually a dull noise, truly sepulchral. The advantages to be derived from a mill in this place render the proprietor insensible to the horrors which surround him. It can only be a regard for pecuniary interest which enables him to live undisturbed by the noise of the waters which dash over the rocks. The lean-

ness of the sheep and cattle attest to the poverty of the soil. The miserable garden, from which the productions seem forced; fields where the scantiness of the grain leaves the soil exposed; plains incapable of producing a middling sized oak; such is the melancholy aspect presented by the country from Baltimorè to Ellicott's Mills.

In time, the Ellicotts erected iron-smelting furnaces, forges, rolling mills, and nail factories in their stretch of the Patapsco Valley. Another mill was added later for the production of copper sheathing. The Ellicotts sold or leased land to other entrepreneurs who established a paper mill, an oil mill, and a carding mill. After reading an article in a horticultural journal and conducting their own experiments with plaster, the Ellicotts instructed the surrounding planters in the use of lime as a fertilizer to restore the exhausted soil. They imported blocks of gypsum from Nova Scotia and ground it for fertilizer. They constructed bridges and a road east to Baltimore at their own expense and, with the assistance of Charles Carroll and other planters, they built a road west to Frederick, opening the new wheat country of the interior to Ellicotts Lower Mills. In 1804 the Baltimore and Frederick Turnpike was established though the Lower Mills, supplanting the old Frederick Road through the Upper Mills. The turnpike was soon linked with the Ohio Valley by the National Road through Cumberland and Wheeling, so that by 1818, when the Ellicotts' settlement on the Patapsco had a population of about three thousand people, Maryland's most important land thoroughfare to the West passed through the Lower Mills.

During the same period, granite quarrying became a major industry in the vicinity of the Lower Mills. Between 1806 and 1821 granite for Baltimore Cathedral—at the time one of the nation's most significant structures because of its large size and distinguished neoclassic design—was hauled from Ellicotts Lower Mills along the Frederick Turnpike in huge wagons drawn by nine yoke of oxen.

Ellicotts Lower Mills received another boost in 1827, when the Baltimore & Ohio Railroad was incorporated by several leading Baltimore merchants and bankers. They feared that the Erie Canal, which in 1825 linked Lake Erie at Buffalo with the

Hudson River at Albany, and the newly planned Chesapeake and Ohio Canal, with its eastern terminus in Washington, D.C., would each divert commerce away from Baltimore. The first leg of the experimental railroad was laid up the Patapsco Valley, and Ellicotts Lower Mills was selected as its inland terminus until the line could be extended farther west.

During the next forty years Ellicotts Lower Mills continued to grow and prosper, although in the aftermath of the financial panic of 1837, the Ellicotts at the Lower Mills, "trading under the name of Jonathan Ellicott & Sons, being embarrassed in their circumstances and largely indebted to many individuals" (as recited in the deed of trust), were forced to convey the flour mill to trustees for the benefit of their creditors. Colonel Charles Carroll III acquired the mill in partnership with Charles A. Gambrill, who eventually became the firm's principal. The mill continued to be owned by the C. A. Gambrill Manufacturing Company until 1923, and during that period it was rebuilt at least twice after being destroyed by flood or damaged by fire. Most of the currently existing structure, still in use as a flouring mill, dates from 1917. It stands across the river from the town and is flanked by huge grain silos.

In 1840 Ellicotts Lower Mills was selected as the site of the courthouse for the new Howard District of what was then Anne Arundel County. In 1851 it was made the county seat when Howard County was organized. The Lower Mills became Ellicott City with the granting of a municipal charter in 1867. The next year, however, much of the city's industry was destroyed in a devastating flash flood, as described in Chapter 16. Although some of the mills were rebuilt, many were not, and the community never fully recovered its former importance as an industrial center. After a long period of stagnation from the late 1800s to the mid-1900s, the town now prospers chiefly as a locus for specialty retailing, antique stores, restaurants, and county government.

OELLA, which in physical terms remains an enclave of mill housing surrounding the former textile plant, is located across the Patapsco River 0.7 mile upstream from Ellicott City. Like Ellicott City, it is discussed here only to round out the catalogue of important Patapsco Valley industrial sites—but if you do not already know Oella, take a look the next time you are in the vicinity. The best access is from Frederick Road on the Baltimore County side of the bridge at Ellicott City.

Oella got its start in 1808 when the founders of the Union Manufacturing Company of Maryland purchased land from the Ellicotts and started selling stock. By October 1809, the first textile mill had been completed. In 1811 the company employed over 300 workers and had its property resurveyed under the name of "Oella," which the patent said was "in commemoration of the first woman who applied herself to the spinning of cotton on the continent of America." However, the identity of this mysterious (or fabled) Oella has yet to be discovered.

The Union Dam, now breached at its western end, is located below the Route 40 bridge about 1.5 miles upstream from the mill. From the dam a millrace—it was constructed by slaves hired out by their owners and is said to be one of the country's longest races feeding a single mill—runs along the eastern bank of the river to Oella, creating a vertical drop at the mill of nearly 50 feet. The mill generated its own power until the construction of Liberty Dam in the early 1950s diminished the flow of water.

For a time the Union mill at Oella was among the nation's largest makers of cotton goods, but in 1889 financial difficulties forced its sale to William J. Dickey of the Dickeyville mills, who proceeded to manufacture a variety of woolen and cotton fabrics at his Oella plant. In 1918 the three main mill buildings and a warehouse burned down, but these structures were replaced by a new mill that was later expanded several times and still stands. The plant prospered during World War II, employing (as of January 1945) 382 people working in three shifts. Production for 1945 was 445,471 yards of woolen cloth of which 60 percent was for military coats. Operations at Oella reached their peak in the 1950s, when the plant employed 500 workers producing fancy woolen fabrics for men's sports coats and suits. In the 1960s, however, the upsurge in imported textiles and synthetics engulfed domestic woolen manufacturers. The decline at Oella became even more precipitous with the advent of double-knit fabrics that could not be produced on the machinery used there. The plant closed in 1972.

For the decade following the mill's closing, the future of Oella even as a residential community was in doubt because there was no public water or sewer system. Raw sewage from the mill housing was pumped into leaky septic tanks, and for a period Baltimore County considered condemning much of the mill housing. During the mid-1980s however, the county installed water and sewer lines through the rocky terrain at a cost of more than $5 million. Now the community, where mill employees lived for generations, is becoming gentrified as the old housing is restored, new luxury residences are built, and a variety of retail enterprises and artisans occupy the mill.

≈   ≈   ≈   ≈

AUTOMOBILE DIRECTIONS: The trail follows the **Patapsco Valley** between the McKeldin Area and Dogwood Road west of Baltimore. (See **Map 1** on page 5, where the McKeldin trailhead is represented by •14 and the Dogwood Road trailhead by •15. For more detail, refer to **Maps 19 and 20** on pages 166 and 167.)

To the McKeldin trailhead: Please turn to page 145 for automobile directions, then refer to the walking directions starting on page 165 at right.

To the Dogwood Road trailhead from Interstate 695 (the Baltimore Beltway): Leave I-695 at Exit 16 for Interstate 70 west toward Frederick. Go 4 miles, then follow the directions in the next paragraph.

To the Dogwood Road trailhead from Interstate 70: Leave I-70 at Exit 87B for **Route 29** north to Route 99. At the T-intersection with Route 99, turn right toward Rogers Avenue. Go 0.6 mile, then turn left onto Old Frederick Road. Follow it 1.5 miles to the bridge across the Patapsco River. (This site, now vacant except for the railroad, was formerly Ellicotts Upper Mills, as described on pages 156-157). After crossing the bridge and turning sharply left, continue along the river for 0.5 mile, in the process passing Johnnycake Road intersecting from the right. At a T-intersection with Dogwood Road, turn left across a small bridge and then left again into the parking area at the entrance to Alberton Road. Do not block the gate.

≈　　≈　　≈　　≈

WALKING: Maps 19 and 20 on pages 166 and 167 show the 9-mile path along the **Patapsco Valley** between the McKeldin Area in the west and Dogwood Road in the east. The easiest way to do the whole trip is to divide it in two. On one day start at the McKeldin Area. After fording the Patapsco's North Branch, walk downstream to Woodstock Road and back, for a round-trip of 6 miles. On another day start at Dogwood Road and walk upstream to the bridge at Woodstock Road and back for a round-trip of 12 miles. Directions for walking downstream from the McKeldin Area start at the bottom of this page. Directions heading upstream from Dogwood Road start on page 170.

Of course, if you decide to walk the whole distance one way, you will have to make special arrangements regarding cars. With a companion you can do a shuttle, leaving one car at the end and then driving to the start in another car, which you can fetch after you are done.

Please note that if you plan to hike all the way from one end of the trail to the other, you should start at the McKeldin Area so that you can be sure, near the outset, that there is not too much water to ford the North Branch of the Patapsco River. Usually, there is very little water, but it would be a dismaying experience to walk all the way upstream from Dogwood Road only to discover at the end that you could not safely cross the river into the McKeldin Area. For more information, please read the introduction to this chapter on page 151.

Walking downstream (west to east) from the McKeldin Area to Dogwood Road: From the ranger station and central parking lot at the McKeldin Area, pass to the right of the nearby lavatories and children's playground. Angle slightly right downhill across the lawn to an intersection located at the right-hand end of another parking lot. Continue downhill along a road toward distant basketball courts. Just before reaching the basketball courts, turn left onto a gravel road and follow it into the woods and then to the right downhill.

Turn right at a trail junction at the bottom of the valley. With the North Branch of the Patapsco River on the left, follow the trail downstream half a mile.

MAP 19 — Patapsco Valley State Park between the McKeldin Area and Dogwood Road

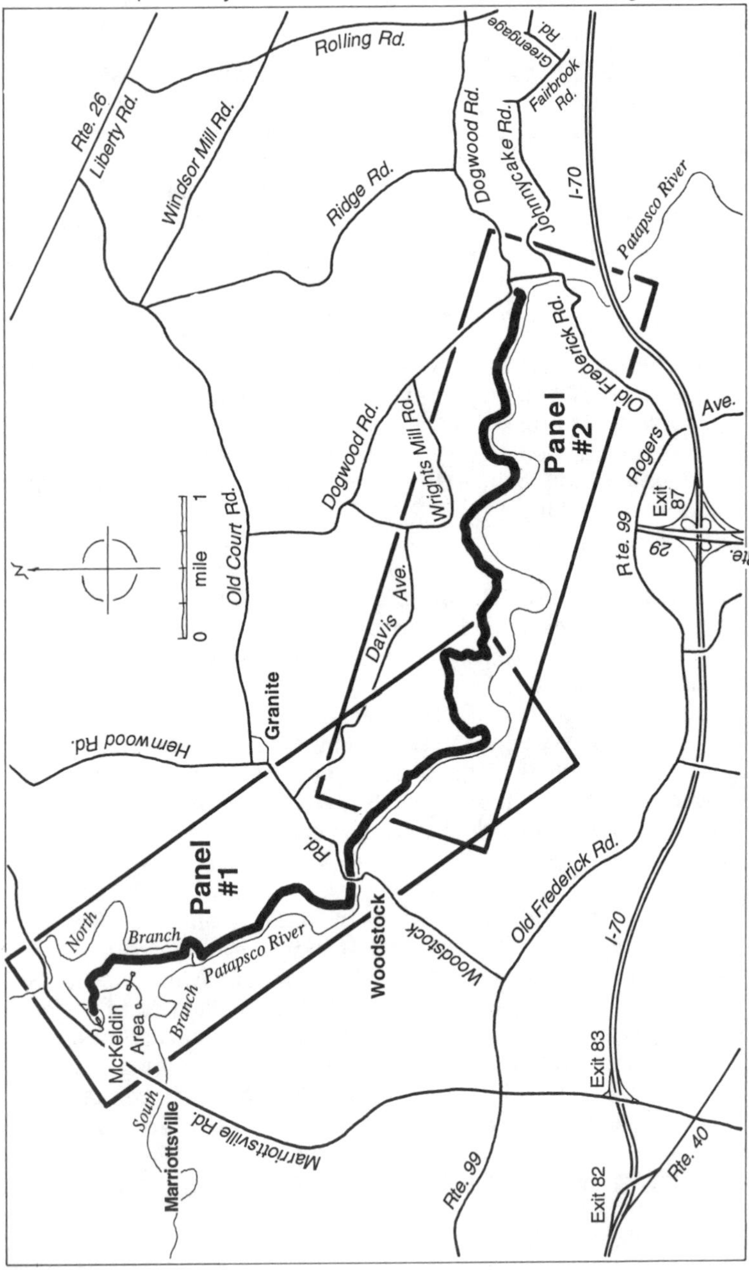

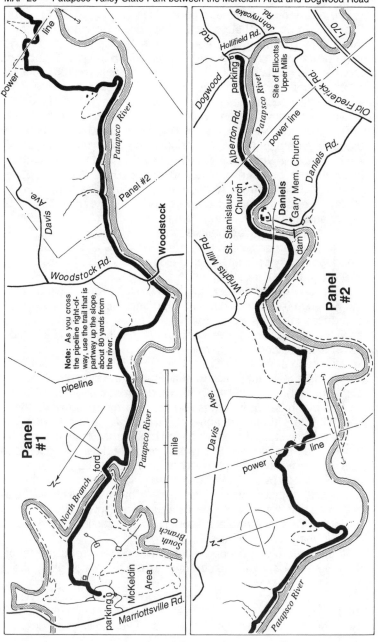

Panel #1

power line

Patapsco River

Davis Ave.

Panel #2

Woodstock

Woodstock Rd.

Note: As you cross the pipeline right-of-way, use the trail that is partway up the slope, about 80 yards from the river.

pipeline

Patapsco River

North Branch   ford

South Branch

McKeldin Area

parking

Marriottsville Rd.

N

1

mile

0

Panel #2

Johnnycake Rd.

Hollifield Rd.

Dogwood Rd.

Alberton Rd.

parking

Patapsco River

Site of Ellicotts Upper Mills

I-70

Old Frederick Rd.

power line

Daniels Rd.

St. Stanislaus Church

Daniels

Gary Mem. Church

Wrights Mill Rd.

dam

Davis Ave.

power line

N

Patapsco River

The next task is to locate a good place to ford the North Branch. To do this, I suggest the following: Continue until the trail and river bend sharply right. This is the signal to turn around and retrace your steps 60 yards. Descend to the river bank and cross at the shallows. Climb the opposite bank and turn right on a narrow path. Follow this faint track 340 yards through the woods, until you arrive at a wider trail by the main river. Turn left and continue downstream, with the Patapsco River on the right.

The next landmark is a pipeline right-of-way, which you should cross on a path partway up the slope, about 80 yards from the river. If instead you find yourself on level land at the foot of the slope next to the river, retrace your steps 70 yards, then turn right onto a higher trail. After crossing the pipeline right-of-way, this trail leads gradually up a ravine and along the rim of the valley past trails intersecting from the left. Eventually, descend to a T-intersection near the river and turn left downstream.

After passing under the long, curved bridge at Woodstock Road, go nearly one mile, then descend half-right. Cross a stream and continue along the river.

Later, pass a trail descending from the left-rear. Continue as the riverside trail climbs half-left, then descends, climbs again and descends once more. Eventually, follow the trail as it veers away from the river, makes a U-turn to the left, and climbs to the rim of the valley. (If you do not make the proper turn, you will know it soon enough, because the riverside trail peters out.)

Turn right at an intersection at the top of the slope, within sight of a house and barn. Continue down and up again. This section of the trail more or less borders a large meadow on the left. After leaving the meadow behind, continue to an intersection, and there turn right downhill on a path that leads to a power-line right-of-way. Follow the trail right downhill under the transmission lines, across a stream, and steeply uphill. Turn left into the woods by a pair of power-line pylons, then turn right downhill after just 40 yards. As the path begins to climb again, it becomes very rough and gullied. Pass a trail intersecting from the right. Continue straight through an intersection at the top of the hill, then descend steeply.

At the bottom of the slope—only a few dozen yards in front of the railroad—bear left and continue as the trail winds along the side of the valley.

After again descending to the railroad, cross the tracks. With the railroad on the left, go 100 yards, then veer half-right along the river bank and through the woods. Eventually, pass near

the dam at Daniels, where the fall of water is audible on the right. Continue under a railroad bridge and along the river as it curves past Daniels, located on the opposite bank. Very little is left of the original stone buildings. Now there are mostly concrete-block structures of recent vintage, although the Gary Memorial United Methodist Church still stands on the hill in the distance.

After passing a trail intersecting from the left—it leads uphill 225 yards to the ruins of St. Stanislaus Kostka Church shown on page 150—continue downstream on old Alberton Road, now closed to cars. Pass a gate and a house and continue to another gate by the small parking lot at Dogwood Road.

Walking upstream (east to west) from Dogwood Road to the McKeldin Area: From the small parking area at the intersection of Dogwood Road and Alberton Road, follow Alberton Road past a gate, a house, and another gate. After a mile, pass a gravel path intersecting from the right-rear. (It leads uphill 225 yards to the ruins of the St. Stanislaus Kostka Church, shown on page 150.)

Continue upstream on the riverside path, which curves past the former mill site at Daniels, located on the opposite bank. Very little is left of the original stone buildings. Now there are mostly concrete-block structures of recent vintage, although the Gary Memorial United Methodist Church still stands on the hill in the distance.

Pass under a railroad bridge and follow the trail as it gradually curves right past the Daniels dam, where the fall of water is audible on the left. Continue as the trail becomes a narrow dirt path which eventually rejoins the river.

Before long the trail emerges from the woods and follows a path alongside the railroad. Go about 100 yards and then, after crossing a small bridge, turn right across the tracks. Head left on a rough track that climbs obliquely up the side of the valley, with the river on the left. Eventually, the trail descends to the level of the railroad, then turns right steeply uphill. Pass straight through a trail junction at the top of the hill, then down a gullied trail past a path intersecting from the left. After climbing to a T-intersection, turn left to a power-line right-of-way.

Turn right and follow a trail along the wide swath below the transmission lines. Descend and climb steeply. Partway up the hill—about a hundred yards below the next pair of power-line pylons—fork left into the woods. Climb steeply to a trail intersection, then bear left and continue through the woods at the rim of the valley. For awhile the trail more or less borders a large meadow on the right.

At an intersection near a house and barn, the trail splits. Fork left downhill, then curve sharply right at the foot of the slope in order to continue upstream next to the river. Pass a trail leading steeply uphill to the right. Eventually, at the mouth of a tributary valley, cross a stream and then join an old road leading left along the river.

Pass under the long, curved bridge at Woodstock Road and continue upstream half a mile with the river on the left. The easiest way to identify the next turn is as follows: Continue until you find yourself at a dead-end by the river, then retrace your steps 120 yards and turn steeply uphill on a gullied path. At the rim of the valley, curve gradually left past trails intersecting from the right, then descend along a ravine. Cross a pipeline right-of-way and continue upstream near the river.

Eventually, the trail reaches the confluence of the North and South Branches of the Patapsco River. During periods of low water, you may be able to ford the North Branch here. Under most conditions, however, it is better to cross farther up the North Branch, as follows: Retrace your steps 140 yards downstream along the main river, looking for a faint track leading left. Follow it 340 yards —in the process, you will join the North Branch—then descend the river bank and cross the shallows.

After fording the North Branch of the Patapsco River, ascend the bank to a white-blazed trail and follow it right. With the North Branch on the right, go half a mile upstream to a major intersection, then turn left uphill. At the top of the slope, follow a gravel track to a paved road. Turn right uphill and follow the road 100 yards to an intersection. From there continue straight uphill across the grass toward children's play apparatus and the central parking lot by the ranger station at the McKeldin Area.

16

PATAPSCO VALLEY STATE PARK

Avalon and Orange Grove

Avalon and **Orange Grove** are two areas of Patapsco Valley State Park southwest of Baltimore. The route outlined on **Map 21** on page 181 starts at Avalon and follows the paved **Grist Mill Trail** upstream along the Patapsco River to the swinging bridge at Orange Grove. Within the next few years, the Grist Mill Trail may be extended to the industrial hamlet of **Ilchester**, as shown by the dotted line. But for now cross the Swinging Bridge at Orange Grove and continue upstream to the **Bloede Dam**. The round-trip distance from Avalon to the dam and back is 4.5 miles (7.2 kilometers).

In addition to the easy riverside path, there are many trails that climb up and down along the side of the Patapsco Valley. All are shown on a map that you can get at the ranger station as you enter the park. In some sections, maintenance of these trails is problematic, but one short spur that you can count on is the blue-blazed **Cascade Trail** leading uphill from Orange Grove to an attractive cascade.

The park is open daily from 10:00 A.M. to sunset. It is closed on Thanksgiving and Christmas. An admission fee is charged April through October. All pets are prohibited. The park is managed by the Department of Natural Resources, Maryland Forest, Park and Wildlife Service; telephone (410) 461-5005.

For automobile directions to the trailhead at Avalon, please turn to page 182. Walking directions are on page 183.

BETWEEN WOODSTOCK and tidewater at Elkridge, the Patapsco River falls more than 200 feet in a distance of 17 miles. The potential of this stretch of river for water power was not lost on the ironmongers, millers, textile manufacturers, and other early industrialists of the eighteenth and nineteenth centuries. Entrepreneurs built many dams and factories in the narrow valley, notably at Elysville (now Daniels), Ellicotts Upper and Lower Mills, Oella, Ilchester, Orange Grove, and Avalon. At some places the old works still stand, and at Ellicott City and Ilchester there are mills, descended from earlier enterprises, that still operate. Other areas, however, are just stretches of wooded valley where, except for a few ruins or faint remnants, whole factory villages have been torn down or obliterated by fire and flood. In some places the names of these company towns survive only in local roads or as designations for different sections of Patapsco Valley State Park.

AVALON is one of these lost towns. It got its start in the 1760s when Caleb Dorsey, ironmaster and owner of Elkridge Furnace (established in 1755), built a forge upstream from his furnace for fashioning implements from the approximately 1,000 tons of pig iron that he produced annually. According to the nineteenth-century memoirs of Martha Ellicott Tyson (a descendant of the Ellicotts of Ellicott City), Dorsey's Forge produced crowbars prior to the American Revolution. Most other tools were imported, as was intended under the British mercantile system by which the colonies were to provide raw materials—including pig iron—to England and to purchase finished goods in return.

During the Revolution, William Whetcroft of Annapolis, who had received a government loan voted by Maryland's revolutionary legislature, leased the Avalon forge. Whetcroft made cast-iron parts for muskets that were assembled in Annapolis. Whetcroft also built a rolling and slitting mill, and by 1777 his Patapsco Slitting Mill was producing nails. This was the first nail factory in Maryland; apparently it was quite primitive, since the nails had to be headed one at a time by hand. Whetcroft's lease with Caleb Dorsey's son Edward (known as Iron Head Ned) stipulated that Dorsey would raise his forge dam at Avalon an additional foot and dig a race to Whetcroft's mill for water power to run the bellows and other machinery. In exchange, Whetcroft would not only pay rent for use of the site but would also buy all of his raw iron from Edward Dorsey, who later purchased the Whetcroft mill for himself.

In 1815 two members of the enterprising Ellicott family purchased the forge and slitting mill at auction. By 1820 the Ellicott ironworks—one at Avalon (the name was first used by the Ellicotts) and another a few miles upstream at Ellicott City—were listed together in the census as having between them four rolling mills, six pairs of rollers with the necessary furnaces, and twenty-four nail machines, each capable of cutting 1,200 nails per minute. The works employed fifty men and thirteen boys and used 800 tons of iron annually to make not only nails but also iron bars, sheets, and plates.

During the next half-century, the Avalon ironworks were repeatedly sold and expanded. In 1845 the nail factory burned. Three years later a new mill started rolling rails for the Baltimore & Ohio Railroad. After being pulled down and rebuilt on a larger scale in the early 1850s, the factory reached its peak in about 1856, producing 44,000 kegs of nails from forty-four steam-driven machines. A panoramic depiction of Avalon in 1857 shows two long open-sided buildings resembling train sheds side by side, standing parallel with the river on the north bank near the present-day park automobile bridge at Avalon. Brick piers supported the roofs. Four tall smoke stacks rose between the mill sheds. One building bore a sign saying "Rolling Mill 1855" and the other a sign saying "Puddling Mill Built 1853." ("Puddling" means simply to work viscous metal.) Around the factory was a small village, including a church, a school, stores, and about thirty mill houses.

The ironworks at Avalon continued in operation until July 24, 1886, when a monstrous flood swept down the Patapsco Valley. There appear to be no eyewitness accounts of what happened at Avalon that morning, but the events at nearby Ellicott City, as recalled by Charles F. Kreh, who was there at the time, give some idea:

> At about 9:15 o'clock the mail train from Baltimore arrived, and at that hour there was little evidence or intimation of impending disaster in the Patapsco. Only a lowering of the clouds and an unusual darkness, together with some fierce bolts of lightning, appeared to cast their shadows before them and to indicate the coming of a storm. But, as yet, few if any had thought of what was in

store for them. Soon, however, came reports of terrible cloudbursts in various places west of the Ellicotts. The Baltimore train left the station and had only reached Union Mills about a mile distant, when it was met by an avalanche of water. The bounds of the river were already broken and only the weight of the train held it to the tracks. Fortunately for the passengers, it stood close by the mountain side, and they were thus enabled to clamber up and return to the city.

Hardly had a few minutes elapsed before the mad waters (in all their intensity and fury and without any warning) burst upon the good people of Ellicotts living along the river course on the Baltimore County side, and almost in a twinkling their homes were surrounded and all avenues of escape cut off. Then began scenes that almost beggar description, many of them pitiful and heartrending. The waters, filled with logs and trees and debris of all kinds, arose as if by magic and seemed to gloat in their power of fierce destruction. Opposite the railroad station across the Patapsco stood a row of houses, some brick, some frame and others stone, extending over a space of about 1,000 feet from the bridge to the mill structure . . . and in a remarkably short time these were seen to begin to crumble from the beating of the waves against them. Now could be seen the dwellers breaking through the roofs from house to house and barely escaping the collapse of their homes. The last house in the row was a brick building owned by William Partridge and in this, thirty-odd persons sought refuge. Many were the prayers that went up to the Most High from those looking on from the opposite shore that this house might be spared, but it was not to be, and soon all were engulfed and swallowed up in the angry waters. School children, who had come across the river in the early morning, stood on the banks and saw their parents go to their watery graves.

The flood crest reached 40 feet above normal. At Ellicott City thirty-two buildings fell. Workers fled the factories as the riverside industries were inundated. The massive Granite Cotton Mill just upstream from Ellicott City collapsed into the torrent, taking with it one man who had been too slow to leave. Bodies from Ellicott City were recovered near Baltimore, 15 miles downstream. Those of one man and his wife and child were found snared in the top of a tree. In all, about fifty people drowned that morning in the Patapsco Valley.

At the Avalon ironworks, the chimneys collapsed and flood-borne debris smashed nearly all the machinery. The *American and Commercial Advertiser* for July 25, 1868, reported that "the Patapsco washed entirely through the lower portion of the large nail factory at Avalon . . . and the machinery at the works was damaged to a very great extent, and the stock on hand carried away. The houses of the workmen, surrounding the factory and like it situated on low ground, were inundated, the water reaching the second story of some of them. It is not known that any lives were lost at this place, but many families lost all their household property."

After the flood, some Avalon residents returned to their company-owned houses, but the ironworks never operated again. The machines were sold for scrap, and what was left of the factory was torn down. By the end of the nineteenth century, even most of the tenant dwellings had vanished. Today only two stone houses survive, of which the more conspicuous is the former mill superintendent's residence located on Gun Road above the railroad crossing. The other is now the Avalon visitor center.

Since 1868 the Patapsco Valley has experienced lesser floods (as it always had) on a more or less regular basis. Tropical Storm Agnes in 1972, however, was of a different order of magnitude; it was comparable to the flood a century earlier. Beginning June 21, the storm lumbered across Maryland in three days of almost constant rain. Over $1,800,000 in damage occurred in Patapsco Valley State Park alone. At Avalon, the high water washed out the northeast end of the old ironworks dam over which the river used to flow. (Damaged by the 1868 flood, this dam had been rebuilt in 1901 by the Baltimore County Water and Electric Company, which until 1928 operated a filtration plant at Avalon.) Now the dam, bypassed by the river, is barely visible opposite Lost Lake in a thicket of trees that have grown up since the 1972 flood. At the same time, the river destroyed the automobile bridge at Avalon, swept away shelters, and pulled down the Swinging Bridge at Orange Grove.

Between Ilchester and Avalon the current ate away long stretches of River Road and the B&0 railbed. The large sanitary sewer that runs down the valley was ruptured in four places.

Since 1972 the Maryland Park Service has gradually repaired much of the damage. The Swinging Bridge has been replaced and River Road has been reconstructed between Avalon and Orange Grove. New rest rooms and picnic shelters have been constructed. For information about the use and reservation of these shelters, call the park office.

ORANGE GROVE, located at the present-day Swinging Bridge two miles upstream from Avalon, is the site of another vanished company village. The mill and hamlet that formerly stood at Orange Grove survived the flood of 1868, but they have vanished since just the same. Only a few traces remain, chiefly massive stone walls that once were part of the C. A. Gambrill Manufacturing Company's Mill C, which in the second half of the nineteenth century was said by the management to be the largest flour mill east of Minneapolis. Two of the mill's better known brands of flour were Orange Grove and Patapsco Superlative Patent. The Gambrill firm marketed its flour products throughout the mid-Atlantic region and eventually as far away as the West Indies, Europe, and South America.

The first flour mill at Orange Grove was constructed in 1856, when George Worthington and George Bayly brought land there on both sides of the river. According to the deed, the property included parts of tracts know as "Talbot's Last Shift," "Small Bit," "Joseph and Jacob's Invention," and all of "Vortex." It is thought that the new mill and its company village became known as Orange Grove because of the Osage-orange trees that were common in the area. In 1860 Worthington and Bayly sold the entire property to the C. A. Gambrill Manufacturing Company, which had also taken over the Ellicott family's flour mill farther upstream. In 1882 the Gambrill company, trading under the name of Patapsco Flouring Mills, opened a third mill in Baltimore and gave letter designations to the three plants. The one at Ellicott City was Mill A, the Baltimore plant was Mill B, and Orange Grove was Mill C.

In 1873 the Gambrill company added a Corliss steam engine and boilers to supplement water power at Orange Grove. In 1880 output was 171,381 barrels of flour. Three years later the company replaced millstones with modern steel rollers, and output increased further. By 1900 the mill building, which measured 150 by 175 feet, had six stories, four of brick topped by two more of frame and metal siding. A massive rectangular grain elevator 100 by 150 feet and eight stories high flanked the mill on its upstream side, and on the downstream side there was a tall, tapering, square smokestack and a three-story structure housing the Corliss engine, coal bins, and a dynamo that generated electricity to light the mill and the nearby superintendent's house.

The entire mill complex was crowded onto a shelf of land between the railroad and a high retaining wall along the river. There was so little room to spare that the former Gun Road (now the Grist Mill Trail) used to pass through the building in an arched passageway. Because the mill and elevator were set into the hillside, trains picked up flour at the fourth story, which was even with the floor of a box car on the siding. Gondolas dumped coal into a chute that is still discernible as a stone lintel and boxlike foundation opposite the end of the swinging bridge. A wooden dam about 10 feet high and slightly curved against the pressure of the impounded water created a millpond stretching upstream as far as Ilchester.

According to the memoirs of a former Orange Grove resident—Thomas LeRoy Phillips, whose father was superintendent of the mill from 1891 to 1904—"the subdued rumble of the mill was heard from early Monday morning to late Saturday evening; the muffled roar of water pouring over the high wooden dam was unbroken; and long freight trains rolled by day and night." William A. Clayton, the day engineer in the early 1900s, was so impressed by the mill's steam engine that he named one of his sons Corliss.

On the west bank of the river, across from the mill, a small company-owned village of seven houses stood along the Patapsco where a parking lot and rest rooms are now located. There was also a combination one-room school and church. As now, a pedestrian suspension bridge spanned the river. It was snagged and pulled down by an ice jam in January 1904, and again washed out by Tropical Storm Agnes in 1972. A hand pump provided water for the community. Itinerant grocers and butchers with horse-drawn carts supplied some food; other shopping entailed a short train ride to Ellicott City, Elkridge, or Baltimore on one of the twelve passenger trains that stopped daily at Orange Grove. On every third Sunday church services were conducted by a itinerant reverend who also preached at Elkridge and at Locust Chapel near Ilchester.

The mill at Orange Grove operated until May 1, 1905, when it was gutted by fire. Rebuilding was not worthwhile. Baltimore's flour trade was in decline, and anyway, the advent of steam engines made access to water power of minor importance, especially when balanced against the risk of flooding. At Orange Grove the Gambrill Manufacturing Company tore down the mill's masonry walls, except where they support the railroad, as seen today. On the opposite side of the river, the stone abutment of the old wooden dam is still visible during the leafless season about 100 yards upstream from the Swinging Bridge.

ILCHESTER is located 1.5 miles upstream from Orange Grove. Now consisting of a dam, a paper mill, and a few stone and frame mill houses up the side of the valley, Ilchester is an unpretty but stirring sight for the simple reason that the factory still runs. The gentrification that has overtaken Ellicott City and Oella is totally absent.

In the 1820s, George and William Morris, two Scottish brothers from Philadelphia, established their Thistle Mills here for making cotton print. A flour mill owned by the Ellicotts already existed on the opposite bank, wedged between the railroad and the river. The name *Thistle* still survives in Thistle Road, which links Frederick Road with the river just beyond the upstream end of the mill complex. In 1850 the mill employed 71 male and 106 female workers. Its water-powered looms produced 1.3 million yards of sheeting and drill annually. By 1900 the mill had been converted to spinning silk. About 300 hands were employed, and the *Baltimore Sun* said that Thistle made "goods that rival the silk works of France." In 1920, however, new owners operating as the Thistle Cotton Mills, Inc. retooled the plant to manufacture automobile tire fabric. Then in 1928 the Bartgis brothers of Baltimore moved their paper carton

MAP 21 — Avalon and Orange Grove Areas of Patapsco Valley State Park

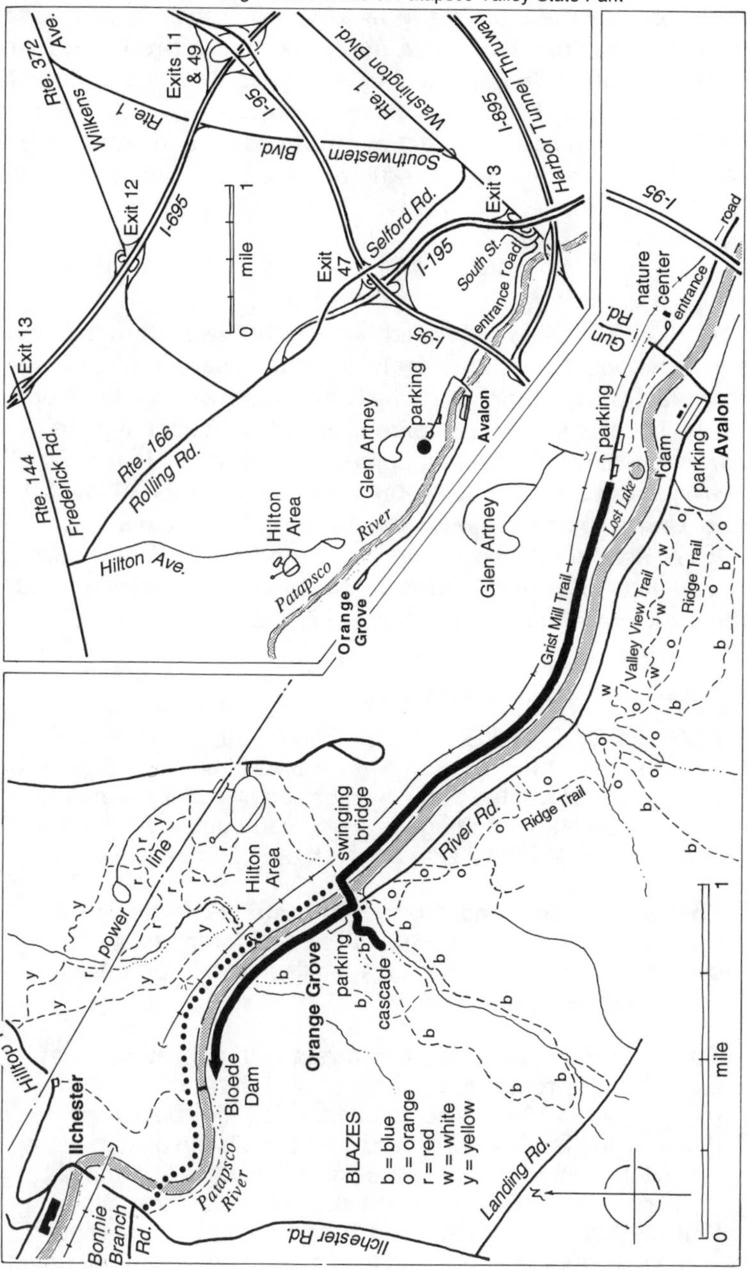

181

business into the old Thistle factory, which has since passed through other hands. The Agnes flood and a fire in 1972 inflicted $1 million in damage, but the works were rebuilt within the old stone walls. The factory now recycles wastepaper to produce paper board, the kind of cardboard used in cereal boxes. Most of the old mill houses—at one time there were thirty-five dwellings crammed along River Road and up Hilltop Road—have been torn down.

THE BLOEDE DAM is located halfway between Orange Grove and Ilchester. It was built in 1906 by the Patapsco Electric and Manufacturing Company, which generated power here until 1924. Named for the company's president, Victor Bloede, the dam was among the first reinforced concrete dams in the United States, and the first to house generators within its hollow interior. **Under no circumstances should you enter the dam.**

River Road used to continue upstream from the dam, but the floodwaters of Tropical Storm Agnes in 1972 carved deeply into the bank, eradicating some stretches of the road.

≈   ≈   ≈   ≈

AUTOMOBILE DIRECTIONS: The trail that is described below starts at the **Avalon Area of Patapsco Valley State Park**, which is located about 8 miles southwest of Baltimore. (See •16 on **Map 1** on page 5. For greater detail, refer to the corner panel of **Map 21** on page 181.)

To the Avalon Area from Interstate 695 (the Baltimore Beltway): Leave I-695 at Exit 11B for Interstate 95 south toward Washington. Go 1.6 miles, then follow the directions in the next paragraph.

To the Avalon Area from Interstate 95: Leave I-95 at Exit 47A for **Interstate 195** east toward BWI Airport. After merging onto I-195 eastbound, take Exit 3 for Route 1 (Washington Boulevard) toward Elkridge. At the bottom of the ramp, turn right toward the state park. Immediately, turn right again onto South Street and left into Patapsco Valley State Park. Follow the entrance road 1.2 miles to a T-intersection. Turn right for Glen Artney and the Lost Lake Historic Area. After just a few dozen yards, turn left and go 0.4 mile to the Grist Mill Recreation Trail at the end of the road. (**Do not** turn right through the big arch leading to the Glen Artney picnic area.)

≈ ≈ ≈ ≈

WALKING: Map 21 on page 181 shows an easy route starting at the **Avalon Area of Patapsco Valley State Park**. The round-trip distance from the Avalon Area to the Bloede Dam and back is 4.5 miles.

Start by following the **Grist Mill Trail** to Orange Grove. After crossing the Swinging Bridge, turn right alongside the parking lot. With the river on the right, continue upstream to the Bloede Dam, then return by the way you came.

Before recrossing the Swinging Bridge, you may want to follow the blue-blazed **Cascade Trail** uphill 330 yards to an attractive cascade. The Cascade Trail starts opposite the bridge.

Finally, the Grist Mill Trail may be extended along the north bank of the Patapsco River to Ilchester, as shown by the dotted line. In part it will follow the old railbed used by the B&O before the present-day tunnel was built. Just before reaching Ilchester, the trail will cross the Patapsco River on a pedestrian bridge supported in part by the stone abutments of the B&O Patterson Viaduct, destroyed by the flood of 1868.

17

GWYNNS FALLS TRAIL

Located in southwest Baltimore, the Gwynns Falls Trail is shown on **Map 22** on page 197. The trail starts near the boundary with Baltimore County and follows Gwynns Falls downstream. The first section—Phase I—stretches 3 miles (4.8 kilometers) through Gwynns Falls • Leakin Park. Phase II, scheduled for completion in 2002, will continue 3 miles more to Carroll Park. When Phase III is finished, the trail will go yet another 3 miles to the Inner Harbor. Another fork will head south to Middle Branch Park.

The Gwynns Falls Trail is open daily from sunrise to sunset. Dogs must be leashed. The trail is managed by the Baltimore City Department of Recreation and Parks; telephone (410) 396-0440.

For automobile directions to the Gwynns Falls Trailhead at Winans Meadow, please turn to page 195. Walking directions start on page 196.

THE FIRST PHASE of the Gwynns Falls Trail follows, in part, the Millrace Path, so-called because it is in fact an old millrace that was filled in to form a walkway at the beginning of the twentieth century. A photograph taken in 1915 shows the Millrace Path as a meticulously groomed promenade about 15 feet wide, along which stroll men and women in their Sunday finery. Winding high along the side of the valley, the path is now a hike-bike trail, bordered by immense yellow-poplar, oak, and beech trees, with views out over the stream to the opposing hillsides. This is one of my favorite places. It demonstrates the special appeal of utilitarian works, including old wagon roads, railroads, and canals—in short, paths with a past—that have been converted to recreational use.

Prior to the time when it was filled in, the millrace started at a dam upstream from Windsor Mill Road. Maintaining a constant elevation, it followed the valley slopes for three miles—an extraordinary distance—to a series of flour mills called Calverton Mills or Five Mills. As can still be seen today, the race was in places supported by stone retaining walls high above the river, and in other places its way was blasted past shoulders of rock. By the time it reached the vicinity of what is now Hilton Parkway, where the first mill was located, the watercourse was about 80 feet above the level of Gwynns Falls. The next four mills were sited at progressively lower elevations farther downstream, so that each mill could use water that had passed over the waterwheel of the one next above it. The tailrace of the first mill became the headrace of the second, and so on until the fifth mill was reached at a site not far upstream from present-day Edmondson Avenue. Built of stone, all five mills were merchant operations, meaning that their owners bought wheat and sold flour in great quantities, rather than merely grinding grain for farmers in exchange for a share of the product, as was done at small country mills.

Farther downstream, the Ellicott family had a group of three flour mills at Frederick Road, to which water was fed by a race that started below Edmondson Avenue. (The Ellicott millrace was filled in to create lower Ellicott Driveway, also part of the Gwynns Falls Trail.) Still farther downstream were two gristmills belonging to the Carrolls: Millington Mill at present-day Carroll Park Golf Course, and Mount Clare Mill below it. The Baltimore Iron Works, located on Gwynns Falls just before tidewater, also used the stream to power its forging and casting operations. There were yet other mills of various sorts on Gwynns Falls and its tributaries above the Calverton site, notably the Powhatan Woolen Mills near Woodlawn, the Ashland Mill at present-day Dickeyville, the Tschudi Paper Mill, Old Windsor Mill (a flouring mill on present-day Windsor Mill Road) and a gristmill at Franklintown. The Old Holly Mill upstream from Calverton was replaced by Hugh Gelston's Calverton Carpet Factory that operated during the middle of the nineteenth century. And overlooking the valleys of Gwynns Falls and Dead run were the estates and mansions of some of Baltimore's leading citizens.

The many gristmills at Gwynns Falls and the large scale of the Calverton and Ellicott enterprises reflects Baltimore's national preeminence as a grain and flour port at the beginning of the nineteenth century. Wheat from central Maryland and south-central Pennsylvania was brought to mills located within the Fall Zone near the tidewater port. Flour was shipped to other cities along the East Coast and to the Caribbean, South America, and even Europe. Although completion of the Erie Canal in 1825 channeled an immense flow of farm products into New York and enabled its port to surpass Baltimore's in wheat (as in every other category), flour-milling in the vicinity of Baltimore remained an important industry throughout most of the nineteenth century. Eventually, however, competition from modern mass-production roller mills established in Minneapolis during the 1870s and '80s led to the abandonment of old, water-powered, burrstone mills at Baltimore and elsewhere.

The Calverton Mills were founded in 1813, and by 1820 all five mills were in operation under different owners. According to the 1820 Manufacturers' Census, the first mill house was four stories tall, measured 50 by 45 feet, and had three pairs of 6-foot burrs powered by two waterwheels, each 16 feet in diameter and 9 feet wide. Operated by nine men, it ground between 35,000 and 50,000 bushels of wheat annually. The other four mills each had four pairs of burrs. All five mills appear to have still been running in 1850, but in 1864 the uppermost one burned. Unable to compete with the "new process mills," the lowermost Calverton mill closed in about 1876 and burned in 1888. The mill on Calverton Lot No. 4 burned in 1879 while undergoing repairs. An 1899 photograph of Walbrook Mill on Calverton Lot No. 2 shows a massive, austerely handsome structure of four full stories set into the hillside above Franklintown Road, and topped by two levels of dormer windows projecting from a peaked roof.

In an article for *The Maryland Monthly Magazine* in 1907, George E. Tack described a walking excursion up the Gwynns Falls Valley and mentioned that only two of the Calverton mills still stood: "The mills are built of the gray rock found in these hills, and are now deserted save the lower portion of one. . . . [T]hey seem to look wistfully out of their darkened window frames across the verdant valley, like giants that have outlived their days of usefulness. . . ." Neither mill is shown in the city's 1914 topographic atlas, which labels the millrace as "Mill Race Walk."

Mr. Tack—who is listed as a poet in a 1911 city directory—followed the old millrace upstream to Windsor Mill Road:

> It is a beautiful scene, where lofty trees stretch their strong arms over our heads, and through the gold-gleamed aisles the summer birds call in liquid tones to each other. Across the valley the Gelston Hills loom up against the orange sky, and along the stream the woods wear a purple veil. There are several quarries along the winding Franklin road, and during the noon hour blasting is carried on, which at a distance sounds like a bombardment between two hostile armies.
>
> To the left is the Winans estate. . . . All through this section are homes of prominent Maryland families, and the old tulip and oak and maple woods have been the trysting places of the happy lovers of other days. . . .
>
> This is a beautiful old valley, all the year round. The spring and summer seasons have their charms, with their birds and flowers; and autumn, with its gold and russet skies, and haze that hangs like a radiant veil over all the face of nature; and in the winter season, when the fields and woods are draped in ermine robes, . . . we may hear the click of the steel skates as the young people, and their elders move over the frozen surface of the falls.

Although Mr. Tate's flowery prose is no longer fashionable, the interesting fact remains that the Gwynns Falls Valley west of Hilton Parkway has changed little since his day, except to become more wooded and even more quiet than it was.

MR. TATE'S DESCRIPTION mentions in passing "the homes of prominent Maryland families," and in particular the estate of Thomas DeKay Winans, Baltimore's rolling stock magnate. Called Crimea, the property had been developed with a train-load of rubles. Winans' massive, almost cubic stone mansion was built shortly before the Civil War and still overlooks the valley of Dead Run above the Gwynns Falls Trailhead at Winans Meadow. Directions to Crimea, which is now part of Gwynns Falls • Leakin Park, are on pages 198-199.

Named for the Ukrainian Riviera, Crimea was Winans' dacha—his summer home and winter hunting lodge. His intown residence was Alexandroffsky, formerly located in a private walled park east of present-day Union Square and described in various accounts as "palatial," "magnificent," "exotic," and "fabulous." Two cast-iron lions that used to guard Alexandroffsky were removed when it was razed in 1927 and now stand near the feline cages at the zoo in Druid Hill Park.

The story of Winans' Russianisms and his Russian millions starts with his father, Ross Winans, a prominent inventor in the early days of the Baltimore & Ohio Railroad. After traveling abroad with a group of experts sent by the B&O to study the English railroad system in 1828, Ross Winans worked on the adaptation of English engines and rolling stock to the steep grades and tight curves of the new American railroads. He reduced the friction of railroad wheels by fusing them with the axle so that the entire massive assembly revolved as a unit, with the axle turning in grease-packed boxes. This arrangement, with some modifications, is still in use around the world. Winans put the flange of the wheels on the inside edge and invented the swivel wheel truck and coned wheels with beveled treads to help trains negotiate curves. He was the first to use horizontal pistons on his *Crab* locomotives, and in time he built increasingly powerful engines, such as the *Camel* and the *Mud Digger*, to pull the B&O over the Allegheny Mountains. In 1835 Ross Winans and a partner assumed management of the B&O locomotive and rolling stock shops at Mt. Clare under an arrangement allowing them to sell equipment to other lines, provided that the B&O had first call. Then, in 1844 Ross Winans left the B&O and set up his own shop, where he built the *Carroll of Carrollton*, a locomotive said to be so fast for its day that its full potential speed could never be tested because the railbeds were not sufficiently straight or evenly graded for the engine to be fully opened.

All of which brings us to the Russians, who in the late 1830s were embarking on their own railroad program. Czar Nicholas I had ordered the construction of a line between St. Petersburg and Moscow. Two Russian engineers came to the United States in 1839 to study American railroads and rolling stock, and they eventually recommended to the Russian government that George

W. Whistler, a civil engineer trained at West Point (and incidentally father of the artist James McNeill Whistler), be hired to superintend construction of the new Russian line. Major Whistler knew Ross Winans; he and Winans has served together on the B&O commission to England, and Whistler had helped survey the B&O route to the Ohio River. Whistler thought highly of Winans' locomotives and abilities. At Whistler's suggestion, Ross Winans was offered a contract in 1842 to set up a shop in Russia to manufacture rolling stock in partnership with the Philadelphia firm of Harrison and Eastwick, which had been recommended by the two Russian engineers. Ross Winans declined on the grounds that he was too old, but he persuaded Whistler and the Russians to accept his two sons, Thomas and William, both of whom had worked under Ross in positions of responsibility.

In 1844 Harrison and Eastwick closed their Philadelphia locomotive shop and shipped their equipment to Alexandroffsky near St. Petersburg, where they were joined by the Winans brothers. A new shop was established and the partners embarked on an immensely lucrative contract to supply two hundred locomotives and seven thousand cars for the new Russian railroad, dubbed "the harnessed samovar" by the local populace. In 1850 the contract was expanded to include more equipment and ongoing maintenance. William Winans also designed and built iron bridges for the railroad, which was being laid out by Major Whistler. The Americans are said to have entertained lavishly, and judging from the estates that the Winans later built here and in England, they became accustomed to life in the grand style.

Thomas Winans returned home in 1854, three years after completion of the railroad. He brought with him a Russian wife of Italian and French ancestry and a fortune estimated at $2 million, which, of course, was a huge sum for those days. William Winans stayed in Europe and never returned to the United States. Nor did Major Whistler, who had encountered constant difficulties and delays in the construction of the railbed. Weakened by cholera, he died in 1849 before the line was completed.

Following his return to Baltimore, Thomas Winans designed and had constructed at his father's shop a streamlined "cigar ship." It was completely cylindrical and tapered to a point at each end like a submarine but was limited to surface travel. This design was intended to increase speed and economy by minimizing water resistance and top-heaviness in high winds and seas. Four of Ross Winans' locomotive engines powered a turbine-like wheel that completely circled the ship's waist, supposedly allowing the application of much more force than the midship paddle wheels of conventional steamers of the day. The ship was launched on October 6, 1858, at Winans Cove in South Baltimore, but despite what newspaper accounts said were successful test runs nothing came of the design.

Another unusual venture of the Winans—in this case Ross Winans—was the repair at the outset of the Civil War of a steam-powered, self-propelled armored cannon—in short, a primitive tank. Invented and built by Charles S. Dickinson of Ohio, the gun was supposed to throw two hundred balls per minute from a revolving set of cupped arms, "just like so many hands throwing baseballs," according to William H. Weaver, a journalist and witness when the gun was tested at the Winans' factory. In less than a minute, according to Weaver (who may just have been making the most of a good story), the weapon demolished a brick wall buttressed with a pile of timbers three feet thick. An ardent and outspoken supporter of the Confederacy, Ross Winans attempted to send this gun to the South, but the weapon was intercepted by federal troops, who could not make it work. According to Mr. Weaver, a key piece of the mechanism had been removed before the gun was shipped and was to be sent only if the weapon reached its destination. In any case, Ross Winans was imprisoned briefly at Fort McHenry. After his release he was jailed again when he tried to send a shipload of arms to the Confederacy.

Unlike his father, Thomas Winans was content to let the war take its own course. In the 1850s he had purchased a large tract of land in the vicinity of Gwynns Falls and Dead Run, and in 1860 he built the Crimea mansion, pictured on page 193 and showing a touch of Russia in the ornate carvings at the corners of the cornice. The Crimea mansion was reached by a long entrance drive that climbed the hill from Franklintown Road at the bottom of the valley. A semicircular masonry parapet halfway down the bluff (and now enveloped in woods) was once decorated with a battery of dummy cannons, supposedly erected to resemble the Russian batteries at Balaklava, or according to another story, to deter passing Union troops from molesting the estate. A large undershot waterwheel on Dead Run pumped springwater to the house, and a gasworks manufactured gas for the principal residence. Near the main dwelling is the "Honeymoon House," which Winans built for his daughter when she married. The estate also has a caretaker's house, a wooden Gothic chapel, a large stone stable, and a vegetable cellar and ice house set into the slope at the bottom of the valley, near the Gwynns Falls Trailhead at Winans Meadow. The ground floor of the main house now serves as park headquarters. Although Baltimore City has no money to restore the Crimea mansion (as some have talked of doing), funds should be allocated immediately to arrest deterioration of the exterior.

In 1866 Thomas Winans returned to Russia, where he served as president of the firm of Winans, Whistler, and Winans, managers of the St. Petersburg and Moscow Railroad under an eight-year contract with the Russian government. The Whistler in the firm's name was another son of the former superintendent and also the Winans' brother-in-law, having married Julia Winans while working in Ross Winans' Baltimore shops. After the management contract had run only two years, however, the Russian government took over the work and released the firm, paying it a settlement of several million dollars. Thomas Winans returned home and divided his time between his houses (he had one also at Newport, Rhode Island), travel, and various charities until his death in 1878.

IN 1904 THE OLMSTED BROTHERS, Boston's pre-eminent land planning firm and consultants to many eastern cities, presented their *Report upon the Development of Public Grounds for Greater Baltimore*. The Olmsted report recommended development of a comprehensive park system based on stream valleys and adjacent lands in the vicinity of the city, as has since been done at the Patapsco Valley, Gunpowder Falls, Herring Run, and Gwynns Falls, and to a lesser extent at Jones Falls, Stony Run, and other streams within the city. Gradually, Gwynns Falls • Leakin Park has been pieced together by a series of purchases

made between 1904 and the present. The last major acquisition was in 1969, when the 100-acre Windsor estate on Windsor Mill and Wetheredsville roads was purchased. A few more acres have been added from time to time since then.

In 1941 the valley portion of the Crimea estate was purchased for a city park from Thomas Winans' heirs, and seven years later the city bought the balance. In both instances the purchase money was provided from the bequest of J. Wilson Leakin, an attorney who had died in 1922. Leakin had left several downtown properties to the city with the stipulation that the proceeds from their rental and eventual sale be used for the acquisition and improvement of a new city park. For years different neighborhood groups and municipal agencies wrangled about where the park should be located. Even after the first Crimea tract was purchased, Mayor Thomas D'Alesandro favored selling the property in 1947 because he thought it inaccessible, but instead the park was expanded in 1948 by the purchase of the Crimea grounds above the valley, with access from Windsor Mill Road.

During the 1960s and '70s the big park at Gwynns Falls was nearly wrecked by the eastward extension of Interstate 70 into Baltimore. The plan specified that about 12 percent of the park (130 acres) would be taken by the highway itself. The eight-lane expressway was to slice through the Crimea section in a trench that would be covered for part of its length. Continuing eastward, the highway would follow the crest of the ridge between the valleys of Gwynns Falls and Dead Run to the confluence of the two streams. It would then cross the central valley on a long, high bridge, and from there would follow the park's south slope to and across Hilton Parkway before reaching another new highway that was to be built westward from downtown Baltimore along Franklin and Mulberry streets. From the interchange with the Franklin-Mulberry spur, Interstate 70 would continue south to join Interstate 95. Without question the sight and sound of such a highway would have completely dominated all of Gwynns Falls • Leakin Park, turning it into little more than something nice to look at from the expressway.

In 1973 and '74, when the highway proposal received city, state, and tentative federal approval, implementation of the plan appeared to be imminent. Interstate 70 was in fact built from the Baltimore Beltway to the western boundary of the park, where the highway abruptly ends, as can be seen today. The 1.5-mile Franklin-Mulberry highway, now a grandiose, entrenched segment of Route 40 just west of Martin Luther King Boulevard, was built at a cost of more than $100 million—a sum so stupendous that many people feared that the expenditure would become a compelling justification to finish the job by extending the highway through the park. At Interstate 95 near the exit for Caton Avenue, ramps that ended in air were built in anticipation of linking with Interstate 70. Even the right-of-way through the western part of the city was purchased.

And then the project gradually faded away. The plan to put the highway through the park faced overwhelming opposition from park users and area residents. The project had been delayed by litigation, and more litigation was a certainty. Leaders of Baltimore's business community, who for years had urged that the park highway was needed as a link in the truck route between the port and the Midwest, changed their opinion, concluding that Interstate 95 and the Beltway provided adequate access to Interstate 70 west of the city. Money set aside for the park highway was reallocated to other transportation projects.

Is the park highway really dead? For the foreseeable future, it appears so. Most of the right-of-way has been sold, and the ramps on I-95 that were to join with I-70 have been dismantled at considerable cost.

≈   ≈   ≈   ≈

AUTOMOBILE DIRECTIONS: The Gwynns Falls Trail starts near the western boundary of Baltimore. (See •17 on **Map 1** on page 5. For greater detail, refer to **Map 22** on page 197.) Two approaches to the trailhead at Winans Meadow are described below.

To the Gwynns Falls Trailhead from Interstate 695 (the Baltimore Beltway): Leave I-695 at Exit 16 for Interstate 70 east toward Park & Ride. Go about 1.5 miles to the end of the freeway, then take Exit 94 for Security Boulevard north. From the bottom of the exit ramp, follow Security Boulevard just 0.2 mile, then turn right at an obscure intersection onto Ingleside Avenue and go straight past the Millrace Tavern on Franklintown Road. (If you miss the turn onto Ingleside, turn right onto Forest Park Avenue, then right again toward Franklintown Road. At the bottom of the hill, turn left onto Franklintown Road itself.)

Follow Franklintown Road into Gwynns Falls • Leakin Park for 1.3 miles, then turn left into the entrance for the Gwynns Falls · Trailhead at Winans Meadow.

To the Gwynns Falls Trailhead from Route 40 (Edmondson Avenue) in west Baltimore: Leave Route 40 at the intersection with Winans Way. If you are coming from downtown, Winans way is a right turn after passing Edmondson Village Shopping Center and Old Frederick Road. If you are coming into the city from the west, Winans Way is a left turn after Cooks Lane, Nottingham Road, and Brookwood Road.

Follow Winans Way 0.8 mile as it snakes downhill into Gwynns Falls • Leakin Park. At the bottom of the valley, turn right onto Franklintown Road. Go 0.3 mile, then turn left into the entrance for the Gwynns Falls Trailhead at Winans Meadow.

≈   ≈   ≈   ≈

WALKING and BICYCLING: Map 22 at right shows the **Gwynns Falls Trail**. As this book goes to press, Phase I (consisting of the first 3 miles) has been completed, and Phase II and Phase III are expected to be finished in 2002 and 2003. The plan is for the trail to stretch from the western boundary of Baltimore downstream along Gwynns Falls to the Middle Branch of the Patapsco River near the football and baseball stadiums. Eventually, there will be links to the Inner Harbor and to Middle Branch Park. Also, the trail may be extended westward for a mile to the Park & Ride lot at the end of Interstate 70.

Start at the Gwynns Falls Trailhead at Winans Meadow. Join the paved path that runs alongside the parking lot. With Franklintown Road toward the right, follow the paved path past a trail and bridge intersecting from the left. After nearly half a mile, cross a bridge over Dead Run and bear left onto Wetheredsville Road (now closed to cars). Continue straight to Windsor Mill Road.

At the intersection with Windsor Mill Road, turn right across the bridge over Gwynns Falls. Go 200 yards, then turn right to

MAP 22 — Gwynns Falls Trail

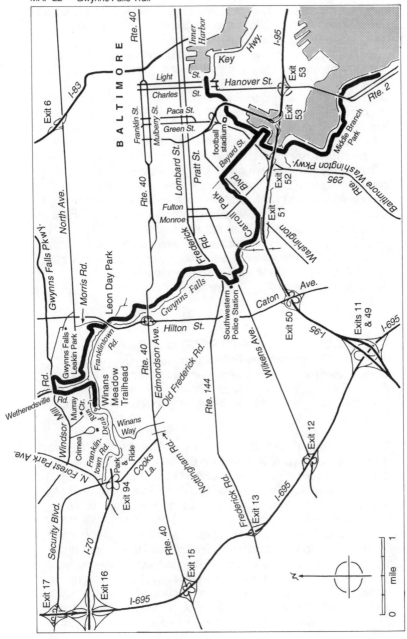

197

continue on the hike-bike trail, which now follows the old Calverton millrace. After awhile, cross a narrow paved road and continue along the constant contour of the hillside.

Eventually, at Morris Street next to Hilton Parkway, the trail makes a hairpin turn to the right downhill. At the bottom of the slope, turn left across Morris Street and pass under Hilton Parkway. Continue alongside Franklintown Road for a quarter-mile to Leon Day Park and on down the Gwynns Falls Valley as far as Frederick Avenue.

At Frederick Avenue, turn right and follow the path across Gwynns Falls, then left past Southwestern Police Station. At Wilkens Avenue, turn left and cross back over the river, then immediately turn right and continue downstream along the riverbank. After crossing one railroad, pass under another at the stone Carrollton Viaduct, then continue through Carroll Park to Washington Boulevard. Bear left and follow the trail more or less parallel with Washington Boulevard, then turn right onto Bayard Street, which eventually crosses Russell Street. Continue to a fork in the trail, where the left spur goes to the Inner Harbor and the right spur runs to Middle Branch Park.

≈   ≈   ≈   ≈

THE CRIMEA and the CARRIE MURRAY NATURE CENTER: These two sites at Gwynns Falls • Leakin Park are located near the Gwynns Falls Trailhead at Winans Meadow. Both are worth visiting. Two approaches by car are described below, but you may find it easier simply to refer to **Map 22** on page 197.

To the Crimea and Carrie Murray Nature Center from Interstate 695 (the Baltimore Beltway): Leave I-695 at Exit 16 for Interstate 70 east toward Park & Ride. Go about 1.5 miles to the end of the freeway, then take Exit 94 for Security Boulevard north. From the bottom of the exit ramp, follow Security Boulevard just 0.2 mile, then turn right onto North Forest Park Avenue. Follow North Forest Park Avenue uphill 0.5 mile to an intersection with Windsor Mill Road. Turn right and follow Windsor Mill Road 0.3 mile to the **Crimea** entrance on the right. Enter the park between stone posts surmounted by cast-iron eagles. Follow the entrance road only 100 yards, then turn left into the large parking lot. From there, walk to the Crimea mansion at the end of the driveway.

For the **Carrie Murray Nature Center**, continue on Windsor Mill Road 0.2 mile past the Crimea entrance, then turn right onto Hutton Road. The nature center is at the end of Hutton Road past the parking lot.

To the Crimea and Carrie Murray Nature Center from downtown Baltimore: Follow Route 40 west past Hilton Parkway and Edmondson Village Shopping Center. After passing intersections with Old Frederick Road, Winans Way, and Nottingham Road, turn right onto Cooks Lane. Follow Cooks Lane (which becomes Security Boulevard) 1 mile to an intersection with North Forest Park Avenue. Turn right onto North Forest Park Avenue and follow it uphill 0.5 mile to an intersection with Windsor Mill Road. Turn right and follow Windsor Mill Road 0.3 mile to the **Crimea** entrance on the right. Enter the park between stone posts surmounted by cast-iron eagles. Follow the entrance road only 100 yards, then turn left into the large parking lot. From there, walk to the Crimea mansion at the end of the driveway.

For the **Carrie Murray Nature Center**, continue on Windsor Mill Road 0.2 mile past the Crimea entrance, then turn right onto Hutton Road. The nature center is at the end of Hutton Road past the parking lot.

18

CYLBURN ARBORETUM

Cylburn occupies 170 acres of meadows and woods on a high plateau above the Jones Falls Valley just south of Northern Parkway. Once a private estate, this property is now Baltimore's arboretum and horticultural center.

The Circle Trail—shown by the bold line on **Map 23** on page 208—follows the rim of the valley for about 1 mile (1.6 kilometers) through the woods. There are also other paths, plus the opportunity to stroll around the grassy grounds among specimen trees that are grouped by families of related species. Behind the mansion are various demonstration gardens. Labels identify hundreds of varieties of trees, shrubs, flowers, and other plants. Over 150 species of birds have been seen here.

The arboretum is open daily from 6:00 A.M. to 9:00 P.M. Dogs must be leashed. **Cylburn Mansion** is open weekdays from 7:30 to 3:30. **The Museum of Birds of Maryland** on the second floor is open Tuesday and Thursday from 10:00 to 3:00. The arboretum is managed by the Baltimore City Department of Recreation and Parks; telephone (410) 396-0180.

For automobile directions, please turn to page 207. Walking directions start on page 209.

STARTED IN 1863, Cylburn was developed during the decade following the Civil War as the country estate of Jesse Tyson, the son of Isaac Tyson, Jr., Baltimore's chrome king. (See Chapter 13.) The gray stone for the mansion was quarried at the Bare Hills west of Lake Roland, where the Tysons had some of their chromite and copper mines.

In 1888 Jesse Tyson married Edith Johns, a Baltimore debutante who in later years Alfred Jenkins Shriver listed in his will as among the ten most beautiful Baltimore women of his era (and all of whom, therefore, were by his testamentary directions painted together in a mural at Johns Hopkins University's Shriver Hall—each woman "at the height of her beauty"). The Tysons entertained frequently and lavishly at Cylburn, where they, their servants, and weekend guests arrived and departed by the Northern Central Railroad; a private carriage road ran from the mansion to Cylburn station, located off what was then Belvedere Avenue. Four years after Tyson's death in 1906, his widow married Lieutenant (later Major) Bruce Cotton, and for decades Cylburn continued to be a showplace where Baltimore society gathered for receptions in the large drawing room or wandered the lawns and gardens that were lit with hundreds of Japanese lanterns during summer musicales. Following Mrs. Cotton's death in 1942, Major Cotton sold the property to the city for a low price with the specific intention that the estate be made a city park. The grounds and gardens—cared for in part by volunteers from the Cylburn Arboretum Association—are very attractive, and the mansion too is well worth seeing, although the grandeur of the interior is somewhat faded.

IF YOU WANT TO LEARN to identify trees, the large variety of labeled specimens at Cylburn Arboretum provides excellent practice and an enjoyable excursion at all times of year. Oak, hickory, and yellow-poplar (also called tuliptree) and to a lesser extent maple, beech, and ash dominate the scene, as is typical in eastern Maryland. Dogwood, sassafras, and mountain laurel are also widespread in the understory.

Learning to identify trees is not difficult. Every walk or automobile trip is an opportunity for practice. Notice the overall forms and branching habits of the trees, and also the distinctive qualities of their twigs, buds, bark, leaves, flowers, and fruits or seeds. These factors are the key identification features that distinguish one species from another. Finally, when using a field guide, check the maps or descriptions that delineate the geographic range within which a tentatively identified tree or shrub is likely to be found.

Some trees, of course, have very distinctive and reliable forms. Familiar evergreens like balsam fir and eastern redcedar have a conical shape, like a dunce cap, although in dense stands redcedar tapers very little and assumes the columnar form of the

Italian cypress, which it somewhat resembles. The deciduous European linden, frequently used as a street tree, is also more or less conical in shape, but with wider-spreading lower branches than the evergreens mentioned above. Elm displays a spreading form like a head of broccoli. A full-bodied egg-shape is characteristic of sugar maple and beech, although both will develop long, branchless trunks in crowded woods, as do most forest trees competing for light. The vertically exaggerated cigar shape of Lombardy poplar—a form called fastigiate—and the pendulous, trailing quality of weeping willow are unmistakable. (Both Lombardy poplar and weeping willow have been introduced to North America from abroad.)

Branching habit, an important clue to some trees, is observable even at a distance. White pine, for example, has markedly horizontal branches with a slight upward tilt at the tips, like a hand turned with its palm up. Norway spruce (another imported species) is a very tall evergreen—sometimes reminding me of a pagoda—with long, evenly-spaced, festoon-like branches. The slender lower branches of pin oak slant downward, while those of white oak and red oak are often massive and horizontal, especially on mature trees growing in the open. The lower branches of the horsechestnut (yet another European import) also droop but then curl up at the tips in chunky twigs. Elm branches spread up and out like the mouth of a trumpet. The trunk of the mature honeylocust diverges into large branches somewhat in the manner of an elm. Even the reviled *ailanthus* or tree of heaven, which in many East Coast cities springs up in dense groves of spindly, spiky saplings wherever earth has been disturbed, eventually develops a spreading form somewhat like an elm or honeylocust. (The thickets of small trees along the embankments of the Jones Falls Expressway are mostly *ailanthus*.)

A good botanist or forester can identify trees by their twigs alone—that is, by the end portion of the branch that constitutes the newest growth. During winter the shape, color, size, position, and sheathing of buds are important. For instance, beech buds are long and pointed, tan, and sheathed with overlapping scales like shingles. Sycamore and magnolia buds are wrapped in a single scale. The twigs of horse chestnut are tipped with a big, sticky, brown bud, while those of silver maple, and to a lesser extent red maple, end with large clusters of red buds. Some oaks, such as white oak, have hairless terminal buds, while other species, such as black oak, have hairy end buds.

Aside from buds, other characteristics of twigs are the size, shape, and position of leaf scars marking where the leaf stems were attached. The scars can be circular, polygonal, crescent, or even heart-shaped, and they also show different numbers of bundle scars or vascular dots. One fundamental factor is the distinction between *opposite* and *alternate* scars. The location of leaf scars in opposite pairs along the twigs (as with maples) distinguishes a wide variety of trees and shrubs from those with leaf scars arranged alternately, first on one side and then on the other (as with oaks).

Yet other twig characteristics are color, thorns, odor, hair, and pith. For example, most maple twigs are reddish brown, but the twigs of striped maple and mountain maple are greenish. Thorns and spines are significant because relatively few trees have them, notably honeylocust, black locust, Hercules-club, prickly-ash, buckthorn bumelia, devils-walkingstick, Osage-orange, American plum, some crabapples, and the many varieties of hawthorn. *Ailanthus* twigs, which show huge heart-shaped leaf scars, have a rank odor when broken open, and the twigs of sweet birch (also called black birch) have a strong wintergreen odor. Most oaks have hairless twigs, although some species such as blackjack oak are distinctly hairy. As for pith, it can be chambered, solid, spongy, or of different colors, depending on the species. Oak and hickory are common forest species in the Baltimore region, but only the pith of white oak in cross section forms a star. All of these distinguishing features can best be appreciated simply by examining the twigs of different species.

Bark is not always a reliable clue for identifying trees, as the color and texture of bark change with age or from trunk to branches to twigs. Often the distinctive character of bark is seen only in the trunks of large, mature trees. Bark can be smooth, furrowed, scaly, plated, shaggy, fibrous, crisscrossed, or papery. Some trees, of course, may be clearly identified by their bark. The names *shagbark hickory* and *paper birch* speak for themselves. Striped maple has longitudinal, whitish stripes in the smooth green bark of the younger trees. The crisscrossed ridges of white ash, the light blotches on sycamores, and the smooth gray skin of beech are equally distinctive. Birches and some cherries are characterized by horizontal lenticels like random dashes.

Most people notice leaves, particularly their shape. The leaves of the gray birch are triangular; ginkgo, fan-shaped; catalpa, heart-shaped; sweetgum, star-shaped; beech, elliptical (or actually pointed at each end); and black willow narrower still and thus *lanceolate*. Notice also the leaf margin or edge. Is it smooth like rhododendron, wavy like water oak, serrated like basswood, or deeply lobed like most maples? And how many lobes are there? Yellow-poplar, for example, has easily recognized four-lobed leaves shown on page 200; maples have three- or five-lobed leaves. Also, are the lobe tips rounded like white oak or pointed like red oak? Or maybe, as with sassafras and red mulberry, the same tree has leaves that are shaped differently, the most distinctive being those with a single asymmetrical lobe creating a leaf outline like a mitten. In some trees, such as the bigleaf magnolia with its tobacco-like foliage, the sheer size of the leaves is significant. Sycamores have leaves resembling sugar maples or red maples, but usually bigger and coarser.

Some leaves such as those of the Japanese maple, horsechestnut, and Ohio buckeye are *palmately* compound, meaning that they are actually composed of leaflets radiating from the end of the stem. In the fall the whole compound leaf may drop off the tree as a unit, or the leaflets may fall off individually, and then finally the stem. Other leaves, such as ash, hickory, and sumac, are *pinnately* compound, being composed of leaflets arranged in opposite pairs along a central stalk. With pinnately compound leaves growing from the top of a branchless trunk, the saplings of *ailanthus* resemble little palm trees. Still other leaves are *bipinnately* compound, somewhat like a fern. The leaflets grow from stalks that, in turn, spread from a central stalk. Honeylocust, Kentucky coffeetree, and the ornamental imported silktree are examples.

Although the needles of evergreens are not as varied as the leaves of deciduous plants, there are still several major points to look for, such as the number of needles grouped together. White pine has fascicles of five; pitch pine, loblolly pine, and sometimes shortleaf pine have fascicles of three; and jack pine, red pine, Virginia pine, Austrian pine, and sometimes shortleaf pine have fascicles of two. Needles of spruce, hemlock, and fir grow singly, but are joined to the twig in distinctive ways. Spruce needles grow from little woody pegs, hemlock needles from smaller bumps, and fir needles directly from the twig, leaving a rounded pit when pulled off. Spruce needles tend to be four-sided, hemlock flat, and fir somewhere in-between. The needles of larch (also called tamarack) grow in dense clusters and all drop off in winter. The needles of baldcypress also drop off—hence its name.

Flowers are a spectacular, though short-lived, feature of some trees and shrubs. Three variables are color, form, and (less reliably) time of bloom. Allegheny serviceberry (also called shadbush), with small, white, five-petaled flowers, is among the first of our native trees to bloom, sometimes as early as March in the Baltimore region. As members of the rose family, cherries, peaches, plums, pears, apples, and hawthorns all have flowers with five petals (usually pink or white) in loose, white clusters, typically blooming in April. The blossoms of flowering dogwood, which also appear in April or early May, consist of four white, petal-like bracts, each with a brown notch at the tip, while the flowers of alternate-leaf dogwood consist of loose, white clusters. These are a few of our native species commonly thought of as flowering trees, but the blossoms of other native species are equally distinctive, such as the small but numerous flowers of red maples, appearing with forsythia in March or early April, or the tuliplike flowers and durable husks of yellow-poplar, appearing in May and early June. Unlike most trees, witch-hazel—which produces small, yellow, scraggly flowers—blooms in fall or winter.

Finally, the seeds or fruit of a tree are a conspicuous element in summer and fall, sometimes lasting into winter and spring. Even if a tree is bare, the fruits and seeds (or for that matter, the leaves) can often be found littered on the ground around the trunk. Nobody who sees a tree with acorns could fail to know that it is an oak, although some varieties, such as willow oak and shingle oak (also known as northern laurel oak) are deceptive. Distinctive nuts are also produced by beech trees, horsechestnuts, hickories, and walnuts. Some seeds, like ash and maple, have wings; such winged seeds are termed *samaras*.

Others, such as honeylocust, Kentucky coffeetree, and redbud, come in pods like beans and in fact are members of the same general legume family. The seeds of birches and alders hang in catkins that in some species develop into conelike strobiles. Sweetgum and sycamore form prickle-balls (as do the shells of horsechestnut and buckeye). Eastern cottonwood and quaking aspen produce seeds that are wind-borne by cottonlike tufts. And, of course, brightly colored berries and fruits are produced by many species, such as crabapples, dogwood, holly, hawthorn, and hackberry. The female ginkgo has pale pink, globular, and remarkably foul-smelling fruit. Among needle evergreens, spruce and pine cones hang from the twigs, while fir cones stand upright like stubby candles, and the small hemlock cones grow from the twig tips.

In conclusion, the trick to tree identification is to consider, either simultaneously or in rapid succession, a wide variety of features of which the ones discussed here—form and branching habit, twigs, buds, bark, leaves, flowers, and fruits or seeds—are the most obvious. Don't get hung up pondering any single ambiguous or inconclusive feature; move on to consider other clues.

≈   ≈   ≈   ≈

AUTOMOBILE DIRECTIONS: Cylburn Arboretum is located in north Baltimore. (See •18 on **Map 1** on page 5. For greater detail, refer to the corner panel of **Map 23** on page 208.) The entrance to the arboretum is on Greenspring Avenue 0.3 mile south of Northern Parkway and 0.7 mile north of Coldspring Lane. Directions are as follows:

To Cylburn Arboretum from Interstate 83 (the Jones Falls Expressway): Leave I-83 at Exit 10B for Northern Parkway westbound. Follow Northern Parkway west only 0.3 mile, then turn left onto Cylburn Avenue toward Sinai Emergency Center. Follow Cylburn Avenue uphill 0.5 mile to Greenspring Avenue. Turn left onto Greenspring Avenue, then immediately turn left again into Cylburn Arboretum. Follow the entrance road 0.3 mile, then park on the left.

≈   ≈   ≈   ≈

MAP 23 — Cylburn Arboretum

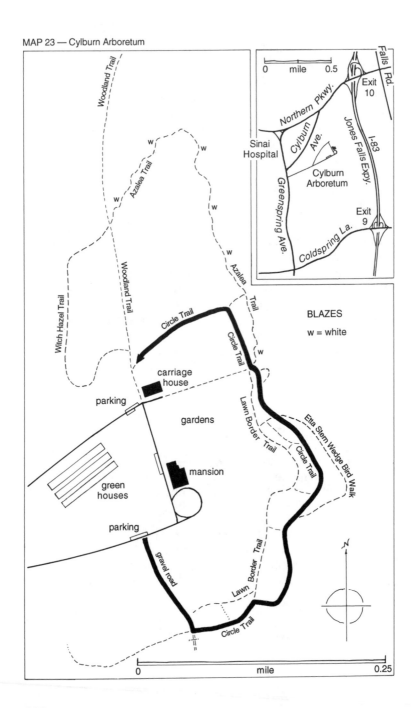

WALKING: Map 23 at left shows the trails at **Cylburn Arboretum**. The bold line is the mile-long **Circle Trail**, which leads to other trails and various gardens behind the mansion.

Start your walk on the rutted gravel track that descends from the entrance road opposite some parking bays for cars and buses. This spot is marked by a sign saying "official vehicles only" and is located about 100 yards before the entrance road reaches the circular drive in front of the mansion.

Follow the gravel track downhill toward the woods. When you enter the woods, turn left in front of a chainlink gate onto a wide footpath (the Circle Trail). Follow the Circle trail along the rim of the bluff. After about 125 yards, turn right to continue on the Circle Trail, which eventually brings you around to the rear of the mansion, where you can join the **Woodland Trail** or the **Azalea Trail** or explore the gardens. For a still longer walk, you can return to your car by circling back clockwise along a path (the **Lawn Border Trail**) that follows the edge of the grass next to the woods.

19

NORTH POINT STATE PARK
and FORT HOWARD PARK

Map 25 on page 221 shows **North Point State Park**, located southeast of Baltimore. The bold lines trace two walks, both of which start at a parking lot near the park entrance.

Heading south to a big jetty that projects into Chesapeake Bay is the **hike-bike path**, which passes through woods and fields. From the waterfront, return by the way you came. The round-trip distance is 3 miles (4.8 kilometers). Near the jetty is the **wading beach**—a term used by the park authorities to emphasize that the site is not intended for swimming. There are no changing facilities and no lifeguards.

The other route shown on Map 25 is the **Black Marsh Trail**, which follows the former Bay Shore trolley bed to the circular **Wetlands Trail**. There are several spurs along the way. The round-trip distance is 3.5 miles (5.6 kilometers). If you want, you can connect from the Wetlands Trail to the hike-bike path, as shown by the short dotted line.

North Point State Park is open daily from 6:00 A.M. to sunset May through October. A small admission fee is charged. During the rest of the year, the park is open free of charge from 8 A.M. to sunset. It is closed Thanksgiving and Christmas. Dogs must be leashed and are not permitted in the vicinity of the visitor center or beach. The park is managed by the Department of Natural Resources, Maryland Forest, Park and Wildlife Service as part of Gunpowder Falls State Park; telephone (410) 477-0757.

Just 1.8 miles down the road from North Point State Park is **Fort Howard Park**. This is more of a picnic park than a walking park, but the waterfront fortifications are well worth exploring, as is made easy by a network of paved paths shown on the corner panel of **Map 24** on page 220. These trails total perhaps 1 mile (1.6 kilometers).

Fort Howard Park is open daily from sunrise to sunset, except during October, when it is altogether closed. Dogs must be leashed. The park is managed by the Baltimore County Department of Recreation and Parks; telephone (410) 887-7529.

For automobile directions to North Point and Fort Howard, please turn to page 218. Walking directions are on pages 219-222 (North Point) and on page 223 (Fort Howard).

NORTH POINT is where five thousand British troops landed in the fall of 1814 for their abortive march on Baltimore. Major General Robert Ross, commander of the British land forces, had announced his intention to use Baltimore—that "nest of privateers" in his words—as his headquarters during the coming winter. He said that with the city as his base, his army would go where it pleased through Maryland.

Two years previously, the youthful United States had declared war on England. In a petition to President Jefferson, Baltimore had urged war with France also, on the grounds that her conduct was "scarcely less atrocious than that of England." Since 1793 Great Britain and France, at that time the world's two most powerful nations, had been locked in a protracted global war, and both countries regularly confiscated American merchant ships and cargoes in an attempt to prevent supplies from reaching the enemy. The United States itself engaged in the same practice during the Civil War, but in the early 1800s most Americans saw the seizures as a piratical violation of their neutrality.

Ire toward England was intensified starting in 1805 by the British navy's practice of stopping merchant vessels in United States coastal waters and removing all sailors whom the English determined or merely surmised were British subjects. Great Britain did not recognize the process by which Englishmen might become naturalized Americans, and in any case, the Royal Navy was sorely in need of seamen. Also, the "war hawks," a group of congressmen from the frontier states, openly urged that war with Great Britain would provide the opportunity for the United States to seize Canada and its lucrative fur trade, to end the Indian menace in the Ohio Valley, where massacres and conspiracies were said to be incited by British agents, and to throw open more land for settlement.

The War of 1812, however, did not go as planned by the Americans. Successive attempts to invade Canada failed miserably. At Baltimore, the British blockade of Chesapeake Bay reduced the export trade to almost nothing. Among shipowners, only the privateersmen made substantial profits through the seizure and sale of English merchant ships. Commissioned by the federal government as private warships and operated as money-making ventures, Baltimore's privateers captured about a third of all enemy vessels that were taken during the war. After being seized, the ships were sailed to American ports, where they and their cargoes were sold through judicial condemnation by admiralty courts.

In the spring of 1814, Great Britain and its allies finally forced the abdication of Napoleon. England then turned its attention to the United States. The London newspapers announced that an expeditionary force of seasoned troops and sailors was being readied. "The seat of the American government, but more particularly Baltimore, is to be the immediate object of attack. . . . Terms will be offered to the American government at the point of the bayonet."

In mid-August the British force appeared in Chesapeake Bay, where the English had already seized Tangier Island as a base of operations. Baltimore gained time while the British marched from Benedict on the Patuxent River to Washington, which they captured on August 24, 1814. This event was enormously exaggerated in England, where the brief occupation of the national capital—a straggling, swampy place of 8,000 inhabitants—was said by the British press to be equivalent to the fall of London. *The Times* of London declared, "The world is speedily to be delivered of the mischievous example of the existence of a government founded on democratic rebellion." After only one day in Washington, where they burned the government buildings, the "modern Goths"—as one indignant American writer called the British—marched back to their ships.

Meanwhile, Baltimore dug in. The previous year a half-million dollars had been raised by subscription among the residents for the defense of the city because no aid came from Washington. Fort McHenry had been strengthened and other shore batteries constructed. A line of earthworks over a mile long was thrown up to the east of the city at Hampstead Hill, across land now occupied by Highlandtown, Patterson Park, and Johns Hopkins Hospital. This was to be the main line of resistance.

Work on the fortifications continued until Sunday, September 11, when three alarm guns in the courthouse square and the ringing of bells announced the arrival of the British squadron at North Point, 12 miles southeast of Baltimore at the mouth of the Patapsco River. After the militia had mustered, Major General Samuel Smith, to whom the city had assigned its defense, sent General John Stricker with 3,185 men out Philadelphia Road to reconnoiter and to delay the enemy's advance. By that evening Stricker had reached the narrow neck of land between the head of Bear Creek and the Back River, about halfway between Baltimore and North Point. He deployed his men there, except for a contingent of cavalry and riflemen who were sent ahead toward a farm owned by Robert Gorsuch.

At three o'clock the following morning, five thousand British soldiers rowed ashore in the dark at North Point. Their landing place at the tip of the peninsula was chosen because the Patapsco was thought to be too shallow for the larger ships to go farther upstream. The battle plan called for the smaller boats to push past Fort McHenry and to attack the city at the same time as the assault by land.

As light came on, the British army advanced up North Point Road toward Baltimore. Eventually, they stopped to rest while General Ross and his retinue left the road in order to get something to eat at the Gorsuch farm. According to Robert Gorsuch's grandson, the elder Gorsuch was forced not only to provide breakfast for General Ross and eight other officers but also to eat and drink a sample of every dish that he served before the British would touch it. Talking of the coming battle while he ate, General Ross purportedly boasted that he would "eat his supper in Baltimore, or in Hell."

Meanwhile, John Stricker (according to his account of the 12th of September) learned from his horse scouts that "the enemy in small force was enjoying itself at Gorsuch's farm." Two hundred and thirty infantry, some cavalry, and a cannon were immediately pushed forward. Stricker reported:

> This small volunteer corps had not proceeded scarcely
> half a mile before the main body of the enemy showed it-

self, which was immediately attacked. The infantry and riflemen maintained a fire of some minutes and returned with some loss in killed and wounded; the cavalry and artillery, owing to the disadvantageous ground, not being able to support them.

The skirmish was more critical than the Americans thought. On the British side, an eyewitness account was provided by the Reverend Mr. Gleig, the military chaplain. He had been waiting with the main British force while General Ross breakfasted at the Gorsuch farm. After an hour the troops started to move again, but they had not traveled more than a mile when the "sharp fire of musketry was heard in front, and shortly afterward a mounted officer came galloping to the rear, who desired us to quicken our pace for that the advance guard was engaged." Gleig continued:

> At this intelligence the ranks closed, and the troops advanced at a brisk rate, and in profound silence. The firing still continued, though from its running and irregular sound, it promised little else than a skirmish; but whether it was kept up by detached parties alone, or by the outposts of a regular army, we could not tell because, from the quantity of wood with which the country abounded, and the total absence of all hills or eminences, it was impossible to discern what was going on at the distance of a half a mile from the spot where we stood.
>
> We were already drawing near the scene of action, when another officer came at full speed toward us, with horror and dismay in his countenance, and calling loudly for a surgeon. Every man felt within himself that all was not right, though none was willing to believe the whispers of his own terror. But what at first we would not guess at, because we dreaded it so much, was soon realized; for the aide-de-camp had scarcely passed when the General's horse, without its rider, and with the saddle and housing stained with blood, came plunging onwards. In a few moments we reached the ground where the skirmishing had taken place, and beheld General Ross laid by the side of the road, under a canopy of blankets, and apparently in

the agonies of death. As soon as the firing began he had ridden to the front, that he might ascertain from whence it originated and, mingling with the skirmishers, was shot in the side by a rifleman. The wound was mortal; he fell into the arms of his aide-de-camp, and lived only long enough to name his wife, and to commend his family to the protection of his country. He was removed towards the fleet, but expired before his bearers could reach the boat.

It is impossible to conceive the effect which this melancholy spectacle produced throughout the army. . . . All eyes were turned upon him as we passed, and a sort of involuntary groan ran from rank to rank from the front to the rear of the column.

Nonetheless, the British pushed on until they ran into General Stricker's main force. A battle of an hour and a half followed. As the British troops advanced at a walking pace, the Americans fired what Gleig described as a "dreadful discharge of grape and canister shot, of old locks, pieces of broken muskets, and everything else which they could cram into their guns." After firing one volley, part of the American line retreated without orders. As the British soldiers approached nearer and nearer, firing as they came, General Stricker was forced to pull his troops back to the main line of fortifications outside the city.

The next day, after a bivouac at the North Point battlefield, the British continued slowly toward Baltimore, hindered by the trees which the retreating Americans had cut down across the road during the night. Rain fell all day and it was not until evening that the British covered the seven miles to Hampstead Hill, where they stopped in front of the American fortifications. Gleig reported:

It now appeared that the corps which we had beaten yesterday was only a detachment, and not a large one, from the force collected for the defense of Baltimore. . . . Upon a ridge of hills which concealed the town itself from observation stood the grand army, consisting of twenty thousand men. Not trusting to his superiority in numbers, their general had there entrenched them in the most formidable manner, having covered the whole face of the heights with breastworks, thrown back his left so as to rest it upon a strong fort, erected for the protection of the river, and constructed a chain of field redoubts which covered his right and commanded the entire ascent. Along the line of the hill were likewise fleches and other projecting works, from which a cross fire might be kept up; and there were mounted throughout this commanding position no less than one hundred pieces of cannon.

The new British commander, Colonel Arthur Brooke, tried to outflank the defenses by moving his troops to the north, but the Americans kept between the British and the city. Brooke then decided to try a night attack, provided he could receive support from the navy. But, as reflected in our national anthem, the English ships were repulsed at Fort McHenry, and Brooke eventually determined that attack would be futile. In the early morning, while their ships continued the unsuccessful bombardment of Fort McHenry, the British began their retreat, which was not discovered by the Americans until daylight. The American troops were so worn out from the two days of watching and waiting, much of it in the rain, that General Smith decided not to counterattack. By the next day, the British had returned to their ships and were gone.

After the retreat, the Baltimore newspapers dubbed the British the "night-retrograders." In England, however, *The Times* of London described the repulse at Baltimore and the contemporaneous naval defeat of the British at Plattsburg on Lake Champlain as a "lamentable event to the civilized world."

WHEN YOU VISIT North Point State Park, you may wonder how this waterfront site could have remained undeveloped up to the present day. The fact is, however, that the area near the jetty was formerly occupied by a day-trippers' beach resort called Bay Shore Park, which operated from 1906 to 1950. Built by United Railways and Electric Company, the amusement park was served by the company's trolley running to and from Baltimore. Structures included a large bathhouse, a two-story restaurant with broad, shaded porches, and a dance pavilion. According to a description in *The Sun* that appeared when the park opened, "At night thousands of electric lights . . . produced a superb effect." Among the amusement rides were the Whirladrome and the Thingamajic roller coaster, plus the Kiddie Koaster and a carousel. An advertisement in 1922 described the park as a "beautiful white temple of recreation set in the green frame of friendly trees; cooled by the vagrant north winds; courted by the great Chesapeake which, better to win your heart, puts on the white plumage of the breaking surf—Bay Shore, heart of Baltimore's heart; renewer of youth—the promise of summer."

In 1947 Bethlehem Steel Corporation, reacting to rumors that U.S. Steel was looking for a tidewater site for a steel mill that would compete with Sparrows Point, bought the amusement park, which it operated briefly but then shut down. Bethlehem Steel held the site until the state of Maryland purchased the 1,310-acre tract for $5.4 million in 1987.

A few relics of Bay Shore Park remain. There is a large jetty and at its base a trolley shed where passengers got off and on. Nearby is a fountain. Part of the trail through Black Marsh follows the former trolley roadbed, which at one point passes an old reinforced-concrete power station that supplied electricity to the trolley line and park.

≈   ≈   ≈   ≈

AUTOMOBILE DIRECTIONS: North Point State Park and **Fort Howard Park** are located about 12 miles southeast of Baltimore at North Point, where the Patapsco River joins Chesapeake Bay. (See •19 on **Map 1** on page 5. For greater detail, refer to **Map 24** on page 220.) Two approaches, one from Baltimore and the other from Interstate 695 (the Baltimore Beltway), are described below.

To North Point and Fort Howard from Baltimore: Follow Route 40 (Orleans Street and Pulaski Highway) east from downtown. After passing under three railroad bridges within a half-mile, bear right up the ramp for Erdman Avenue (and also Interstate 895). Immediately, bear left for Erdman and go 6.7 miles as Erdman Avenue becomes Route 151 (North Point Boulevard). After passing under Interstate 695, turn left at a traffic light onto North Point Road toward Edgemere and Fort Howard. Go 1.9 miles through Edgemere, then turn left into **North Point State Park**. Follow the entrance road 0.5 mile to a parking lot on the left.

To reach Fort Howard Park, simply continue past North Point State Park for 1.8 miles. The entrance to Fort Howard Park is on the left at the end of North Point Road.

To North Point and Fort Howard from Interstate 695 (the Baltimore Beltway): The access route described below is not the most direct. However, it entails very little extra distance and has the advantage of avoiding abrupt maneuvers and the confusing snarl of highway ramps at Sparrows Point.

Leave I-695 at Exit 41 for Cove Road. From the Beltway's Outer Loop, turn *left* at the top of the ramp toward Route 151; from the Inner Loop, fork *right* on the ramp toward Route 151. Go to the intersection with Route 151 at a traffic light, then turn left and follow Route 151 south 2.4 miles. After passing under Interstate 695, turn left at a traffic light onto North Point Road toward Edgemere and Fort Howard. Go 1.9 miles through Edgemere, then turn left into **North Point State Park**. Follow the entrance road 0.5 mile to a parking lot on the left.

To reach Fort Howard Park, simply continue past North Point State Park for 1.8 miles. The entrance to Fort Howard Park is on the left at the end of North Point Road.

≈   ≈   ≈   ≈

WALKING AT NORTH POINT STATE PARK: Map 25 on page 221 outlines two out-and-back routes, both starting at the parking lot near the entrance. One spur is a **hike-bike path** leading through fields and woods to the water's edge near the old Bay Shore Amusement Park and jetty. The other spur, which itself has several smaller prongs, leads through **Black Marsh** to the circular **Wetlands Trail**.

To get started toward the shore and jetty, pick up the hike-bike path where the entrance road turns left just beyond the parking lot. Paved with gravel, the path runs parallel with the entrance road at first, but then turns right alongside the distant woods. The way is self-evident. Near the end, the trail splits. Bear right to swing past the shore and through the trolley shed, then turn right to the jetty. Nearby is the visitor center.

MAP 24 — North Point State Park and Fort Howard Park

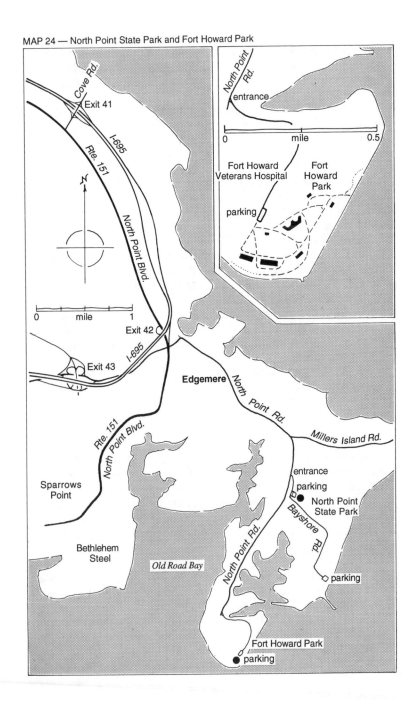

MAP 25 — North Point State Park

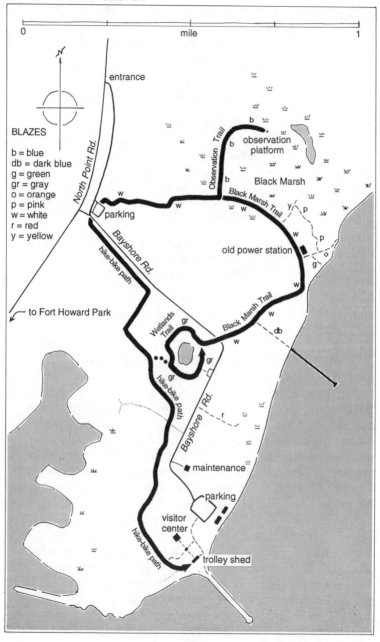

BLAZES

b = blue
db = dark blue
g = green
gr = gray
o = orange
p = pink
w = white
y = yellow

To get started toward Black Marsh, follow the white-blazed **Black Marsh Trail** from the end of the parking lot. At first the trail may be soggy and overgrown in places, but it soon joins the old Bay Shore trolley bed, where the trail improves greatly. At an intersection with the blue-blazed **Observation Trail**, turn left and follow this spur to an observation platform at its end, where there is a good vantage point overlooking the marsh.

After returning to the intersection of the Observation Trail and Black Marsh Trail, turn left to continue along the white-blazed trolley bed, at one point passing the former power plant, where the orange-blazed **Power House Trail** leads to the water's edge. Eventually, the trolley bed reaches the entrance road. Cross the road to continue around the loop of the gray-blazed **Wetlands Trail**, then return by the way you came.

To combine the two trails described above, you can use a short path linking the hike-bike path with the Wetlands Trail. This link is shown on the map by a dotted line.

≈

≈ ≈ ≈ ≈

≈

JUST SOUTH of North Point State Park is Fort Howard Park, located at the actual tip of North Point. Like Mayan ruins overrun by jungle, several massive structures lie half-buried in the tangled brush and woods. All are of concrete, empty, strangely abstract, like the imaginary buildings in the drawings of M. C. Escher. These are the fort's old bunkers and huge amphitheater-like gun pits, which during the first two decades of this century helped to guard the water approach to Baltimore.

Built at the end of the nineteenth century during the Spanish-American War, Fort Howard never saw combat then, nor did it during World War I, when Forts Smallwood, Armistead, and Howard formed Baltimore's line of coastal defense against attacks that never came. The Fort Howard garrison, however, was said to maintain a high standard of proficiency. The *Baltimore Sun* for October 14, 1908, reported that the Howard gunners had been credited with hitting, nine times out of ten, a target that was being towed in the shipping channel nearly three miles away. The fort's guns included two batteries of 12-

inch mortars that fired projectiles weighing 1,000 pounds. The mortars were housed in the largest firing pits. Another emplacement held two 12-inch disappearing rifles (i.e., modern rifled guns—not smoothbores) that were raised for firing and lowered behind the revetment walls for loading. Four other emplacements (only three of which survive) housed 6-inch, 5-inch, and 4.7-inch rifles and 3-inch rapid-fire guns.

In 1941, long after the guns had been removed, the fort was decommissioned as obsolete. The bunkers, barracks, officers' houses, and land were turned over to the Veterans Administration for development of present-day Fort Howard Hospital. Twenty-five years later, the area occupied by the concrete revetments was returned to the Army for use by the intelligence school at Fort Holabird. During the Vietnam War, a mock Vietnamese village was constructed in the underbrush among the old coastal batteries.

Fort Holabird was closed in 1972, and the next year the 62-acre parcel at North Point was deeded to Baltimore County by the General Services Administration under the federal government's Legacy of Parks program, by which surplus federal property is donated to local governments with the provision that the land be used for recreation. The hospital grounds, however, are not part of the park and are not open to visitors.

≈   ≈   ≈   ≈

AUTOMOBILE DIRECTIONS FROM NORTH POINT STATE PARK TO FORT HOWARD PARK: Turn left out the entrance at North Point State Park and follow North Point Road south for 1.8 miles to the end, where Fort Howard Veterans Hospital is on the right and Fort Howard Park is on the left. Fork left for the park and follow the curving entrance drive 0.5 mile to the parking lot.

≈   ≈   ≈   ≈

WALKING AT FORT HOWARD PARK: The park has a network of paved paths shown on the corner panel of **Map 24** on page 220. The site is so small that you can easily explore the entire installation of scattered gun emplacements that have been enveloped by woods since the fort's abandonment.

20

BWI TRAIL and the BALTIMORE & ANNAPOLIS TRAIL PARK

Maps 26 and 27 on page 234 and 235 show the circular **BWI Trail** and the linear **Baltimore & Annapolis Trail Park**. Located south of Baltimore, these two paved hike-bike paths are linked to each other.

The circuit around Baltimore Washington International Airport is 11 miles long (17.6 kilometers). In some sections the path cuts through woods and wetlands; in other places it is merely a glorified sidewalk near local roads. Along the way are two excellent vantage points for watching jetliners take off and land.

The Baltimore & Annapolis Trail Park is 13 miles long (20.8 kilometers). It follows the old Baltimore & Annapolis Railroad, providing a cross-sectional view of suburban Anne Arundel County, from Glen Burnie in the north, past Marley Station Mall and Severna Park, to wooded ravines and even a few horse farms in the south near the Severn River.

The BWI and B&A trails are open daily from sunrise to sunset. The headquarters parking lot at Earleigh Heights Road, however, does not open until 7:00 A.M. Dogs must be leashed. On both trails, you must cross roads frequently, so use caution at all places where cars may be present.

Both the BWI Trail and the B&A Trail are managed by the Anne Arundel County Department of Recreation and Parks. The trail's headquarters are located where the B&A Trail crosses Earleigh Heights Road at milepost 7; telephone (410) 222-6244.

For automobile directions, please turn to page 233. Walking directions start on page 236.

BEFORE CONSTRUCTION of Baltimore Washington International Airport, Baltimore's municipal air facility was 360-acre Harbor Field, now part of the Dundalk Marine Terminal.

Developed during the early 1930s, Harbor Field was inadequate from the beginning. Material was dredged from the harbor to create land, which slowly settled even after the airport had been built. As commercial airliners became larger and faster, the short, uneven runways at Harbor Field were increasingly substandard.

In 1943 Mayor Theodore McKeldin appointed a committee to study Baltimore's aviation needs. The resulting report recommended construction of a new and much larger airport at Friendship Church in Anne Arundel County, eight miles south of the city. Among the advantages of the proposed site, which ultimately encompassed 3,200 acres, was the possibility of acquiring enough land to accommodate several stages of airport expansion. Few homes would be affected and land values were not excessive. The thick mantle of Coastal Plain clay, sand, and gravel provided good drainage and could easily be regraded, leveled, and compacted. Because the site was distant from water and had at an average elevation of 130 feet, there was far less ground fog than at other East Coast airports, almost all of which were at sea level next to tidewater. And adjacent to the site was the new Baltimore Washington Parkway, which provided excellent access from north and south.

In 1945 Baltimore's voters approved a bond issue of $6 million to construct the new airport, as authorized by the state legislature. After a master plan was completed, city residents approved another $6 million, and the federal government provided $3 million because the airport would in part serve the nation's capital. Construction began in 1947, and three years later Friendship International Airport, as it was called, opened for service. President Harry Truman was among those who spoke at the dedication ceremony. Incorporating technology invented or improved during World War II, Friendship was hailed as a model of what a forward-looking airport should be. Captain Eddie Rickenbacker, at that time head of Eastern Airlines but better known as a World War I ace, termed the facility "the first modern airport which has really been engineered and thought out."

In 1972 the State of Maryland bought Friendship from Baltimore for $36 million and two years later started a $70 million program of improvements, including construction of the present-

day terminal, completed in 1979. The state also inaugurated the new name of Baltimore Washington International Airport in order to emphasize the large region that was served. In 1991 a $29-million parking garage was completed in front of the terminal, and near the end of the decade the $140-million International Pier opened.

The 1990s also saw construction of another, rather more primitive transportation feature at the airport: the hike-bike BWI Trail. It is a good way to appreciate the immensity of the airport and to enjoy the spectacle of jets taking off and landing.

STRETCHING SOUTH from the circular BWI Trail is the linear Baltimore & Annapolis Trail Park, which follows the bed of the former Baltimore & Annapolis Railroad.

The B&A Railroad was chartered in 1880 under the name Annapolis & Baltimore Short Line Railroad. The route crossed the Severn River on a long bridge, then followed the river's north shore through what are now Arnold, Severna Park, Pasadena, Harundale, Glen Burnie, Ferndale, Linthicum, Baltimore Highlands, and Westport to Baltimore. The sobriquet "Short Line" was a bit of self-promotion, intended to inform customers that the new railroad provided a shorter, faster route than the Annapolis & Elk Ridge Railroad, which since 1840 had operated along the Severn's south shore, linking Annapolis, Crownsville, and Odenton with Annapolis Junction north of Laurel, where passengers transferred to and from the Baltimore & Ohio line linking Washington and Baltimore.

After a period spent raising capital and acquiring the right-of-way, the Short Line company started construction in 1886, at times employing more than a thousand black and immigrant laborers to grade the roadbed and lay tracks. Pulled by steam locomotives, trains started running in March 1887, traversing a region between Baltimore and Annapolis that was wholly rural in character. There were no towns: just scattered churches, schools, and country stores that served as the focal points of loose farm communities. Most agricultural products—chiefly vegetables and fruit—were transported by boat to market in Baltimore. Much of the region was not even cultivated. Its sandy soil had been exhausted by tobacco farming during the eighteenth century, and since then large areas had reverted to piney woods.

The railroad helped gradually to change all that. Before automobiles came into widespread use in the 1920s and '30s, the railroad served as the main locus of commercial activity and transportation in this part of Anne Arundel County. Trains carried mail and groceries, dry goods, coal, kerosene, and feed to general stores that were established at sidings up and down the line. Truck farmers shipped fresh produce by train to Baltimore. Canneries and lumber yards were built along the railway. In the vicinity of the Patapsco River and at Pasadena, pits were established from which sand and gravel were shipped out by railroad. The line helped to bring into being a variety of small hotels and taverns—some with dance floors—located on the Severn and Magothy waterfront or by the railroad. Owners of vacation homes also came and went by train.

The A&B Short Line—reorganized in 1894 as the Baltimore & Annapolis Short Line Railroad Company—promoted excursions to Annapolis and to Bay Ridge on the Chesapeake, reached by an extension of the rail line eastward from the state capital. Escaping the summertime miasma of Baltimore, passengers enjoyed the breeze and scenery of the train ride, especially as the coaches crossed the half-mile-long bridge over the Severn River. The railroad company also promoted excursions to the small turn-of-the-century resort of Round Bay on the Severn, which was owned by the railroad's principal shareholder. A short spur ran to the resort, which later was converted into a waterfront residential community.

Construction of the railroad fueled land speculation up and down the line. Areas near the railway were bought and subdivided by real-estate companies. Although lots sold slowly at first, some new towns were successful. In 1889 a development that became Glen Burnie was platted by the Glenn family, which over the course of the nineteenth century had acquired extensive holdings in northern Anne Arundel County. Glen Burnie became a commuter town that by 1925 had about two thousand residents. The small summer community of Briarcliff on the Severn was established in 1896. The Severn River Company started selling lots at Severna Park in 1906. (The brick station at Severna Park was built in 1919.) Commuting to work by train became a way of life both for year-round suburbanites and for those who seasonally closed their houses in Baltimore and moved to summer cottages on the Magothy and Severn Rivers. South of Severna Park, the land for Pines-on-the-Severn was subdivided in the early 1920s. Many modest summer cottages, long since converted to year-round residences, are now pricey waterfront or waterview homes. At some early subdivisions, however, only a few houses were built, and at others the streets and dwellings altogether failed to materialize.

In 1907 The Maryland Electric Railways Company (which owned no other railroad) acquired control of the Baltimore & Annapolis Short Line and by the following year completed installation of overhead wires from which self-propelled cars drew power. An electric substation was built at Jones Station Road next to the railway. (Painted white, the boxlike brick structure now houses a shop run by the archaically spelled Ann Arrundell County Historical Society, where browsers are welcome.) In 1914 the railroad was converted from alternating to direct current, which entailed building a larger power house that still stands next to the trail a few hundred feet north of Jones Station Road. Electrification enabled the railroad to provide a smoother, quieter, cleaner ride for its growing clientele of passengers. The steel cars had large windows with shallowly arched stained glass transoms, plus a second tier of elliptical clerestory windows. Inside, the cars were paneled with mahogany, and the seats were covered with green plush.

In 1921 the Short Line merged into the Washington, Baltimore, & Annapolis Electric Railroad Company, which since 1908 had operated trains between Baltimore and Washington with a spur to Annapolis that in part followed the old Annapolis & Elk Ridge right-of-way. The WB&A was a model of modern efficiency. According to one newspaper account, its operations were studied by a delegation of Japanese engineers who were preparing to build electric railroads in their own country. At its peak the railroad system carried more than five million passengers annually (1,750,000 on the former Short Line). Up to seventy trains a day left Baltimore for either Washington or Annapolis. On the Short Line route, passenger coaches ran hourly throughout the day and evening and more frequently during rush hours.

By the end of the 1920s, however, the number of riders was declining as automobile use increased. In 1931, as the nation sank into the Great Depression, the WB&A entered receivership. Granted a tax exemption by the state and a voluntary reduction in wages by its employees, the company continued in business until 1935, when the tax exemption was terminated and the Maryland Public Service Commission authorized the receiver to auction the company's assets for scrap. The Washington-Baltimore route and the line along the south shore of the Severn were abandoned, but the former Short Line along the Severn's north shore was acquired by a group of investors newly incorporated as the Baltimore & Annapolis Railroad.

Although the B&A survived the depression and even prospered during World War II, when rationing of gasoline and tires restricted automobile use, the railroad quickly lost riders to automobiles and buses in the postwar years. Ritchie Highway had been completed in 1939, and by 1948 the Baltimore & Annapolis Railroad was itself operating buses that supplemented its worn out, money-losing trains. The buses were not significantly slower than the train, which took 55 minutes and made thirty stops during the 22-mile trip to Annapolis. Convinced that the company could not make money by operating passenger trains and that bus service provided an adequate alternative to the railroad, the Maryland Public Service Commission allowed the B&A—by then rechristened by some riders as the Bumble & Amble or the Bounce & Agitate—to terminate passenger rail service in 1950. In its decision, the commission wrote that the B&A had "not been maintained as a first-class railroad; the roadbed needs constant attention; the rails are worn and would have to be replaced if passenger service is continued; the cars or trains are antiquated, decrepit and unattractive as a means of travel; schedules are slow, and there is no inducement, save that of necessity, for anyone to travel by rail. While not yet dead, it is moribund."

What was noxious to some, however, was nostalgic to others. After the discontinuation of passenger service was announced, newspapers ran evocative valedictions. In the *Baltimore Evening Sun* for December 14, 1949, Richard K. Tucker wrote that the "ancient, rattling electric train suddenly became like an old friend, more valued despite a myriad of faults than something new and strange."

The deep Anne Arundel County woods in the springtime and autumn somehow didn't look the same from the windows of a cramped and speeding bus. Grown men who had recalled shooting imaginary Indians from the open windows of the B&A as small boys somehow couldn't find any nostalgia in a tangle of auto traffic. And traversing the broad Severn River at sunset over the old wooden B&A trestle was an experience ten times more memorable than crossing the bridge in a parade of honking automobiles.

More than that, there was a comforting old country store atmosphere to the worm leather seats, the ancient overhead lamps with their scallop-edged white glass shades, the dark wood fittings rubbed by generations of county travelers, and (something the buses will never have) the roughed metal strips beside the window for striking the big wooden matches carried from country kitchens. The cars, more often than not, were pungent with the odor of cigar and pipe smoke.

Did B&A commuters really miss the train? They had a chance to demonstrate their preference anew in 1961, when passenger service from Harundale north into Baltimore was resumed on an experimental basis for a few weeks, then dropped because of lack of riders.

Freight service, however, continued on the Baltimore & Annapolis line. During the 1950s and '60s, a lone 70-ton diesel switcher making at most one trip each weekday hauled boxcars and gondolas to and from factory sidings and sand and gravel pits. Occasionally the train delivered coal to the Naval Academy—until the old trestle over the Severn, with a swing-span drawbridge at the middle, was condemned in 1968. Freight service south of Severna Park stopped in 1969. After the flood rains of Tropical Storm Agnes in 1972 fragmented the line by damaging bridges at the Patapsco River, Saw Mill Creek, and Marley Creek, the B&A sought permission from the Interstate Commerce Commission (which had jurisdiction because the B&A handled freight that traveled among states) to shut down the railroad altogether. The petition was first denied and then, in 1976, granted only for the section of the line south of Dorsey Road at the northern edge of Glen Burnie. In the meantime, no trains ran. But after the Patapsco River bridge was rebuilt in 1976, freight service resumed from Baltimore to Dorsey Road, and in 1987 the old Short Line—by then *very* short—celebrated its 100th anniversary. At that time, the company operated one train three days a week over 6.5 miles of track. It had six full-time employees, six part-time employees, and the same diesel locomotive (now at the Baltimore & Ohio Railroad Museum) that the B&A had bought new in 1950. But the railroad company also had a gold mine in its right-of-way, which in 1991 the Mass Transit Administration purchased for $9 million for its new light rail line terminating at Dorsey Road.

As for the B&A right-of-way south of Dorsey Road, abandoned and derelict, it was purchased in 1980 for just $1.3 million by the Anne Arundel County Department of Recreation and Parks. Since 1985 the county has spent more than $12 million on new bridges, parking lots, grading, landscaping, paving, fences, and other work (including restoration of the Earleigh Heights ranger station) to create and improve the very popular linear park seen today.

≈   ≈   ≈   ≈

AUTOMOBILE DIRECTIONS: The **BWI Trail** and the **Baltimore & Annapolis Trail Park** are located south of Baltimore. Together, they form one long interconnected hike-bike path. Two access points—**Sawmill Creek Park** and the **B&A Trail Headquarters** at Earleigh Heights Road—are shown as •20a and •20b on **Map 1** on page 5. For more detail refer to **Maps 26 and 27** on pages 234 and 235. Directions to the two access points from Interstate 695 (the Baltimore Beltway) and from the vicinity of Annapolis are as follows:

SAWMILL CREEK PARK is located on the eastern spur of the BWI Trail near the juncture with the Baltimore & Annapolis Trail. This is a good place to start for a circuit around the airport or for a down-and-back trip on the old railroad right-of-way to Annapolis.

To reach Sawmill Creek Park from Interstate 695 (the Baltimore Beltway), take Exit 4 for Interstate 97 south toward Annapolis. After about 2 miles, leave I-97 at Exit 15 for

MAP 26 — Overview: BWI Trail and Baltimore & Annapolis Trail

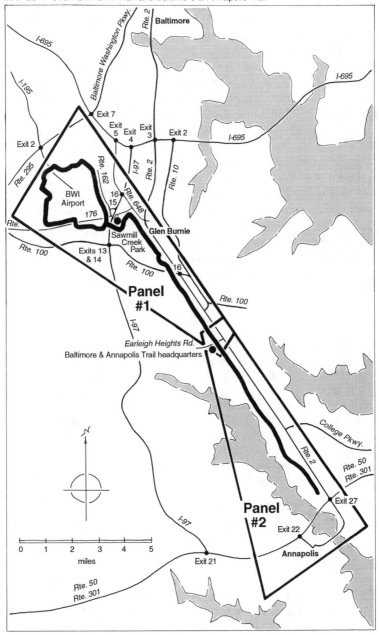

234

MAP 27 — BWI Trail and Baltimore & Annapolis Trail

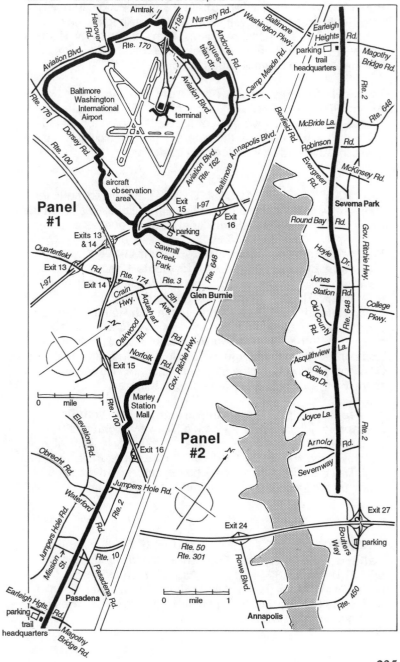

Route 162 (Aviation Boulevard). At a T-intersection, turn left onto Route 162 and follow it south just 0.3 mile to an intersection with Route 176 (Dorsey Road). Turn left and follow Route 176 east 0.4 mile, then turn right at a traffic light onto Eckman Lane leading into Sawmill Creek Park.

To reach Sawmill Creek Park from the vicinity of Annapolis, follow Route 97 north to Exit 15A for Route 176 (Dorsey Road) east toward Glen Burnie. At the bottom of the exit ramp, go just 0.1 mile, then turn right at a traffic light onto Eckman Lane leading into Sawmill Creek Park.

THE B&A TRAIL HEADQUARTERS are located near the midpoint, where the trail crosses Earleigh Heights Road. On the maps, this point occurs where Panel #1 and Panel #2 overlap.

To reach the trail headquarters from I-695 (the Baltimore Beltway), take Exit 2 for Route 10 south toward Severna Park. Follow Route 10 south 6.5 miles, taking care **not to exit** onto Route 100 eastbound toward Gibson Island. When Route 10 ends at a T-intersection with Route 2, turn left and follow Route 2 south toward Severna Park. Go only 1.2 miles, then turn right onto Earleigh Heights Road. Follow Earleigh Heights Road for just 0.3 mile, then turn left into the B&A Trail parking lot by the park headquarters. If there is no room, try the lot on the opposite side of the road.

To reach the trail headquarters from the vicinity of Annapolis, follow Route 2 (Ritchie Highway) north past College Parkway and Severna Park. Turn left onto Earleigh Heights Road and follow it for just 0.3 mile, then turn left into the B&A Trail parking lot by the park headquarters. If there is no room, try the lot on the opposite side of the road.

≈   ≈   ≈   ≈

WALKING and BICYCLING: The BWI Trail and the **Baltimore & Annapolis Trail** are outlined on **Maps 26 and 27** on pages 324 and 235. As shown on the maps, the two trails join at the intersection of Route 176 (Dorsey Road) and Route 648 (Baltimore Annapolis Boulevard). Be careful at the frequent road crossings.

For an 11-mile circuit around BWI Airport starting at Sawmill Creek Park, locate the paved path at the back of the park and follow it right. Immediately after crossing Route 97, turn left toward the Thomas Dixon, Jr. Aircraft Observation Area. From there continue clockwise around the loop. At about the halfway point, fork left to pass the Andover Equestrian Center. Eventually, you will arrive back at the bridge over Route 97. Cross the bridge, then turn left to follow the paved path back to Sawmill Creek Park.

For the Baltimore & Annapolis Trail starting at Sawmill Creek Park, locate the paved path at the back of the park and follow it left for 0.6 mile to the northern end of the B&A Trail. From there the paved path stretches south 13 miles along the old railroad bed through Glen Burnie, Pasadena, Severna Park, and Arnold. The southern end of the B&A Trail is at Boulters Way. Bicyclists may want to continue downhill on the road shoulder, then right on Route 450 and across the Severn River into Annapolis.

For the Baltimore & Annapolis Trail starting at the park headquarters on Earleigh Heights Road, you have a choice of heading north or south. The distance to the trail's northern end at Dorsey Road (where it joins the BWI Trail) is 6.3 miles. The distance to the trail's southern end at Boulters Way is 7 miles. The entire round-trip distance up and down the B&A Trail and around the circuit at BWI is 38 miles.

21

SAVAGE PARK and SAVAGE HISTORIC MILL TRAIL

Map 28 on page 243 shows **Savage Park**, located between Jessup and Laurel southwest of Baltimore. Three miles long (4.8 kilometers), the route shown by the bold line passes through deep woods and valleys at the confluence of the Little and Middle Patuxent Rivers.

After hiking at Savage Park, you may want to stop by at nearby **Savage Mill**, also shown on the map. The handsomely restored mill buildings now house several eateries and a wide variety of shops selling antiques, crafts, art, and other specialties. In front of the mill is the nation's only remaining **Bollman Truss Bridge**, commonly used by railroads in the nineteenth century. From the bridge, the **Savage Historic Mill Trail** leads to the former dam, as indicated by the dotted line. The distance round-trip is 1 mile (1.6 kilometers).

Savage Park, the Bollman Truss Bridge, and the Savage Historic Mill Trail are all administered by the Howard County Department of Recreation and Parks; telephone (410) 313-4700. They are open every day from 7:00 A.M. to dusk. Dogs must be leashed.

The seven-building complex at Savage Mill is open daily starting at 10:00 A.M. The mill closes at 6:00 P.M. Sunday through Wednesday and at 9:00 P.M. Thursday, Friday, and Saturday.

For automobile directions to Savage Park, please turn to page 241. Walking directions start on page 242. Directions to the Savage Historic Mill Trail are on page 244.

THE SAVAGE MANUFACTURING COMPANY was chartered in 1822 to build and operate a cotton works downstream from a series of cascades on the Little Patuxent River. Headed by Amos Williams and his three brothers, the enterprise was named for John Savage, a director of the Bank of the United States who loaned the Williamses $20,000 to start the new company. The first building was a tall stone structure that still stands with its gable end facing Foundry Street. By 1825 the cotton works had 120 looms and 1,000 spindles powered by a 30-foot waterwheel. The main product was canvas, used chiefly for sails. In addition to erecting and running the cotton factory, the firm operated a grist mill that came with the site and also a foundry and machine shop to make replacement parts for the looms.

In 1859, on the eve of the Civil War, the Baldwin family of Anne Arundel County acquired the mill. From a business point of view, their timing was superb. The war created an immense demand for canvas tents and cannon covers. After the war the enterprise continued to prosper and the factory grew into the large complex seen today. Starting in 1880, steam power supplemented waterpower, and a year later an 80,000-square-foot addition was built adjoining the original stone mill. The company also erected a separate wheelhouse containing a horizontal water turbine, still in place. The most recent addition, constructed in 1916 to help fill government contracts during World War I, is the long building now entered from the main parking lot. Containing 123,000 square feet, it held looms called "Big Berthas" that weighed up to 27 tons. In 1918 the company undertook an electrification program. Built on piers above the river, a power plant housed a steam turbine and generator. The water turbine too was connected to a 750-kilowatt generator. Even in the 1920s, the company still made sail cloth and also cotton duck for tarpaulins, tents, awnings, fire hose, industrial belting, and canvas bags. After the doldrums of the Great Depression, production reached an all-time peak during World War II, when 350 employees operated 72 carding machines, thousands of spindles for plying thread, and 194 looms that turned out 4 million pounds of cloth monthly.

Adjacent to the mill complex is the residential area where many of the mill's employees lived with their families in company-owned houses, some of which still stand along Baltimore and Washington streets, within hearing of the factory bell that regulated the workday. At the head of Baltimore Street is Savage Mill Manor, the superintendent's residence. Starting early in the twentieth century, the company undertook a series of improvements to its town, including construction of a water system, sanitary sewer, and a lighting plant. The company provided garbage collection and snowplowing and it also ran stores that sold groceries, dry goods, coal, and cordwood. In 1921 the firm built the Carrol Baldwin Memorial Community Hall, where movies were shown weekly. By 1945 the company leased houses to 98 families, some representing the third generation to work at the mill. The top rent was $15 per month, and some houses rented for $8.90 monthly. The average wage was 90 cents per hour. Benefits included modest coverage for medical expenses, lost wages from sickness or accidents, and a small life insurance policy.

Following World War II, the market was flooded with surplus canvas. As the demand for new cotton duck plummeted, employment at Savage Mill declined drastically. Although the mill made some specialized products, such as heavy filter duck for the petroleum industry, biscuit duck for bakeries, and even netted bags for commercial laundries, the Savage Manufacturing Company went out of business in 1947. In that year Harry Heim, a manufacturer of Christmas tree ornaments, bought nearly the entire town for $450,000. Heim, whose name mean "home" in German, conceived a Yule village that he called Santa Heim, Merryland, where during the holiday season visitors could see Santa's helpers at work in the factory—but the project flopped. In 1950 the mill was bought by the Winer family, owners of National Industries. National made commercial furniture at Odenton and used the buildings at Savage mainly for warehousing and sales. Ephraim Winer, the head of the business, for decades promoted the idea of renovating Savage Mill as a sort of museum supported by dozens of small shops, and this plan came to pass in 1988 with the opening of the present-day Historic Savage Mill.

≈   ≈   ≈   ≈

AUTOMOBILE DIRECTIONS: Savage Park is located about 15 miles southwest of Baltimore. (See •21 on **Map 1** on page 5. For greater detail, refer to the corner panel of **Map 28** on page 243.)

To Savage Park from Interstate 695 (the Baltimore Beltway): Leave I-695 at Exit 11B for Interstate 95 south toward Washington. Go about 10 miles, then follow the directions in the next paragraph.

To Savage Park from Interstate 95: Leave I-95 at Exit 38A for **Route 32** east toward Fort Meade. Go 1.2 miles, then take the exit for **Route 1** south toward Laurel. At the bottom of the exit ramp, turn right and go just 0.5 mile, then turn right again onto Gorman Road. Follow Gorman Road 0.4 mile, then turn right onto Foundry Road, which immediately leads past the **Savage Historic Mill Trailhead**, the **Bollman Truss Bridge**, and **Savage Mill**, all on the left. For now, however, I suggest that you continue to **Savage Park**, as follows.

Go past the mill and past intersections with Washington Street on the right and left, then turn right onto Baltimore Street. Go one block, then turn left onto Savage-Guilford Road. After 0.7 mile, turn left onto Vollmerhausen Road and follow it 0.5 mile to the entrance and parking lot for Savage Park on the left.

≈   ≈   ≈   ≈

WALKING: The bold line on **Map 28** at right shows a 3-mile route at **Savage Park** along the Middle Patuxent and Little Patuxent Rivers. The trails are marked by colored blazes.

Start by following the paved path into the woods. Continue as the paved path becomes an unpaved trail marked with red-blazes. Twice pass a green-blazed trail intersecting from the left. Stay on the red-blazed trail as it descends to the Middle Patuxent River.

At the bottom of the slope (and about 70 yards from the river), fork left to follow the red-blazes. Continue downstream with the river on your right. Eventually, at a trail junction, continue straight up log stairs on the red-blazed trail. At a T-intersection, turn right and follow the red-blazed trail 225 yards to an intersection with the green-blazed trail that you passed earlier.

Turn sharply right onto the green-blazed trail. After a few dozen yards, bear left to stay on the green-blazed path, then left again past an overlook high above the river. Continue in and out of a tributary ravine as the trail gradually descends. At the river's edge, continue downstream.

After half a mile, turn sharply left to continue on the green-blazed trail. The Little Patuxent River may be audible on the right; after awhile it comes into view. Eventually, make a hairpin

MAP 28 — Savage Park and the Savage Historic Mill Trail

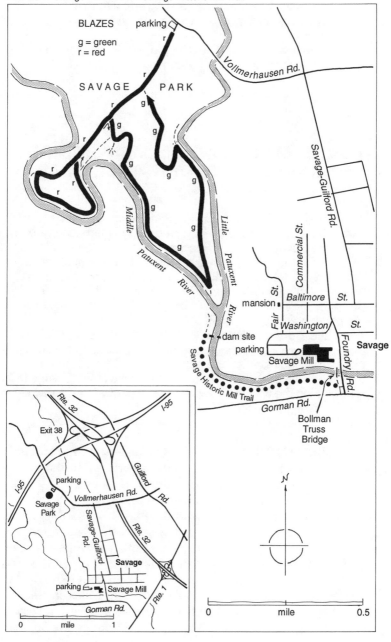

turn to the left to stay on the green-blazed trail, which climbs obliquely along the side of the valley. At the top the trail curves gradually right.

Continue to a T-intersection with the red-blazed trail and follow it right to return to the parking lot.

≈
≈   ≈   ≈   ≈
≈

SAVAGE MILL, the BOLLMAN BRIDGE, and SAVAGE HISTORIC MILL TRAIL

To reach these sites from Savage Park, return by the way you came—i.e., right out the parking lot onto Vollmerhausen Road, right onto Savage-Guilford Road, and then right onto Baltimore Street. For the large parking lot behind **Savage Mill**, follow Baltimore Street across Foundry Street, uphill past former mill housing, left onto Fair Street in front of Savage Mill Manor (formerly the mill superintendent's house), and then right into the parking area at the head of Washington Street.

For the **Bollman Bridge** and **Savage Historic Mill Trail**, park on the shoulder of Foundry Street by the automobile bridge. As indicated by the dotted line on **Map 28** on page 243, the trail leads half a mile to the remnants of the Savage Mill dam. Along the way, the river drops steeply over large rocks.

≈   ≈   ≈   ≈

THE BOLLMAN TRUSS BRIDGE at Savage is the nation's only surviving example of this type of all-iron bridge. It is shown in the photograph on page 8. The design was patented in 1852 by engineer Wendel A. Bollman of Baltimore, whose job title was Master of Road for the Baltimore & Ohio Railroad. Featuring standardized caste-iron parts that were easily transported and assembled, the design blends principles of truss and suspension bridges. Descending diagonally from the tops of the iron columns, the many spindly truss-rods are somewhat redundant in case one or two should break under tension as trains crossed the span. More durable than wooden trusses, which were subject to fire and rot, and far cheaper than masonry bridges, the Bollman

Truss aided the rapid expansion of American railroads during the mid-1800s. After the Civil War, however, larger locomotives and heavier loads exceeded the capabilities of the Bollman design. The last Bollman truss was built in 1873. Eventually, nearly all Bollman bridges were either replaced by stronger spans or abandoned.

The Bollman Bridge at Savage originally stood on the B&O's main line, but it was disassembled and re-erected here in 1887 when a spur of the B&O was built to serve Savage Mill. Before that, materials had to hauled by ox-team to and from Savage Station a mile away—or all the way to and from Baltimore before the B&O's Washington Branch and Savage Station opened in 1835.

22

NATIONAL WILDLIFE VISITOR CENTER
at the Patuxent Research Refuge

Located about half way between Baltimore and Washington, the **National Wildlife Visitor Center** features outstanding exhibits that focus on different habitats, environmental issues, and research methods and results. A large window overlooking Lake Redington is equipped with spotting scopes, binoculars, and even sound equipment for viewing and hearing waterfowl and other birds and animals. For walkers there are several short trails totaling about 4 miles (6.4 kilometers).

The bold line on **Map 29** on page 257 traces a circuit of 2 miles (3.2 kilometers) around Cash Lake. From late fall through spring, however, the Cash Lake loop is closed, at least in part, to avoid disturbing wintering waterfowl and nesting ducks, so during that period you may want to try some of the other trails shown on the map. There is also a tram that runs around Lake Redington on a regular weekend schedule, spring through fall.

The building and grounds at the National Wildlife Visitor Center are open daily from 10 A.M. to 5:30 P.M. Dogs must be leashed. The tram road around Lake Redington is off limits to walkers.

The Patuxent Research Refuge and the National Wildlife Visitor Center are managed by the U.S. Fish and Wildlife Service within the Department of the Interior. Telephone (301) 497-5760 for information, including the schedule of films, educational programs, and events.

For automobile directions, please turn to page 256. Walking directions are on pages 256-259.

WITH ITS VARIED HABITATS—piney and deciduous woods, meadows, streams, freshwater marsh, small ponds, and larger lakes—the National Wildlife Visitor Center is among the better places in the Baltimore region to see a wide assortment of birds. More than 260 species of waterfowl, land birds, and migrating shorebirds have been recorded here—or about 85 percent of all species that occur regularly near Baltimore.

Even for fledgling birders, identifying the many species that nest in the Baltimore region or pass through during migration is easier than might at first be thought. Shape, size, plumage, and other physical characteristics are distinguishing field marks. Range, season, habitat, song, and behavior are other useful keys to identifying birds.

Range is of primary importance for the simple reason that many birds are not found throughout North America or even the eastern United States, but only in certain regions such as the Atlantic and Gulf coasts. For example, Baltimore orioles and Bullock's orioles are two species that closely resemble each other (for a period they were even thought to be two races of the same species), so it helps to know that the latter is not seen near Baltimore. Good field guides provide range maps based on years of reported sightings and bird counts. Of course, bird ranges are not static; some pioneering species, such as the glossy ibis and house finch, have extended their ranges during recent decades. Other birds, such as the ivory-billed woodpecker, have lost ground and died out.

Season is related to range, since migratory birds appear in different parts of their ranges during different times of year. The five species of spot-breasted thrushes, for instance, are sometimes difficult to distinguish from each other, but usually only the hermit thrush is present in the Baltimore region during the winter. In summer the hermit thrush is rare near Baltimore, but the wood thrush is common and indeed nests at the National Wildlife Visitor Center. Swainson's thrush and the gray-cheeked thrush are seen during migration in spring and fall. Again, the maps in most field guides reflect this sort of information, and a detailed account of seasonal occurrence often is contained in local bird lists maintained and disseminated at some of the parks and wildlife sanctuaries discussed in this book.

Habitat, too, is important in identifying birds. Even before you spot a bird, its surroundings can tell you what species you are likely to see. Within its range a species usually appears only in certain preferred habitats, although during migration some species are less particular. (In many cases, birds show a degree of physical adaptation to their preferred environment.) As its name implies, the marsh wren is seldom found far from cattails, rushes, sedges, or tall marsh grasses; if a wrenlike bird is spotted in such a setting, it is unlikely to be a house wren or Carolina wren or one of the other species commonly found in thick underbrush or shrubbery. Ducks can be difficult to identify unless you tote a telescope; but even if all you can see is a silhouette, you can start with the knowledge that shallow marshes, ponds, and streams normally attract few diving ducks (such as oldsquaw, canvasbacks, redheads, ring-necked ducks, greater and lesser scaup, common goldeneye, and buffleheads) and that large, deep bodies of water are not the usual setting for surface-feeding puddle ducks (American black ducks, gadwalls, mallards, common pintails, American widgeons, wood ducks, northern shovelers, and blue-winged and green-winged teals).

Some of the distinctive habitats that different bird species prefer are open oceans; beaches; salt marsh; mud flats; meadows; thickets; various types of woods; and creeks, ponds, and lakes. The area where two habitats join, called an *ecotone*, is a particularly good place to look for birds because species peculiar to either environment might be present. For example, both meadowlarks and wood warblers might be found where a hay field abuts a forest. All good field guides provide information on habitat preference that can help to locate a species or to assess the likelihood of a tentative identification.

Song announces the identity (or at least the location) of birds even before they are seen. Although some species, such as the red-winged blackbird, have only a few songs, others, such as the mockingbird, have an infinite variety. Some birds, most notably thrushes, sing different songs in the morning and evening. In many species the basic songs vary among individuals and also from one part of the country to another, giving rise to regional "dialects." Nonetheless, the vocal repertory of most songbirds is sufficiently constant in timbre and pattern to identify each species simply by its songs.

Bird songs, as distinguished from calls, can be very complex. They are sung only by the male of most species, usually in spring and summer. The male arrives first at the breeding and nesting area after migration. He stakes out a territory for courting, mating, and nesting by singing at prominent points around the area's perimeter. This wards off other males of his species and simultaneously attracts females. On the basis of the male's display and the desirability of his territory, the female selects her mate. Experiments suggest that female birds build nests faster and lay more eggs when exposed to the songs of males with a larger vocal repertory than others of their species, and the relative volume of their songs appears to be a way for males to establish status among themselves.

In a few species, including eastern bluebirds, Baltimore orioles, cardinals, and white-throated sparrows, both sexes sing, although the males are more active in defending their breeding territory. Among mockingbirds, both sexes sing in fall and winter, but only males do in spring and summer. Some birds, such as canaries, have different songs for different seasons.

Birds tend to heed the songs of their own kind and to ignore the songs of other species, which, after all, do not compete for females nor, in many cases, for the same type of nesting materials or food. In consequence, a single area usually includes the overlapping breeding territories of several species. From year to year such territories are bigger or smaller, depending on the food supply. Typically, most small songbirds require about half an acre from which others of their species are excluded.

Bird calls (as distinguished from songs) are short, simple, sometimes harsh, and used by both males and females at all times of year to communicate alarm, aggression, location, and existence of food. Nearly all birds have some form of call. Warning calls are often heeded by species other than the caller's. Some warning calls are thin, high-pitched whistles that are difficult to locate and so do not reveal the bird's location to predators. Birds also use mobbing calls to summon other birds, as chickadees and crows do when scolding and harassing owls and other unwanted visitors. Birds flying in flocks, like cedar waxwings, often call continuously. Such calls help birds migrating by night to stay together.

The study of bird dialects and experiments with birds that have been deafened or raised in isolation indicate that songs are genetically inherited only to a very crude extent. Although a few species, such as doves, sing well even when raised in isolation, most birds raised alone produce inferior, simplified songs.

Generally, young songbirds learn their songs by listening to adult birds and by practice singing, called *subsong*. Yet birds raised in isolation and exposed to many tape-recorded songs show an innate preference for the songs of their own species. Probably the easiest way to learn bird songs is to listen repeatedly to recordings and to refer at the same time to a standard field guide. Most guides describe bird vocalizations with such terms as *harsh, nasal, flutelike, piercing, plaintive, wavering, twittering, buzzing, sneezy,* and *sputtering.* Although these terms are somewhat descriptive, they do not take on real meaning until you have heard the songs on records or in the field. Incidentally, bird recordings that are played slowly demonstrate that the songs contain many more notes than the human ear ordinarily hears.

Shape is one of the first and most important aspects to notice once you actually see a bird. Most birds can at least be placed in the proper family and many species can be identified by shape or silhouette, without reference to other field marks. Some birds, such as meadowlarks, are chunky and short-tailed, while others, such as catbirds and cuckoos, are elegantly long and slender. Kingfishers, blue jays, tufted titmice, Bohemian and cedar waxwings, and cardinals are among the few birds with crests.

Bird bills frequently have distinctive shapes and, more than any other body part, show adaptation to food supply. The beak can be chunky, like that of a grosbeak, to crack seeds; thin and curved, like that of a creeper, to probe bark for insects; hooked, like that of a shrike, to tear at flesh; long and slender, like that of a hummingbird, to sip nectar from tubular flowers; or some other characteristic shape depending on the bird's food. Goatsuckers, swifts, flycatchers, and swallows, all of which catch flying insects, have widely hinged bills and gaping mouths. The long, thin bills of starlings and meadowlarks are suited to probing the ground. In the Galapagos Islands west of Ecuador, Charles Darwin noted fourteen species of finches, each of which had evolved a different type of beak or style of feeding that gave it a competitive advantage for a particular type of food. Many birds are nonetheless flexible about their diet, especially from season to season when food sources change or become scarce. For example, Tennessee warblers, which ordinarily glean insects from foliage, also take large amounts of nectar from tropical flowers when wintering in South and Central America.

In addition to beaks, nearly every other part of a bird's body is adapted to help exploit its environment. Feet of passerines, or songbirds, are adapted to perching, with three toes in front and one long toe behind; waterfowl have webbed or lobed feet for swimming; and raptors have talons for grasping prey.

Other key elements of body shape are the length and form of wings, tails, and legs. The wings may be long, pointed, and developed for swift, sustained flight, like those of falcons. Or the wings may be short and rounded for abrupt bursts of speed, like those of accipiters. The tail may have a deep fork like that of a barn swallow, a shallow notch like that of a tree swallow, a square tip like that of a cliff swallow, or a rounded tip like that of a blue jay.

Size is difficult to estimate and therefore not very useful in identifying birds. The best approach is to bear in mind the relative sizes of different species and to use certain well-known birds like the chickadee, sparrow, robin, kingfisher, and crow as standards for mental comparison. For example, if a bird resembles a song sparrow but looks unusually large, it might be a fox sparrow.

Plumage, whether plain or princely, muted or magnificent, is one of the most obvious keys to identification. Color can occur in remarkable combinations of spots, stripes, streaks, patches, and other patterns that make even supposedly drab birds a pleasure to see. In some instances, like the brown streaks of American bitterns and many other species, the plumage provides camouflage. Most vireos and warblers are various shades and combinations of yellow, green, brown, gray, and black, as one would expect from their forest environment. The black and white backs of woodpeckers help them to blend in with bark dappled with sunlight. The bold patterns of killdeers and some other plovers break up their outlines in much the same manner that warships used to be camouflaged before the invention of radar. Many shorebirds display countershading: They are dark above and light below, a pattern that reduces the effect of shadows and makes them appear an inconspicuous monotone. Even some brightly colored birds have camouflaging plumages when they are young and least able to avoid predators.

For some species, it is important *not* to be camouflaged. Many seabirds are mostly white, which in all light conditions enables them to be seen at great distances against the water. Because flocks of seabirds spread out from their colonies to search for food, it is vital that a bird that has located food be visible to others after it has landed on the water to feed.

To organize the immense variation in plumage, focus on different basic elements and ask the following types of questions. Starting with the head, is it uniformly colored like that of the red-headed woodpecker? Is there a small patch on the crown, like that of Wilson's warbler and the ruby-crowned kinglet, or a larger cap on the front and top of the head, like that of the common redpoll and American goldfinch? Is the crown striped like the ovenbird's? Does a ring surround the eye, as with a Connecticut warbler, or are the eye rings perhaps even joined across the top of the bill to form spectacles, like those of a yellow-breasted chat? Is there a stripe over or through the eyes, like the red-breasted nuthatch's, or a conspicuous black mask across the eyes, like that of a common yellowthroat or loggerhead shrike? From the head go on to the rest of the body, where distinctive colors and patterns can also mark a bird's bill, throat, breast, belly, back, sides, wings, rump, tail, and legs.

Finally, what a bird *does* is an important clue to its identity. Certain habits, postures, ways of searching for food, and other behavior characterize different species. Some passerines, such as larks, juncos, and towhees, are strictly ground feeders; other birds, including flycatchers and swallows, nab insects on the wing; and others, such as nuthatches and creepers, glean insects from the crevices in bark. Woodpeckers peck into the bark. Vireos and most warblers pick insects from the foliage of trees and brush.

All of these birds may be further distinguished by other habits of eating. For example, towhees scratch for insects and seeds by kicking backward with both feet together, whereas juncos rarely do, although both hop to move along the ground. Other ground feeders, such as meadowlarks, walk rather than hop. Despite the children's song, robins often run, not hop. Swallows catch insects while swooping and skimming in continuous flight, but flycatchers dart out from a limb, grab an insect (sometimes with an audible smack), and then return to their perch. Brown creepers have the curious habit of systematically searching for food by climbing trees in spirals, then flying back to the ground to climb again. Woodpeckers tend to hop upward, bracing themselves against the tree with their stiff tails. Nuthatches walk up and down trees and branches head first, seemingly without regard for gravity. Vireos are sluggish compared to the hyperactive, flitting warblers.

Many birds divide a food source into zones, an arrangement that apparently evolved to ensure each species its own food supply. The short-legged green heron sits at the edge of the water or on a low overhanging branch, waiting for its prey to come close to shore. Medium-sized black-crowned and yellow-crowned night herons hunt in shallow water. The long-legged great blue heron stalks fish in water up to two feet deep. Swans, geese, and many ducks graze underwater on the stems and tubers of grassy plants, but the longer necks of swans and geese enable them to reach deeper plants. Similarly, different species of shorebirds take food from the same mud flat by probing with their varied bills to different depths. Various species of warblers that feed in the same tree are reported to concentrate in separate areas, such as the trunk, twig tips, and tree top. Starlings and cowbirds feeding in flocks on the ground show another arrangement that provides an even distribution of food: Those in the rear fly ahead to the front, so that the entire flock rolls slowly across the field.

Different species also have different styles of flight. Soaring is typical of some big birds. Gulls float nearly motionless in the wind. Buteos and vultures soar on updrafts in wide circles, although turkey vultures may be further distinguished by wings held in a shallow V. Some other large birds, such as accipiters, rarely soar but instead interrupt their wing beats with glides. Kestrels, terns, kingfishers, and burrowing owls can hover in one spot. Hummingbirds, like oversized dragonflies, can also hover and even fly backward. Slightly more erratic than the swooping, effortless flight of swallows is that of swifts, flitting with wing beats that appear to alternate (but do not). Still other birds, such as the American goldfinch and flickers, dip up and down in wavelike flight. Some species, including jays and grackles, fly dead straight. Among ducks, the surface-feeding species launch themselves directly upward into flight, seeming to jump from the water, but the heavy diving ducks typically patter along the surface before becoming airborne.

Various idiosyncrasies distinguish yet other species. The spotted sandpiper and northern waterthrush walk with a teetering, bobbing motion. Coots pump their heads back and forth as they swim. The eastern phoebe regularly jerks its tail downward while perching, but wrens often cock their tails vertically. Herons and egrets fly with their necks folded back; storks, ibises, and cranes fly with their necks outstretched. Still other birds have characteristic postures while sitting or flying or other unique habits that provide a reliable basis for identification.

AND NOW for a few practice puzzlers to illustrate and apply some of the points discussed above.

Standing at the edge of thickets early in May, you hear a distinctive song: about eight buzzy notes ascending the chromatic scale, or that is, rising in a series of half tones. This song is enough to identify—what? Finally, you spot a small warbler with an olive back and yellow underparts, streaked black along the sides. The bird bobs its tail. It is the misnamed prairie warbler, which is common in bushy pastures, saplings, and low pines. The palm warbler also bobs its tail, but it is brown above and in spring has a chestnut cap.

At the wooded edge of a pond in summer you observe a small bird that is all brown above and streaked with brown below. A long, pale-yellow stripe runs above each eye. As it walks the bird teeters and bobs. This is a . . . (I'm waiting for you to answer first) . . . a northern waterthrush, whose peculiar gait is shared by the somewhat larger spotted sandpiper, also seen near water.

Soaring overhead in big circles in spring is a bird with broad wings and a wide unbanded tail. It is probably a buteo, but which? Broad-winged hawks have wide white tail bands (i.e., equal in width to the intervening black bands); red-shouldered hawks have narrow white tail bands; mature red-tailed hawks have no tail bands, so this is your bird. Your identification is confirmed by a glimpse of red on the upper surface of the tail as the hawk banks in its flight. You might also see a harrier (or marsh hawk) at the National Wildlife Visitor Center, flying low over the meadow with wings held in a shallow V as it veers from side to side, showing a white spot at the rump just above its long tail. Also present are ospreys, soaring like buteos. From time to time, they hover and then plunge feet first into the water, from which they immediately emerge and fly off, interrupting their wing beats to shudder in mid-flight, like a dog shaking itself.

Imagine that you spot a large, dark, long-legged, long-necked wading bird in the marsh. It has a downward-curved bill. Of course, the vast majority of large, dark waders are great blue herons, but herons have straight bills. So your bird is probably a glossy ibis. The identification is confirmed when the creature flies off with its neck outstretched. Herons and egrets fly with their necks folded back. The whimbrel, too, has a downwardly curved bill and flies with its neck outstretched, but its neck and legs are visibly shorter than those of the glossy ibis.

≈   ≈   ≈   ≈

AUTOMOBILE DIRECTIONS: The National Wildlife Visitor Center is located about 20 miles southwest of Baltimore. (See •22 on **Map 1** on page 5. For greater detail, refer to the corner panel of **Map 29** at right, where the visitor center is shown as the lower of two dots; the upper dot is the refuge's North Tract, featured in Chapter 23.)

To the National Wildlife Visitor Center from Interstate 695 (the Baltimore Beltway): Leave I-695 at Exit 7A for Route 295 (the Baltimore Washington Parkway) south toward Washington. Go about 14 miles, then follow the directions in the next paragraph.

To the National Wildlife Visitor Center from Route 295 (the Baltimore Washington Parkway): Leave the parkway at the exit for Route 197 toward Bowie. Follow Route 197 south 1.7 miles, then turn right onto Powder Mill Road. After 0.7 mile, turn left and follow the Visitor Center's entrance road 1.3 miles to the parking lot.

≈   ≈   ≈   ≈

WALKING: Map 29 at right shows the trails at the **National Wildlife Visitor Center.** The most attractive route is the

MAP 29 — National Wildlife Visitor Center at the Patuxent Research Refuge

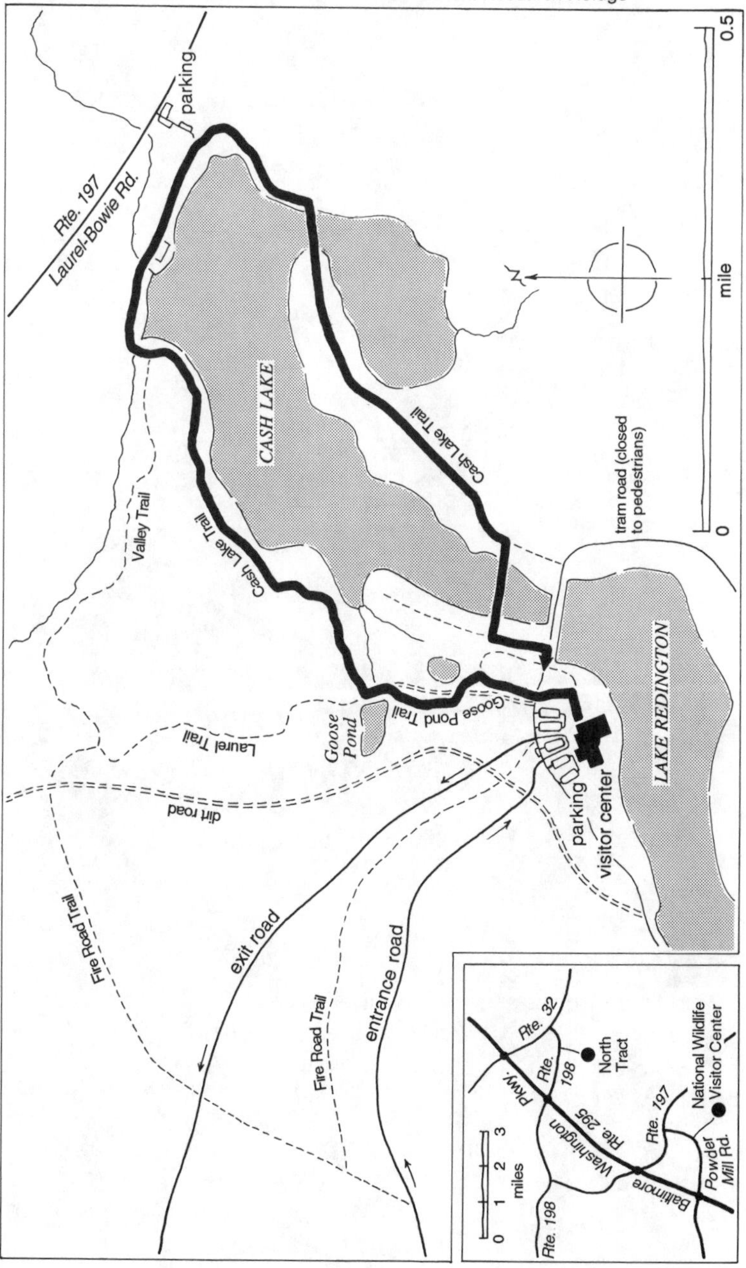

2-mile loop past Goose Pond and around Cash Lake, shown by the bold line.

Start at the main hall of the Visitor Center building. Exit via the Gallery. At a fork in the paved path, bear left. Cross a road and then, where the paved path curves sharply right, turn left onto the unpaved **Goose Pond Trail**.

A few yards beyond Goose Pond, turn right onto the **Cash Lake Trail**. Continue through the woods, with the lake visible to the right. Pass an intersection with the **Valley Trail** and continue across a wooden bridge. Cross a larger bridge over the dam spillway. After passing the fishing pier, continue around the circuit and back to the Visitor Center.

≈　　　≈　　　≈　　　≈

You may also want to visit the nearby **North Tract of the Patuxent Research Refuge**, which is separate from the Visitor Center itself and is featured in Chapter 23.

23

NORTH TRACT of the Patuxent Research Refuge

Located about half way between Baltimore and Washington, the **North Tract of the Patuxent Research Refuge** is huge—nearly 13 square miles. Although most of this area is off limits to visitors, hikers will find plenty of room to stretch their legs.

The *dotted line* on **Map 30** on page 265 shows the **Forest Habitats Nature Trail**, which is 2.5 miles long (4 kilometers).

The *bold line* on Map 30 traces a much longer walk via **unpaved roads** that are closed to all but a few authorized motor vehicles. The total distance is 10 miles (16 kilometers). There is nothing special here—just woods, meadows, and a few cultivated fields—but the overall effect is very pleasant.

The North Tract is open daily, except Thanksgiving, Christmas, and New Years Day, starting at 8:00 A.M. It closes at hours that change with the seasons and that correspond approximately with sunset. Dogs must be leashed.

The Patuxent Research Refuge is managed by the U.S. Fish and Wildlife Service; telephone (410) 674-3304. **Hunting** is permitted in fall to control the deer population, so call beforehand to make sure that the trails are not closed to hikers. Or you can just go on Sunday, when hunting is not allowed.

The North Tract was formerly part of Fort Meade. In the very unlikely event that you spot a metal object that could possibly be an **unexploded shell**, do not pick it up.

For automobile directions, please turn to page 264. Walking directions are on pages 264-267.

THE NORTH TRACT of the Patuxent Research Refuge is one of the few places in this book that lies in Maryland's Coastal Plain. Here, only a few miles downstream from the gorge and rocky cascade at Savage Mill (featured in Chapter 21), the

Patuxent River flows with only minor riffles between banks of clay and sand. There is not a boulder in sight, even in the streambed. The gently undulating land surface has a far smaller range of relief than in the Piedmont. The vegetation too is somewhat different. Growing from the sandy soil, pines are much more abundant among the woods. And along the Patuxent's tributaries there are marshes and swamps. which are almost never found in the Piedmont, except at man-made reservoirs.

The Coastal Plain and Piedmont are two of several physiographic provinces that run parallel with the Atlantic shore in belts of varying width from New York southward almost to the Gulf of Mexico. Starting at the water's edge, the land rises gradually across the Coastal Plain, then more rapidly over the Piedmont. Disregarding soil, most of the Piedmont province is composed of hard crystalline rock, including shist, granite, gneiss, quartzite, serpentine, and gabbro, although occasionally there are areas—both large and small—of relatively soft limestone. The low, broad Frederick Valley is one such area. West of Frederick is the abrupt line of the Blue Ridge, and west of that are the Valley and Ridge province of Washington and Allegany Counties and the high Appalachian Plateau of Garrett County and West Virginia.

Together with the underwater Continental Shelf, the Coastal Plain is one continuous apron of clay, silt, sand, and gravel eroded from the Piedmont and Appalachian highlands. The Coastal Plain sediments were laid down in relatively recent geologic time—that is, within the last 135 million years. In response to movements in the Earth's crust and fluctuations in climate, the coastal region was sometimes submerged beneath the sea or under shallow inland lakes, swamps, and slowly meandering rivers. Seashells and the bones and teeth of marine animals are common in some layers of sediment. Also contributing to the thick mantle of deposits along the mid-Atlantic coast are immense quantities of rock flour and sand scoured by continental glaciers from regions farther north and carried to the sea by huge rivers of meltwater that today survive in the relatively trivial trickle of the Hudson, Delaware, and Susquehanna rivers. During the last million years, the ocean shore has advanced and receded repeatedly across the coastal sediments as the sea has risen and fallen, depending on how much of the planet's water was amassed in the polar ice caps and in continental ice sheets.

The layers of sediment all dip toward the southeast, as does the underlying bedrock which emerges at the surface in the Piedmont. Although the angle of dip is very slight—generally less than one degree—the sediments have accumulated to a depth of more than a mile beneath the present Atlantic coastline. Even near the boundary with the Piedmont, the coastal deposits are hundreds of feet thick, giving rise to large sand and gravel strip mines in the vicinity of the Patuxent Research Refuge and also near Interstate 95 north of Washington's Capital Beltway.

Marking the transition between the Coastal Plain and Piedmont is the so-called Fall Line, which is not really a sharp line but rather a zone of considerable width. As rivers descend through the fall zone, there is such a concentrated release of energy that often gorges are cut into the Piedmont plateau, as exemplified by the Patuxent and Patapsco Rivers and Gunpowder Falls. Continuing toward the sea across the easily eroded sediments of the Coastal Plain, many rivers have carved wide valleys that now are flooded by the ocean all the way to the boundary with the Piedmont. Baltimore, for example, is located mostly in the Piedmont, but it is lapped by the tidal Patapsco River. Similarly, the tidal Potomac River twists and turns through the Coastal Plain for a hundred miles—from Chesapeake Bay to the edge of the Piedmont just upstream from Washington.

The boundary between the Coastal Plain and Piedmont is sinuous and ill-defined, characterized by a feathering out of the deposits of coastal sand, silt, and clay as they lap up onto the soil and underlying bedrock of the Piedmont. South of Baltimore, the boundary lies in the vicinity of Route 1. Near Washington, the transition very roughly corresponds to the boundary between Montgomery and Prince George's counties. Somewhat surprisingly, however, topography is often not a clue. Despite its name, the Coastal Plain west of Chesapeake Bay is in many places not at all flat. To some extent, the coastal deposits reflect the uneven surface on which they were laid down, particularly in areas close to the Piedmont. Also, because the sedimentary deposits of the bay's Western Shore commonly stand a hundred feet or more above sea level, they have been shaped by stream erosion like any other upland, in some places producing a very unplanar region of ridges and ravines descending steeply to tidewater.

≈   ≈   ≈   ≈

AUTOMOBILE DIRECTIONS: The North Tract of the Patuxent Research Refuge is located about 16 miles south of Baltimore. (See •23 on **Map 1** on page 5. For greater detail, refer to the corner panel of **Map 29** on page 257 and also to **Map 30** at right.)

To the North Tract from Interstate 695 (the Baltimore Beltway): Leave I-695 at Exit 7A for Route 295 (the Baltimore Washington Parkway) south toward Washington. Go about 11 miles, then follow the directions in the next paragraph.

To the North Tract from Route 295 (the Baltimore Washington Parkway): Leave the parkway at the exit for Route 198. Follow Route 198 east toward Fort Meade 1.7 miles. At an obscure intersection, turn right onto Bald Eagle Drive, as the entrance road to the North Tract of the Patuxent Research Refuge is called. After 1 mile, turn left into the parking lot for the Visitor Contact Station. The walks described below assume that you will start from here, **but first sign in at the Visitor Contact Station to obtain a free pass.**

≈   ≈   ≈   ≈

WALKING: Map 30 at right shows the **North Tract of the Patuxent Research Refuge.** Totaling nearly 13 square miles, most of this area is off-limits to visitors. Nonetheless, there are good opportunities for walking. Two routes, one short and the other much longer, are described below.

The Forest Habitats Nature Trail is shown on Map 30 by a dotted line. Winding through mixed deciduous and piney woods, this trail is 2.5 miles long

Start at the Butterfly Garden across the entrance road from the Visitor Contact Station. Enter the woods on the narrow trail,

MAP 30 — North Tract of the Patuxent Research Refuge

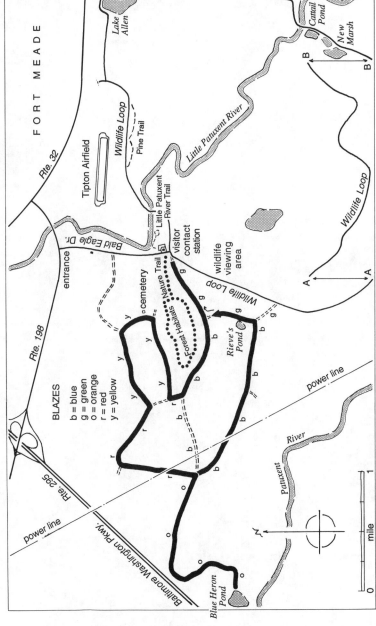

which eventually leads to a T-intersection with the loop portion of the trail. Follow the loop in either direction, but first take a good look at the trail junction so that you will recognize it when you complete the circuit and want to return to the parking lot.

A system of unpaved roads also provides good walking. The bold line on Map 30 shows a route of 10 miles. For a shorter outing, skip one of the loops or the spur to Blue Heron Pond. Closed to all but a few motor vehicles, the roads cut through the woods, occasionally passing fields and meadows. Navigation is made easy by blazes consisting of metal disks showing an arrow on a blue, green, orange, red, or yellow background.

Start by following the entrance road to a T-intersection with Wildlife Loop just beyond the Visitor Contact Station. Turn right and go 60 yards, then continue straight into the woods on a sand-and-gravel road marked with green blazes.

At the first major intersection, stay right for the blue road. At the next junction, turn right onto the red road, then right again onto the yellow road, which leads past an old cemetery. Bear left past a road intersecting from the right.

At a T-intersection with the red road, turn right. Eventually, the red road passes under a power line and reaches a four-way junction. Bear right to follow the orange road through the woods and a large meadow to Blue Heron Pond.

From Blue Heron Pond, return by the way you came to the four-way junction. Bear right to follow the blue road. Eventually, turn sharply left onto the green road, which leads past Rieve's Pond. Finally, at another junction, turn right to stay on the green road, which leads back to the Visitor Contact Station.

INDEX OF SITES AND TRAILS

Avalon and Orange Grove Areas of Patapsco Valley State Park:
automobile directions: 182-183
history:
  Avalon, 174-178
  Bloede Dam, 182
  Ilchester, 180-182
  Orange Grove, 178-180
introduction, 173
map, 181
walking, 183

Baltimore & Annapolis Trail: see BWI Trail

Baltimore-Washington International Airport: see BWI Trail

Big Gunpowder Trail at the Central Area of Gunpowder Falls State Park:
automobile directions, 92
industrial sites, 89-92, 96-97
introduction, 89
map, 93
walking, 92-97

Black Marsh Trail at North Point State Park, 219, 222

Bloede Dam, 173, 182,183

Bollman Bridge, 239, 244-245

BWI Trail and the Baltimore & Annapolis Trail:
automobile directions, 233-236
history:
  Baltimore & Annapolis Railroad, 228-233
  Baltimore-Washington International Airport, 225-228
introduction, 225
maps, 234, 235
walking and bicycling, 236-237

Cash Lake Trail at the National Wildlife Visitor Center, 259

Central Area of Gunpowder Falls State Park; see these headings:
Big Gunpowder Trail
Lost Pond Trail & Sawmill Trail
Sweathouse Branch Wildlands

Cylburn Arboretum:
automobile directions, 207
history (Tyson family), 201-202
introduction, 201
map, 208
tree identification, 202-207
walking, 209

Daniels, 152-156

East Hereford at Gunpowder Falls State Park:
automobile directions, 36
introduction, 33
map, 37
trees and their settings, 33-36
walking, 36-39

Ellicotts Lower Mills, 157-162

Ellicotts Upper Mills, 156-157

Forest Habitats Trail at the North

Tract of the Patuxent
Research Refuge, 261,
264-265

Fort Howard Park (see also
North Point State Park):
211, 222-223

Franklinville, 61, 63, 67

Grist Mill Trail at Patapsco Valley
State Park, 173, 183

**Gunpowder Falls State
Park**; see these
headings:
Big Gunpowder Trail
East Hereford
Hereford Area
Little Gunpowder Trail between
Route 1 and Interstate 95
(including Jerusalem Mill)
Little Gunpowder Trail and Ma &
Pa Trail between Bottom
Road and Pleasantville
Road
Lost Pond Trail and Sawmill Trail
Sweathouse Branch Wildlands
Sweet Air Area
West Hereford

Gunpowder North Trail at the Hereford Area, 13, 21, 23

Gunpowder South Trail:
at East Hereford, 33, 38
at the Hereford Area, 13, 20, 23
at West Hereford, 25, 30-31

Gwynns Falls Trail:
automobile directions, 194-196
Calverton Mills and Millrace
Path, 185-188
Crimea and the Winans family,
188-192; directions to,
198-199
Interstate 70 dispute, 193-194
introduction, 185

map, 197
Murray (Carrie) Center, 198-199
Olmsted Report and park development, 192-193
walking and bicycling, 196-198

Hereford Area of Gunpowder
Falls State Park (see also
East Hereford and West
Hereford):
automobile directions, 20
introduction, 13
map, 21
park development, including
land acquisition and
funding, 14-19
walking, 20-23

Highland Trail at West Hereford,
25, 30-31

Ilchester, 173, 180-182

Jericho Covered Bridge, 61, 63, 67

Jerusalem Mill, 61-62, 65, 67

Little Gunpowder Trail
between Route 1 and
Interstate 95:
automobile directions, 63-64
Franklinville, 63, 64
introduction, 61
Jericho Covered Bridge, 61, 62
Jerusalem Mill, 61-62
map, 66
walking, 65-67

**Little Gunpowder Trail and
Ma & Pa Trail** between
Bottom Road and
Pleasantville Road:
automobile directions, 56-58
introduction, 53
map, 57
Maryland & Pennsylvania Railroad, 53-56
walking, 58-59

Loch Raven:
  automobile directions, 102
  introduction, 99
  map, 103
  recreational use, 99-101
  walking, 102-105

Lost Pond Trail and Sawmill Trail at the Central Area of Gunpowder Falls State Park:
  automobile directions, 84-86
  introduction, 81
  map, 85
  stream erosion, 81-84
  walking, 86-87

Ma & Pa Trail on Little Gunpowder Falls, 53, 59

McKeldin Area of Patapsco Valley State Park:
  automobile directions, 145-146
  introduction, 141
  map, 147
  park history, 141-145
  walking, 146-149

McKeldin Area - Dogwood Road section of Patapsco Valley State Park:
  automobile directions, 164
  history:
    Daniels, 152-156
    Ellicotts Lower Mills, 157-162
    Ellicotts Upper Mills, 156-157
    Oella, 162-164
  introduction, 151-152
  maps, 166, 167
  walking, 165-171

Millrace Path, 185-187

Mingo Forks Trail at West Hereford, 25, 31

National Wildlife Visitor Center:
  automobile directions, 256

bird identification, 247-256
introduction, 247
map, 257
walking, 256-259

North Point State Park and Fort Howard Park:
  automobile directions, 218-219, 223
  Bay Shore Park, 217-218
  British invasion at North Point, 212-217
  Fort Howard, 222-223
  introduction, 211-212
  maps, 221-222
  walking:
    at Fort Howard, 223
    at North Point, 219-222

North Tract of the Patuxent Research Refuge:
  automobile directions, 264
  Coastal Plain and Piedmont, 261-264
  introduction, 261
  map, 265
  walking:
    Forest Habitats Trail, 264
    unpaved roads, 267

Northern Central Railroad (including the York County Heritage Rail Trail):
  automobile directions, 114-121
  history, 107-114
  introduction, 107
  maps, 116-119
  walking and bicycling, 121

Oella, 162-164

Orange Grove Area of the Patapsco Valley State Park (see also Avalon), 173,174, 178-180, 183

Oregon Ridge Park:

automobile directions, 126
introduction, 123
Oregon Furnace, 123-126
walking, 126-129

Panther Branch Trail at East
    Hereford, 33, 38-39

**Patapsco Valley State
    Park**; see these
    headings:
Avalon Area
McKeldin Area
McKeldin Area - Dogwood Road
Orange Grove Area

Patuxent Research Refuge;
    see these headings:
National Wildlife Visitor Center
North Tract

Savage Park and **Savage
    Historic Mill Trail:**
automobile directions, 241-242
introduction, 239
history:
    Bollman Bridge, 244-245
    Savage Mill, 239-241
map, 243
walking:
    at Savage Park, 242-244
    at Savage Historic Mill Trail,
      244

**Soldiers Delight Natural
    Environment Area:**
automobile directions, 136-138
chromite mining, 131, 132-135
introduction, 131
map, 137
serpentine rock, 131-132
Tyson, Jesse, 132-136
trees, grasses, and wildflowers,
    131-132, 135
walking, 138-139

Stanislaus Kostka Church, 154,
    170

Stockdale Trail at Sweathouse
    Wildlands, 79

**Sweathouse Branch Wild-
    lands** at the Central
    Area of Gunpowder Falls
    State Park:
automobile directions, 77
introduction, 69
map, 78
stream erosion and develop-
    ment, 69-77
walking, 77-79
weathering, 70-71

Sweet Air Area of Gunpowder
    Falls State Park:
automobile directions, 48-50
bird names, 41-48
introduction, 41
map, 49
walking, 50-51

Switchback Trail at the McKeldin
    Area of Patapsco Valley
    State Park, 146, 149

West Hereford at Gunpowder
    Falls State Park:
automobile directions, 28-30
introduction, 25
falls, and other local terms, 26
map, 29
walking, 30-31

Wetlands Trail at North Point State
    Park, 219, 222

York County Heritage Rail Trail:
    see Northern Central
    Railroad

IF YOU LIKE THIS BOOK, you might also enjoy some of the other guidebooks listed below. All follow the same format. These guides are widely available at bookstores, nature stores, and outfitters, and also from on-line booksellers.

DAY TRIPS IN DELMARVA
The Delmarva Peninsula, which consists of southern Delaware and the Eastern Shore of Maryland and Virginia (hence Del-Mar-Va, in local parlance), is one of the most fascinating vacation areas on the East Coast. *Day Trips in Delmarva* emphasizes the region's historic towns, scenic back roads, wildlife refuges, undeveloped beaches, and routes for car touring, hiking, and bicycling.

"The best organized, best written, most comprehensive and practical guide to the Delmarva Peninsula"—*Easton Star Democrat* • "An infinitely enjoyable book"—*Baltimore Magazine*

COUNTRY WALKS NEAR WASHINGTON
Dozens of outings explore national, state, and local parks and hike-bike trails located within an hour's drive of the U.S. capital. Each chapter includes an overview, detailed directions, one or more maps (there are sixty in all), and extensive commentary.

"Cream of the local outdoors-guide crop"—*Washington Post* • "The happy union between a utilitarian and historically informative guide"—*Washington Times*

COUNTRY WALKS & BIKEWAYS
IN THE PHILADELPHIA REGION
This guidebook explores the Delaware Valley's parks, wildlife refuges, and trail networks, including eighty-five miles of canal trails along the Delaware River.

COUNTRY WALKS NEAR BOSTON
"An invaluable paperback, profusely illustrated with photographs and maps. . . Possibly the best few dollars you could ever spend"—*Boston Globe* • "My favorite trail guide"—*Boston Phoenix*

COUNTRY WALKS NEAR CHICAGO
"A handy guide. . . . The general information sections— which, if combined, constitute three-fourths of the book—are excellent."—*Chicago Tribune*